FORECLOSED

FORECLOSED

High-Risk Lending,

Deregulation,

and the Undermining

of America's Mortgage Market

Dan Immergluck

Cornell University Press
ITHACA AND LONDON

Copyright © 2009 by Cornell University

First published 2009 by Cornell University Press

Printed in the United States of America
Typesetting: Jack Donner, BookType

Library of Congress Cataloging-in-Publication Data

Immergluck, Daniel.
  Foreclosed : high-risk lending, deregulation, and the undermining of America's mortgage market / Dan Immergluck.
    p. cm.
  Includes bibliographical references and index.
  ISBN 978-0-8014-4772-3 (cloth : alk. paper)
  1. Mortgage loans—United States. 2. Mortgage loans—Government policy—United States. 3. Subprime mortgage loans—United States. 4. Foreclosure—United States. 5. Financial services industry—Deregulation—United States. 6. Housing—Finance—Government policy—United States. 7. Financial crises—United States. I. Title.

  HG5095.I45 2009
  332.1'753—dc22

                                                          2008052549

Cornell University Press strives to use environmentally responsible suppliers and materials to the fullest extent possible in the publishing of its books. Such materials include vegetable-based, low-VOC inks and acid-free papers that are recycled, totally chlorine-free, or partly composed of nonwood fibers. For further information, visit our website at www.cornellpress.cornell.edu.

Cloth printing   10 9 8 7 6 5 4 3 2 1

Contents

Figures

Preface

As the U.S. mortgage crisis unfolded in 2007 and 2008, issues of housing finance and of homeownership policy more generally, became front-page news. This happened, however, not just because many people were losing their homes to foreclosure but because the banking and financial community began to suffer major losses on their investments in mortgage-backed securities and the derivatives associated with them. After some down-playing of the potential scale and impact of the problems spurred by the high-risk lending boom, government officials and regulators eventually saw that decades of deregulation in the financial services industry—accompanied by the aggressive preemption by federal regulators of state regulations—had come home to roost. Moreover, the arguments that mortgage transactions are best left to "free exchange" between borrowers and lenders—with government relying primarily on a weak system of consumer disclosure to prevent excessively risky lending—were called into question. And the social and public cost of mortgage market excesses and failures became painfully obvious as vacant buildings spread, credit markets seized, and national economies collapsed.

This book is an effort to tell a more nuanced story than has been told in many treatments of the recent crisis and, in particular, to place the events in the context of the longer history of institutional mortgage markets in the United States. This history shows that many successful and sustainable developments in these markets were the result of a mixed-economy approach to housing finance that included the substantial involvement of the federal government both in the regulation of home loans and in investing in fair, sustainable, and risk-limiting mortgage products and systems. As the nation moves forward with deciding what to do about mortgage market regulation and government involvement in secondary markets, it is critical that we have a keen knowledge of this history and an understanding of how mortgage markets actually work on the ground, and that we not rely too heavily on theoretical notions from any one narrow ideological or disciplinary perspective.

As this book went to press, there were already several books out on closely related topics and more in the works, but this gave me more motivation to offer what I was sure would be a perspective on the future of mortgage markets, and on the crisis itself, that would not be well represented in many of the popular treatments hitting the business shelves of bookstore chains or in the often narrow perspectives of traditional financial economists. It is important for policymakers, scholars, students, and those interested in taking a deeper look at the issues involved to have an alternative to such fare. Given the magnitude and importance of the crisis and what it means for the future of housing conditions and economic stability and opportunity in the United States, it is hard to argue that there can be too many ideas offered about how to avoid such calamities.

I have benefited greatly from a number of people who read earlier drafts of the book. Kevin Byers read and commented on key chapters on structured mortgage finance and securitization. Ira Rheingold and Ellen Seidman also provided very helpful feedback on sections. Two anonymous reviewers also gave me valuable feedback and suggested important improvements. Notwithstanding the valuable comments contributed by all of these people, any errors or omissions—and all opinions—remain entirely my responsibility. I especially want to thank Peter Wissoker, Susan Specter, and John Raymond at Cornell University Press for all of their efforts and for their support of this project. It was a real pleasure working with them.

Most of all, I want to thank Lilly, Kate, and Anna for putting up with me while I took on this "extra" task. It was not great timing and the intensity of the topic and the seeming unending evolution of the mortgage crisis made it an especially difficult topic to stay on top of and write about. I am so looking forward to gaining back some of that lost time with them.

FORECLOSED

Housing Finance, Ideology, and the Rise of High-Risk Mortgage Markets

This book is about residential mortgage markets and public policy. It describes the development and regulation of institutional mortgage markets—lending by banks, savings and loans, mortgage companies, and other organizations—over the last one hundred years, with a particular emphasis on changes from the 1990s through much of 2008. Unlike many treatments of financial services regulation or policy, however, the perspective of this book is focused very much on the effects of housing finance on homeowners and their neighborhoods and communities. The effects of mortgage market problems on the broader economy became painfully obvious in late 2007 and 2008, and some of those effects will be addressed. However, a good deal of the media attention about housing and mortgage market problems in recent years—especially since the second half of 2007—has focused on the problems of high finance, troubled lenders, and investors. Less attention has been paid to the effects of skyrocketing foreclosures—and their ripple effects—on low- and moderate-income homeowners who have lost homes and seen their credit histories shattered, on renters evicted from foreclosed properties, and on neighborhoods littered with vacant buildings.

A primary audience for this book is the set of policymakers involved at various levels of government and in various roles that touch on mortgage lending regulation, housing finance and development, community development, and related issues. However, it is also aimed at those simply interested in understanding what happened in the late 1990s and, especially, the middle-to-late 2000s to cause the mortgage and housing problems that so weakened communities and the broader economy. And finally, it is aimed at scholars, researchers, and students who would like a long-term, in-depth perspective on U.S. housing finance and the very unsteady and politically determined nature of its development over the last hundred years.

The structure of housing finance markets in the United States has changed time and again over the last century and, especially since the 1930s, has been molded and shaped heavily by public policy—regulation, deregulation, and other forms of intervention and public investment. For the bulk of the twentieth century, most policymakers recognized that housing and housing finance were qualitatively different from other markets and could not be left completely to the free market. Industrialization and urbanization have generally led most countries to this same conclusion and, although nations vary a great deal in the structure of their mortgage markets and regulations, this variation itself shows how mortgage markets are almost always the object of a great deal of social and political influence and construction.

The focus of much of the book is on what I term "high-risk" mortgage markets and products. This terminology warrants some explanation and clarification. The term "subprime lending" dominated newspaper headlines in 2007 and 2008. The popularity of the word caused its usage to be sometimes confused and highly imprecise. Therefore, although I do not avoid the term, I use it in its more traditional form, to define a segment of the loan market that was originally targeted at borrowers with impaired credit (although, in the 2000s, subprime-priced loans were increasingly made to a broader class of borrowers, including many with high credit scores). Because mortgage markets evolved in many different ways since the early 1990s and, especially after 2002, there were many higher-risk and higher-cost products that were aimed at prime borrowers but that exhibited various features that increased their default risks. I generally refer to a broader class of "high-risk" loans that include subprime loans, but also include loans with alternative or "exotic" structures (such as payment-option or interest-only loans) regardless of whether they are defined as subprime. In this category I also include zero down-payment loans and any form of stated-income loan where the income of borrowers is not verified.

The 2007–2008 Mortgage Crisis
and the Deregulationist Policy Movement

The timing of this book is not coincidental. Although its historical breadth will hopefully make it particularly useful beyond the near term, I have a proximate objective of using lessons from the 2007–08 mortgage crisis to promote the principle that sound, affordable, and sustainable mortgage markets require a mixed-economy approach—a public-private partnership if you will—that involves a significant and persistent role for government in the regulation and funding of mortgages. (I will continue to refer to the most recent period of serious mortgage market calamity as the "2007–08 mortgage crisis" even though its associated problems and effects will clearly last well beyond 2008.)

In recent years, the costs of deregulation and the privatization of secondary mortgage markets have been very large and, in many cases, painfully obvious. In early 2008, the mortgage crisis had been estimated at creating direct losses to investors in mortgage-backed securities in the $350 to $420 billion range, but because these losses occur at leveraged financial institutions, their full impact has been estimated at $2 trillion or more (Blundell-Wignall 2008; Greenlaw et al. 2008). By August 2008, write-downs and losses of mortgage-backed securities by commercial and investment banks alone amounted to over $500 billion, without accounting for leveraged impacts, and some were predicting that total write-downs and losses will reach well beyond these levels (Onaran 2008). Gorton (2008) referred to the impacts of the mortgage crisis on credit markets more broadly as the "Panic of 2007," reminiscent of the financial panic a century earlier.

By November of 2008, Roche (2008) argued that as a result of the broader financial crisis—which was spurred but not solely caused by the mortgage crisis—the global financial sector had lost as much as 85 percent of the sector's Tier 1 equity capital, amounting to a loss of more than $4.2 trillion at financial institutions. If the postcrisis values of financial assets were measured more liberally, he argued, such losses were likely to be about half this, but still amounting to over $2 trillion.

But the costs of the crisis went far beyond investors and financial institutions. Homeowners saw their credit records decimated, often after being lured into unfair or excessively risky mortgages without understanding the dangers embedded in the loans. Renters—who clearly had no role in the mortgage process—found themselves given little notice to vacate foreclosed rental properties. Neighborhoods around the country were littered with vacant and abandoned properties that depress the values of nearby homes, that can create havens for crime, and that have the power to undo decades of progress in community development. And the problems were not just confined to the inner city. In some places, entire suburban or exurban subdivisions that had been planned or started at the peak of the high-risk lending boom in the mid-2000s were left half empty or worse. Cities and suburbs have been forced to become custodians of abandoned houses in order to slow the contagion effects of derelict properties.

The problems of high-risk loan markets also spread relatively rapidly into broader mortgage and credit markets and other areas of finance and the economy, some of which, at first blush, had only tenuous connections to mortgages and home buying. The more obviously connected spillovers affected the construction industry and the revenues of local governments, which rely heavily on property taxes. But problems soon spread to sectors such as the auction rate securities market, which provides funding for municipal governments. By the spring of 2008, property values had declined so much that loans that had solid underwriting were experiencing substantially higher levels of default. Even banks that had not engaged in risky lending or in buying the mortgage-backed securities that funded such loans were experiencing problems because they had mortgages on their books (including many home equity loans) that were being affected by steep drops in housing values. These problems weakened the banks' balance sheets and their ability to make mortgages in a market in which many mortgage companies were failing or losing access to their traditional sources of capital.

Among the most critical impacts of the problems caused by high-risk lending and the attendant failure to regulate was the harm done to the government-sponsored secondary-market firms Fannie Mae and Freddie Mac. By the summer of 2008, the long-term solvency of the two government-sponsored enterprises (GSEs) was being questioned and, in early September, the U.S. Treasury Department put the firms into federal conservatorship. The firms' stock price had dropped dramatically since the beginning of the year; because the firms were heavily leveraged, declining stock prices threatened their ability to withstand heavy credit losses. Losses on prime loans had risen steadily in 2008, in part driven by the overall decline in housing prices but also by high-risk features such as "payment-option" structures and other nontraditional loan terms. When prices decline, borrowers experiencing difficulty with repaying their loans find it difficult to avoid foreclosure, as selling or refinancing their houses become difficult. Thus, the problems of the subprime market had spurred price declines (after spurring price increases), which now threatened the bulwarks of the U.S. mortgage market. Thus, the failure to contain and regulate the high-risk mortgage market threatened overall housing prices and the mainstream infrastructure of housing finance.

It is true that the two GSEs had, especially since 2004, increased their exposure to subprime and other high-risk loan products through their investments in mortgage-backed securities. However, the bulk of their own loan purchases and securitizations had remained in the lower-risk segments of the mortgage market. Although they had loosened credit standards for limited amounts of their loan purchases, the bulk of their portfolio and the loans appeared to have been underwritten relatively conservatively, especially when compared to subprime loans and other high-risk alternative products that had so permeated the market by the middle 2000s.

This is not to say that the business model and regulation of the GSEs was adequate. Given the overheated housing markets fueled by high-risk lending, the GSEs' regulator or Congress should have required the firms to reduce their leverage (the ratio of the firm's assets to its owners' equity) to be prepared for large drops in housing values and worsening loan performance. Because the securities issued by the firms had at least an implicit government guarantee, it was incumbent upon Congress to establish a more forceful regime of safety and soundness regulation.

Unfortunately, at the time this book goes to press, some political and ideological opponents of the GSEs are attempting to lay the principal blame for the mortgage crisis on federal investment and intervention in the mortgage marketplace via the agencies. This argument may be used to eventually privatize the bulk or all of operations of the GSEs. The fallacy of this argument is that it was too little—not too much—government intervention that precipitated the problems of 2007 and 2008 and led to the agencies' difficulties. In particular, the severity and spillovers of the mortgage crisis were principally due to a failure to regulate consumer mortgage markets. Stronger regulation of the GSEs—including increasing their reserves and equity requirements as housing prices rose—would have restrained the agencies from beginning to enter those riskier market segments. However, fundamentally it was the damage that the high-risk lenders did to housing values and overall mortgage markets that was the root of the mortgage market failure over this period.

The Failure of Deregulationist Ideology

Contrary to the impression one might have gotten from reading the mortgage crisis headlines in 2007 and 2008, there were many who had anticipated the problems of rising defaults and foreclosures—at least in broad outlines. These included some veterans in the mortgage industry, some policymakers, and, especially, numerous consumer and fair lending advocates. Few could have predicted the precise magnitude or nature of the crisis and, especially, all of the indirect effects that it would have on broader financial markets. However, the risks and costs of essentially deregulated, high-risk lending markets had become clearer during an earlier, but somewhat smaller, boom in high-risk lending in the mid- to late 1990s. For a variety of reasons, the knowledge of the problems and costs of high-risk lending had minimal impact on policymaking. And, while regulators and legislators in office during the more recent 2002–07 high-risk lending boom could have done much more to reduce the eventual fallout, the seeds of the fundamentally flawed market structures and regulatory systems that allowed the crisis to develop had been sowed much earlier, beginning in the early 1980s.

The 2007–08 mortgage crisis has lessons for citizens and policymakers concerned about restructuring mortgage markets and regulation to avoid a repeat of such damaging boom-bust episodes. This is a principal focus of this book. However, there are also lessons for housing policy more generally and, more fundamentally, for questioning a "deregulationist" paradigm that has dominated so much policymaking in the United States over the last thirty years. Especially since the early 1980s, there has been a deliberate and organized movement, aggressively promoted by the financial services sector and by some in Congress and federal regulatory agencies, to reduce public-sector oversight of the financial services sector. These deregulationists have argued that removing regulatory restrictions on the financial system unleashes free market efficiencies. They have applied the simple logic of markets for cookies or pork chops to the market for home loans. In this perspective, less government involvement is almost always seen as a superior model for any form of exchange of goods or services.

In the arena of financial services regulation, the shift over the last thirty years toward increasingly deregulationist policies has been at least as political as any other phase in U.S. history. Some argue that the successes of deregulationist advocates are related, both as a cause and a result, to the increasing concentration of wealth in the United States. In a vicious circle, financial services providers are served well by deregulation and then are able to push for even more deregulation.

Lobbying by the financial industry, however, has not been the only factor supporting deregulation. Hays (1995) and Hoffman (2001) argue that public policies are shaped by more than a simple competition of special interests; they are shaped by the competition of ideas. I believe both interests and ideas have been important in shaping policy in this arena. Campaign finance and the dominance of corporate lobbyists have clearly been important in continuing movement toward the deregulation of mortgage and consumer finance. However, deregulationist, free-market ideology has been accepted even by many who do not have clear financial interests in an unregulated financial system. By the late twentieth century, many policymakers had developed what social scientists call "priors" that include a strong antiregulatory posture. Regulation often became viewed as inherently ineffective or counterproductive.

For most of the history of the United States, the deregulationist ideology did not dominate policy thinking as it did in the late twentieth century and early twenty-first century. Nineteenth-century state government, for example, was heavily involved in licensing and regulating occupations, enforcing health requirements, and constraining trade (Novak 1996). It is true that the regulatory agencies were much less present in earlier eras, when regulation occurred more through legislative action. But, with some possible exceptions, the strongest moves toward a vision of "unfettered" free markets occurred in the last decades of the twentieth century.

One effect of the recent devotion to free markets, however, has been to conceal the highly political nature of banking and credit markets. It has served to mask the extent to which market developments in mortgage finance were derived from a long history of government action and involvement. To hear some analysts describe financial developments, one might gather that private entrepreneurs and lenders developed most of the successful innovations and developments in consumer finance and mortgage markets, while public-sector involvement had only been counterproductive. In fact, government agencies and actions created, subsidized, and institutionalized many of the most successful and sustainable mortgage products and practices since the early part of the twentieth century. This includes the long-term fully amortizing mortgage, private mortgage insurance (especially in its recent forms), and all sorts of standardization and discipline that enhanced the stability of the financial services industry. Meanwhile, many private-sector innovations, such as highly structured and layered securitizations, stated-income and piggyback loans, have proven to be abject failures.

Of course, public policy has aided and abetted some harmful developments as well as positive ones. Specifically, it had a significant role in paving the way for a fundamentally flawed system of structured mortgage finance that was the principal driver of the 2007–08 crisis. But the principal policy approach that encouraged and enabled the boom-bust problems of recent decades consisted largely of deregulation and the preemption of states' power to regulate when they felt that federal regulation was lacking.

A key theme that I hope to convey in this book is that consumer finance markets—and especially mortgage markets—are not well served by a deregulationist paradigm. One would think that the lesson of the mortgage crisis would make this painfully obvious, and it has to some. However, there are still many policymakers and commentators who suggest that moving toward a firmer and more comprehensive regulatory structure will cause more harm than good, that it will excessively impede access to credit for those who need it, and that it will encourage moral hazards and inefficiencies in housing finance. Yet periods of stability and incremental progress toward access to affordable and sound credit and capital have involved a strong, proactive role for the public sector, both in terms of providing and standardizing risk-limiting mortgage products and in terms of providing a regulatory infrastructure that constrains market booms and busts.

The rise of stable mortgage finance markets in the broad middle part of the twentieth century—epitomized perhaps by the long-term dominance of the plain-vanilla thirty-year fixed-rate mortgage—was due to a persistent and substantive role for the federal government. These markets and products were not without the serious and pervasive problems of discrimination and redlining, as described in chapter 2. However, their basic structure constituted a sound base upon which to build a fairer system, and in the late 1960s and into the 1970s a number of federal statutes—the Fair Housing Act, the Home Mortgage Disclosure Act, the Equal Credit Opportunity Act, and the Community Reinvestment Act—were adopted toward this end. Although implementation and enforcement of these laws was frequently lackluster, there were periods when significant progress toward fair, affordable, and sustainable home finance was made, especially in the late 1980s and early 1990s. This progress, however, was soon overwhelmed by a flood of high-risk credit.

This flood of high-risk credit, in turn, was fundamentally enabled by a strong deregulationist push on the part of the financial services industry, as well as many policymakers, to avoid or eviscerate state and federal regulation and constraints that had resulted in a robust, but risk-limiting, mortgage finance system. Especially since the 1980s, deregulationist forces typically dominated the development of consumer and mortgage finance policy, especially in the specific area of consumer protection. Even when some states stepped in to fill the regulatory vacuum, federal policymakers rebuffed them, preempting state consumer protection laws. Deregulation as well as other policies favored the growth of highly complex and engineered systems of residential finance. These policies paved the way for the connection of unrestrained global capital markets to create investment structures designed primarily to speed the flow of high-cost and high-risk credit to local communities, and especially to communities most vulnerable to such costs and risks.

The market structures developed in the absence of government oversight or regulation—although sometimes with specific tax advantages—were able to ignore the very powerful negative spillovers of excessively risky and irresponsible lending. The result was that mortgage lending was treated no differently than markets for most mass-marketed consumer products. There was little thought given to the fundamentally different nature of real estate and housing, or to the impacts of foreclosure on households' long-term economic prospects and on neighborhoods and cities. And, while structured finance greased the wheels of global capital flowing into lower-income neighborhoods, policymakers and financial engineers gave little thought to the "back-end" problems of what would happen if many loans failed and many houses were left vacant.

The Shifting Nature of Institutional Mortgage Markets in the United States

Although there were forms of institutional mortgage lending before the Civil War, mainstream institutional mortgage finance developed more fully in the early decades of the twentieth century. The rise of institutional lending was tied in part to the growing industrialization and urbanization of the country. Rural homesteaders faced lower costs and fewer obstacles to homebuilding than did urban households in industrializing cities where land and building materials were more expensive and labor was more specialized. As cities grew and land became more expensive in the late nineteenth century, most working-class families could not afford to purchase their own house.

At least through the 1970s, no single type of institutional mortgage lender was more critical to the development of safe and sound mortgage lending than the building and loan (B&L), later known as the savings and loan (S&L). Although the earliest B&L dates back to at least 1831, the early B&Ls were quite limited in their extent and were not permanent institutions. In fact, at the turn of the century most mortgage debt was held by individual investors, with institutions holding only just over a quarter of mortgage debt in the United States as of 1892 (Frederickson 1894). The financial roller coasters of the 1890s and first two decades of the twentieth century led to several booms and busts in mortgage markets, some of which are reminiscent of the 2000s. For example, in the 1890s there was a rapid growth in national-scale B&Ls. The traditional B&L, and later the S&L, had been primarily a local savings bank that accepted deposits and used those deposits to make loans to local borrowers. Early B&Ls, in fact, made loans only to depositors, while the S&L model allowed for lending to a wider variety of households in the S&Ls' local area.

The national B&L gathered deposits from many parts of the country and made loans over similarly dispersed geographic areas. By 1893, there were almost three hundred national B&Ls, and their branches spread to every state (Mason 2004). But by the late 1890s, many national B&Ls had failed. These institutions had relied heavily on abusive pricing and terms for large portions of their revenue. Later on, it became apparent that the national B&L industry was riddled with self-dealing and the undue enrichment of officers and executives. In what hopefully will turn out to presage the aftermath of the more recent mortgage crisis, a key outcome of the national B&L failures was that leaders of the B&L industry became aware of the economic benefits provided by government regulation (Mason 2004).

The boom years of the 1920s saw a rapid growth of institutional lenders, including B&Ls, but also of mortgage companies using financing from insurance companies and other investors. By the end of the 1920s, commercial banks gained the ability to make mortgages as well. The late 1920s and the Great Depression saw a major collapse in housing and mortgage markets, but this calamity gave birth to a wide variety of government innovations and essentially shifted the paradigm toward government supervision, regulation, and participation in the mortgage finance marketplace. The system of government-supervised and enhanced mortgage lending that dominated most of the twentieth century and led to the development of standardized and risk-limiting mortgage products—including especially the thirty-year fixed-rate mortgage—was generally a success. A critical exception was the fact that many households and communities were subject to very severe problems of discrimination and redlining. Despite its very significant failures, the mixed-economy system of mortgage finance that developed in the 1930s, which included a substantial public-sector role as standard-setter, market-maker, regulator, and frequent guarantor or investor, provided a reasonable foundation on which to improve.

The very substantial problems of lending discrimination and redlining that permeated this new private-public mortgage marketplace persisted essentially unmitigated until some major policy developments beginning in the late 1960s, including the Fair Housing Act, the Equal Credit Opportunity Act, the Home Mortgage Disclosure Act, and the Community Reinvestment Act. Although these laws all suffered from some structural weaknesses and inconsistent enforcement, they clearly improved access to affordable mortgage credit, especially during periods of more aggressive enforcement.

Just as some progress was being made in the late 1980s and early 1990s in improving the enforcement of fair lending and community reinvestment laws, the subprime lending industry was gaining its first real head of steam. The Home Ownership and Equity Protection Act (HOEPA), which was built from a paradigm of using consumer disclosures as a key policy tool for providing consumer protection, was passed in 1994. But HOEPA did little to actually proscribe abusive or unsound lending practices for the vast majority of mortgages—even the majority of high-risk or high-cost mortgages—because it only had any real teeth for loans priced over very high fee and rate thresholds. In fact, it is arguable the HOEPA helped pave the way for the emergence of the subprime mortgage market by implicitly sanctioning many high-cost and high-risk loans that were not prohibited by the law and that did not reach the HOEPA pricing thresholds. In effect, HOEPA provided lenders with an implicit endorsement for high-risk loans that were priced under—even just under—these thresholds.

The amount of attention that the 2007–08 mortgage crisis received partially obscured the fact that there was an earlier boom in high-risk lending in the mid-to-late 1990s, and that this boom also resulted in high and geographically concentrated foreclosure rates. However, because the overall scale of the subprime market was smaller on a national scale, and especially because this first subprime boom did not cause major losses to the investment community, it received much less press coverage and was essentially ignored during the recent crisis. Also, because the 1990s subprime lending was more concentrated in lower-income and minority markets and was much less extensive in high-cost metropolitan areas such as those in California and Florida, the foreclosure problems of the 1990s were both less severe and affected fewer neighborhoods and cities than did those in the late 2000s.

The first high-risk lending boom, which occurred during the 1995–99 period, primarily involved refinance loans, with little penetration of the home purchase market. This was, in part, due to the fact that subprime lenders in this first boom often made loans with modest loan-to-value ratios, so that the loans were substantially smaller than the market value of the property, in order to reduce the severity of any losses they might have in this emerging segment of the market. Borrowers during this first boom typically had substantial amounts of owner equity in their properties that could be extracted, some of which could be used to finance the fees of mortgage brokers and lenders. Repeated refinancings over short periods of time allowed for large amounts of "equity stripping" to occur. Equity stripping occurs when the homeowner is left with substantially less financial equity in the home after receiving a loan, due to heavy fees and costs incurred in the transaction. During the second high-risk boom, refinance loans still accounted for a very large share of subprime and high-risk loans, but the share going to home purchase activity increased markedly, which fed the growth of housing prices, especially in hot housing markets such as California, Florida, and many parts of the East Coast.

Contrary to the notion that the entire country had somehow overlooked the development of high-risk mortgage lending, the issue of subprime and high-risk mortgage lending had actually been heavily debated since the early 1990s, and especially since the late 1990s, after subprime lending had grown significantly. Federal regulators and Congress chose not to adapt the regulatory infrastructure to high-risk lending. In the 1980s, federal policymakers began overriding states' ability to regulate mortgages and consumer loans—in large part to pave the way for the growth of larger secondary markets and securitization. However, they were doing little to nothing to create a new system of financial regulation, or even expanding existing regulatory resources, for what was to become a rapidly growing set of new and effectively unregulated mortgage lenders that benefited from new secondary-market funding sources. They were also driving a stake in the heart of already struggling savings and loans (which were suffering from other problems) by providing their mortgage company competitors with cheaper secondary-market capital and free rein from a more extensive regulatory regime. Later, in the early 2000s, federal banking regulators affirmatively acted to preempt state efforts to regulate lending when it involved federally chartered institutions or their subsidiaries.

A major problem in the development of mortgage market supervision and regulation in the latter half of the twentieth century was the bifurcation of regulatory supervision, especially in consumer protection, fair lending, and community reinvestment. Banks and thrifts were subject to the Community Reinvestment Act. Moreover, they were supervised by thousands of bank examiners from the four federal federal bank regulators. These examiners conduct regular, proactive exams of the depositories for their compliance with consumer protection and fair lending laws. Although such exams were not always rigorous, there was at least a regulatory infrastructure set up to routinely police lender activities and respond to consumer complaints.

At the same time, the mortgage companies that came to dominate the subprime market were subject to little to no substantive regulatory supervision at the federal level. These firms were not regularly examined by any federal agency, and state regulatory enforcement, if any, was often quite weak. The federal agency with principal authority over enforcing consumer protection laws regarding the fast-growing set of subprime mortgage companies was the Federal Trade Commission, an agency that was not at all equipped for such levels of activity.

This book will illustrate how the unregulated and essentially unrestrained connection of globalized capital markets to local mortgage markets generated systematic transactional failures among a large number of intermediaries involved in the world of private-label securitization. These failures were often driven by conflicts of interest and the concealment of critical information from some parties by others in the credit supply chain. These problems accumulated to dramatically increase the amounts of default risk embedded in these mortgage markets.

For a few years, the "virtuous" cycle of increasing property values in many parts of the country masked the unsustainability of the underwriting of high-risk mortgages. In hot property markets, even when delinquencies and defaults rose, foreclosures were often averted because another lender was ready to step in to refinance the borrower or the borrower could easily sell her house because its value exceeded any loan balance. As long as lenders and their funders were able to keep pushing the envelope on effective debt-to-income ratios through unsustainable gimmicks and loan structures, the virtuous cycle was sustained—at least in nationally diversified investment vehicles. But eventually the gimmicks could not keep fueling the bubbles and, as property values stalled and began to fall, loan distress turned into default, and default turned into foreclosure. The virtuous cycle turned into a vicious cycle. Hot markets became cold and could no longer prop up nationally diversified mortgage-backed securities, which already contained failing loans in slower real estate markets. Moreover, as credit markets pulled back, tightened credit exacerbated the situation even more. Even traditional, low-risk lenders began to experience trouble, especially when property values dropped and borrowers had trouble selling their homes or refinancing even when their credit histories were not particularly weak.

The answers on how to avoid repeating major boom-bust lending market cycles—which we now know can fall even faster than they rise—lie in looking back at some regulatory and financial history. The Panic of 1907, which followed a series of boom-bust cycles since the early 1890s, prompted the creation of the Federal Reserve System in 1913. The Great Depression, which was preceeded by a major downturn in real estate markets, led to a revolution in mortgage finance and consumer banking in the United States. These major institutional developments and paradigm shifts in policymaking certainly were not accomplished without political or ideological resisistance. However, the shifts fundamentally turned on a pragmatic notion that excessive risk in financial markets can spin out of control quickly and can have large, systemic, and essentially irreversible consequences. The 2007–08 mortgage crisis will hopefully spur similar, fundamental systemic reform in policymaking and in reconstituting a meaningful and reliable regulatory infrastructure.

The Organization of the Book

Chapter 1 begins with a brief history of mortgage markets in the United States over the last century. The chapter covers most phases of major change in U.S. mortgage markets through the 1980s, with some emphasis on the New Deal policies that supported the standardization of the risk-limiting and generally affordable thirty-year fixed-rate mortgage. It also describes the development of government-sponsored secondary markets and the growth of structured mortgage finance. The chapter also discusses some of the key federal policies that encouraged the development of secondary markets and, in particular, paved the way for "private-label" securitization. (Chapters 3 and 4 will describe how private-label securitization differs from that of securitization via the GSEs.) A good deal of this policy work involved a strong push toward deregulation, including overriding state consumer protection laws.

Chapter 2 complements chapter 1 by explaining many of the serious and pervasive problems in institutional mortgage markets both before and after the New Deal innovations, including redlining and discrimination. It explains the policy developments, especially beginning in the late 1960s, that were aimed at reducing these problems as well as the successes and limits of these efforts. Chapter 2 also discusses the development of the "dual" regulatory system in which some lenders were subjected to much more regulatory scrutiny and supervision than others.

Chapters 3 and 4 describe and explain the development and growth of high-risk lending markets in the 1990s and 2000s. Chapter 3 discusses the strong racial patterns evident in subprime lending as well as the role of mortgage brokers, information technology, and other related developments. It also documents the qualitative difference in the nature of high-risk lending between the first and second high-risk lending booms, such as the growth of stated-income loans, zero down-payment products, piggyback loans, and others. Chapter 4 particularly examines the reasons why the system of private-label, structured mortgage finance suffered from so many transactional failures and problems and was shown to be effectively unsustainable, at least in the industrial and regulatory context in which it developed. Chapter 4 also includes a brief case study of a large, failed subprime lender—New Century Financial—in order to provide more context to a somewhat complex set of forces and causes.

Chapter 5 examines the economic and noneconomic costs that can arise from high-risk lending. One of the primary reasons that mortgage lending requires higher levels of regulation than most consumer markets is the damage that irresponsible lending can cause, to borrowers, lenders, and investors, and also to parties that had nothing to do with the mortgage transaction—neighborhoods, cities, and broader participants in markets that are indirectly affected. Even if one wants to avoid paternalistic consumer protections, the spillover costs alone are sufficient to justify proscriptive regulation. That is, even if one argues that, other than basic consumer disclosures, borrowers should not be protected from their own mistakes or abusive loans, the costs imposed by high-risk lending on households and communities not party to the loan transaction merit regulatory intervention. Therefore, it is important to understand these costs and how they are distributed. The 2007–08 crisis is particularly instructive here not only because it illustrates the direct costs of high-risk lending but because the scale of the crisis was so large that the indirect effects on neighborhoods, cities, and the broader economy became painfully obvious.

Chapter 6 focuses on the history of public policies since the 1990s that concern high-risk and subprime lending, with a particular focus on policy debates in the late 1990s and early 2000s following the first high-risk boom. It details how, despite a high-profile and serious debate about irresponsible lending and its problems and costs, the regulatory response by policymakers—especially at the federal level—was either exceedingly minimal or actually worked to override state efforts to improve and adapt regulatory systems. Chapter 6 also discusses the major policy responses to the crushing rise in foreclosures beginning in 2007, including both federal and state responses—or lack thereof.

The concluding chapter is focused on future policy developments and directions. The goal of the chapter is not to create a litany of highly detailed and nuanced policy prescriptions. The context for detailed policymaking is constantly changing, and this book is not the appropriate vehicle for engaging in that level of detail. Rather, the chapter begins by laying out a set of broad principles that are intended to lay the groundwork for policy discussions. Following this, the chapter provides some major recommendations for improving the structure of mortgage finance and regulation, while recognizing the perhaps limited political viability of some of these recommendations, at least in the short run. The chapter also provides some limited commentary on some of the measures the Federal Reserve Board took in the summer of 2008 to strengthen Home Ownership and Equity Protection Act (HOEPA) regulations.

The final chapter also covers two nonregulatory policy areas. First, it touches on the challenges and problems facing localities that have neighborhoods peppered—or sometimes flooded—with foreclosed and vacant properties. Given the problems posed by foreclosures and vacant buildings—some of which are discussed in chapter 5—large clusters of these properties, especially in a slow housing market, can do substantial damage to cities and communities. Given the pro-cyclical nature of foreclosures and vacancies (they increase during weak economic times and exacerbate revenue shortfalls) and the contribution of federal policy failures to these problems, there is ample justification for federal support for recovery efforts focused on vacant property problems.

The final area addressed in the conclusion is the need to rethink housing subsidy policies at all levels of government. Especially since the 1980s, federal housing policy has increasingly favored homeownership programs over support for rental housing. Also, unlike in some other countries, in most places in the United States housing policy options are almost completely constrained between supporting traditional homeownership on the one hand or rental housing on the other. In reality there are other tenure options, including limited equity cooperatives, community land trusts, and affordability-restricted housing. In many communities, however, subsidies favor homeownership programs. Although homeownership can be a beneficial option under the right circumstances, other options should be available, especially for lower-income households.

1

U.S. Mortgage Market Development and Federal Policy to the Early 1990s

To understand how the mortgage market problems of the 1990s and 2000s developed, and how fundamentally different these markets functioned compared to earlier periods, it is helpful to look much further back to the evolution of home finance in the United States, particularly the origins and institutionalization of loan products such as the long-term, fully amortizing, fixed-rate mortgage that became the dominant home loan of the twentieth century. The development of this product and the generally stable—but far from perfect—mortgage market that accompanied it was hardly a creature of unfettered private market innovation. Rather, it was the outcome of a fundamentally mixed sector of the U.S. economy, which included and required a persistent role for government as an innovator, an investor, and a regulator. During the 1980s and 1990s, however, policymakers began making explicit choices to move toward a highly deregulated system of housing finance. This left an increasingly large portion of the mortgage market subject to little regulation, shifted substantial amounts of risk from lenders to borrowers, and exacerbated boom-bust cycles in housing prices.

Certainly, U.S. mortgage markets had very serious flaws before the 1990s, especially in terms of continual disparities in access to credit across race and space. However, many of the policy solutions to these problems—especially increased enforcement of fair lending and community reinvestment laws—were just beginning to gain headway in the early to middle 1990s when the first boom in subprime lending came along, largely eviscerating many of the gains made under these policies, which had already been limited by flaws in design and inconsistent enforcement. Notwithstanding strong, repeated signs that deregulation was resulting in serious problems of mortgage abuse, increases in market risk and foreclosures, and disparate access and pricing among different segments of the population, bank regulators and policymakers continued to tout the purported benefits of deregulation and "market innovation" with little scrutiny of these supposed benefits or considerations of the costs.

In this chapter I focus on the development of the government-supervised, risk-limited mortgage market, as well as the creeping move over the last quarter of the twentieth century toward deregulation and increasingly unsupervised market innovations, many of which fed directly into the excesses and abuses of the late 1990s and 2000s. The timeline of mortgage market development and change is not one of bright lines and clear boundaries, although there are certainly periods during which change occurred quite rapidly. Rather, different outside forces—including those based in technology, policy, and demography—were occurring, often simultaneously, and were interacting with each other to produce new financial products and practices, changes in the structure of the financial services industry, and various market opportunities—and often vulnerabilities—among homeowners and would-be homeowners in different parts of the country.

Since at least the early 1920s, the federal government has been a supporting—and sometimes catalyzing or initiating—actor in the promotion of homeownership for a broader segment of society. Beginning with various forms of homeownership boosterism and then moving fairly quickly into intervention and innovation in mortgage markets, Congress and the executive branch became key partners in the development, expansion, and direction of homeownership and mortgage finance.

Pre-Hoover Home Finance

Before the 1930s, many Americans, even many with decent incomes, found it quite challenging to borrow sufficient funds to purchase a home. The homeownership rate at the turn of the century was just above 46 percent and, despite the very large economic expansion of the 1920s, it had climbed to only just under 48 percent by 1930.[1] When compared to the homeownership rate of some other countries, including the United Kingdom, this rate was not particularly low, but this was partly attributable to the relatively rural nature of the United States at the time

---

1. Reliable data on homeownership rates between decennial censuses at the national level are not available for the 1920s. The real estate sector had slowed down in the late 1920s, before the stock market crash of late 1929 (Fisher 1950). Therefore, it is very likely that the homeownership rate in the 1920s peaked before 1930. However, it is unlikely that it hit rates substantially above 50 percent given the substantial barriers to ownership.

(homeownership rates in cities tended to be lower than in rural areas) and to the desire of recent immigrants in the United States to own their own home (Harris and Hamnett 1987). Moreover, up until 1940 the U.S. homeownership rate remained relatively low compared to post–World War II levels.

The structure of homeownership finance certainly played a key role in the relatively limited extent of homeownership before the 1930s. Going further back, to the early nineteenth century, institutional lending for homeownership was relatively rare, and generally dates back to the first terminating building society in 1831 (Fisher 1950; Lea 1996). For the nonaffluent, owner occupancy was usually achieved during this preinstitutional period either through a combination of doing much of one's own construction, extensive household savings, borrowing from individuals, and land contract financing (Weiss 1989). Land contracts are essentially rent-to-own schemes in which the buyer does not gain ownership of the home until he makes many years of what are essentially rent payments. If payments are missed, the buyer is evicted and has no equity in the property and no right to redeem it in any way. Land contract sales were frequently used by land subdividers, who would sell parcels to families on which they could build their own house, and by developer-builders well into the twentieth century. They were also used to transfer property between individuals as a form of seller financing.

It is no coincidence that institutional lending in the United States and in England developed alongside the Second Industrial Revolution and large-scale urbanization in the late nineteenth century and early twentieth century (Mason 2004). Rural homesteaders faced fewer obstacles to home building and ownership than urban households. Land was relatively inexpensive and materials could be harvested off the land for the most part. As cities grew and land values rose, working class and modest-income families could rarely afford to buy land and build a house without some sort of financing over time.

At least through the 1970s, it is arguable that no single type of institutional mortgage lender was more important to the development of government-supervised, risk-limited mortgage markets than the building and loan (B&L), later called the savings and loan (S&L). This is not due solely to the fact that the B&L became a major provider of mortgage credit but also because of its direct and indirect effects on the structure of home finance and the mortgage market itself.

Historians tend to point to the Oxford Provident Building Association, established in 1831 in what is now Philadelphia, as the nation's first B&L

(Hoffman 2001; Lea 1996; Mason 2004). The early B&Ls were actually local "terminating building societies." Those joining a terminating B&L would make regular payments on shares they purchased in the B&L as a form of savings. Once enough capital was accumulated in the B&L to build or purchase a house, the capital was auctioned off to the member willing to pay the highest interest. The resulting payments by the borrower were then distributed to members as dividends. Once everyone had paid for their loans in full, the organization closed its doors.

By the latter half of the nineteenth century, permanent B&Ls began forming. These institutions allowed shareholders to vary the amounts of their contributions more easily and to vary the timing of share payments and withdrawals. They also began the practice of setting up reserve funds—loan loss reserves—to prepare for potential loan defaults and losses.

The primary purpose of early building and loans was not to earn a profit, at least not directly, but rather to promote homeownership. In many cases, local merchants and businessmen helped organize them in order to stimulate residential and economic development. At the same time, many participants and organizers saw the promotion of savings and loans, and the resulting homeownership, as the development of a movement more than an industry (Lea 1996; Mason 2004). Building and loans were local institutions, with members all living in the same area and many of them knowing each other. This social and geographic cohesiveness gave them an informational advantage that kept underwriting costs and defaults low.

Time deposits—the equivalent of certificates of deposit today—were introduced by B&Ls in the late nineteenth century and were offered at fixed terms. This created greater funding and liquidity in the mortgage system and allowed for more pooling of risk. Borrowers and savers benefited from economies of scale as the organizations grew. Yet, once B&Ls began offering deposit services to nonborrowers, they lost some of their inherent peer-lending enforcement advantages. Depositors and borrowers were decoupled–so that losses from defaulting borrowers were spread over more depositors. By 1931, of the twelve million savings and loan members in twelve thousand institutions, only two million had home loans (Hoffman 2001, 154). This created the need for the B&L to act more like a bank and rely more on staff to assess the quality of loans rather than rely primarily on peer pressure. Moreover, providing dividends to depositors became more important than the original goal of maximizing homeownership.

Mutual savings banks were similar in form to the B&L, except that they were organized primarily to encourage thrift and savings among those of modest means, not for making mortgages. They did, however, have a stimulating effect on mortgage lending because many of their assets were invested in mortgages even before they became direct lenders themselves. Mutual savings banks actually preceded B&Ls in the United States, with states chartering them as early as 1816 (Hoffman 2001, 152). Later, in the 1850s, they entered the mortgage market and soon became the largest source of mortgage funds until surpassed by B&Ls in the 1920s (Lea 1996).

Life insurance and mortgage companies were also important providers of mortgages in the late nineteenth century. Mortgage companies made loans and then sold either individual loans (i.e., what would now be called "whole loan" sales) or bonds backed by the loans to investors (Frederickson 1894; Snowden 2008). However, the bonds sold by mortgage companies were not like the mortgage-backed securities that became so common in the late twentieth century. These bonds more closely resembled corporate bonds because they remained general obligations of the originating mortgage company and the underlying mortgages remained on the books of the mortgage company. However, the mortgages were still pledged as collateral for the bonds. By contrast, modern mortgage-backed securities, which dominated mortgage markets in the 1990s and 2000s, were isolated in "special purpose vehicles" separate from the originating mortgage company. The nineteenth-century mortgage companies also often serviced the loans they originated; because the loans remained on their books, they had more reason to be concerned with the quality of the underlying mortgages than is the case with the later mortgage-backed securities of the late twentieth century that allowed lenders to take loans off their balance sheets. This older type of mortgage bond—often called a debenture or "covered" bond—was not a new innovation in the United States; it had been used in France and Germany from at least the early nineteenth century (Lea 1996; Snowden 2008).

But even with the importation of mortgage bond financing, many loans originated by mortgage companies were sold individually to investors and not financed as bonds as late as the end of the nineteenth century. In an 1894 study of both home and farm indebtedness, Frederickson estimated that a large majority of mortgages were held by individuals, and not by institutions (Frederickson 1894). Figure 1.1 shows that institutional investors accounted for a little over a quarter of mortgage debt held in the United States as of 1892.

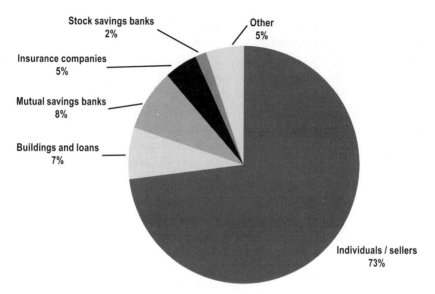

Figure 1.1. Holders of mortgage debt in the United States, 1892.
Source: Frederickson, 1894.

Frederickson also examined more closely the locations of investors in seventeen counties across five largely rural states (Alabama, Illinois, Kansas, Tennessee, and Iowa), finding that 48 percent of the debt in these counties was held by residents of the same state as the property. Mortgage agents or companies often originated mortgages but then quickly sold them—often as "whole" loans to individual investors in nearby areas.

Although the source of most mortgage credit in the late nineteenth century was local, at least three sources were not: insurance companies, national building and loans, and mortgage bond investors. Mortgage companies issuing mortgage bonds grew during the 1890s, but largely failed during the recession of the mid-to-late 1890s. Lea (1996) suggests that mortgage bond investors—even in the case of the older debenture-style bonds—suffered from problems of "asymmetric information" vis-à-vis the mortgage company originator selling the bonds. The originator had an incentive to pass off riskier loans as collateral for its mortgage bonds, as purchasers of individual loans were more likely to scrutinize the details of the underlying loan. As we shall see, this is a recurring problem in the buying and selling of loans after they are originated. The selling party often has an advantage in access to information about the loans compared to the buyer, and has a financial incentive not to reveal this additional information. This problem continued into the securitization era and was exaggerated as securitization structures became more complex and less transparent.

The national building and loans also suffered during the economic downturns of the 1890s (Lea 1996; Mason 2004). By the late 1880s, the national B&L had arrived. These entities were typically formed by bankers and industrialists in large cities. They were for-profit lenders whose stock was often closely held. National B&Ls used agents or promoters to sell shares and formed local branches in smaller cities and rural areas. Thus, they were able to pool savings from across disparate and numerous communities, which by themselves may have lacked sufficient capital to constitute strong local B&Ls. Moreover, unlike many local B&Ls, voting control was allocated by share of outstanding stock, giving wealthy founders more control of these organizations. However, the more aggressive profit-seeking nature of national B&Ls was accompanied by higher operating expenses, which ran at 6 to 11 percent of revenues, compared to just 1 to 2 percent for local B&Ls (Mason 2004).

The growth of the national B&L movement was a rapid one. Almost three hundred nationals existed by 1893, and branches of national B&Ls spread to every state (Mason 2004). Their downfall was even swifter. By the late 1890s, failures mounted rapidly. National B&Ls had relied heavily on excessive and sometimes abusive pricing and terms for large portions of their revenue, on both the lending and deposit sides of the business. Later on, it became apparent that the industry was riddled with self-dealing and undue enrichment of officers and executives. Mason (2004) recalls one Minneapolis national that had assets of $2.1 million but spent $1.2 million in expenses in only seven years of operation and another that had only $170,000 of assets but spent $40,000 annually on operating costs.

Mason (2004) argues that a key positive outcome of the national B&L failures was that leaders of the B&L industry became aware of the economic benefits provided by government regulation. They also realized the importance of the need for capital reserves to protect against falling real estate prices.

Despite the failures of national B&Ls and many bond-funded mortgage companies during the 1890s, institutional lenders as a whole rebounded in the early twentieth century (Weiss 1989). Besides local B&Ls, life insurance companies were also significant lenders and managed to avoid many of the problems of other national-scale lenders. While national banks were restricted from making mortgage loans until the 1920s, state banks had begun entering the market. By 1914, 25 percent of loans and 15 percent of state-chartered bank assets were in real estate (Snowden 1994).

In addition to the first-lien mortgages made by institutional lenders, a good deal of mortgage debt in the pre-Hoover era was made up of second mortgages, many of which were made by builders and developers, or their affiliates, which had an interest in making homeownership more feasible. These parties would make subordinate loans at very high interest rates—as high as 20 percent or more—to homebuyers for a quarter or a fifth of the purchase price. Because the institutional lender often did not finance more than 50 or 60 percent of the price, this still left a very substantial requirement for a down payment from the buyer.

B&Ls grew significantly in the early twentieth century, supported to some degree by state-level regulation that had begun in the late nineteenth century, and maintained their emphasis on homeownership finance. Figures 1.2 and 1.3 show the growth in the number of B&Ls and their cumulative assets, respectively, from 1888 to 1937. The number of B&Ls grew quite quickly in the late 1880s and early 1890s, but the turbulent economic times of the 1890s and the first decade of the 1900s meant that

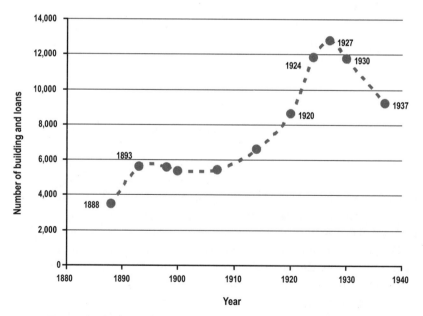

Figure 1.2. Number of building and loans in the United States, 1888–1937.
Source: Mason, 2004.

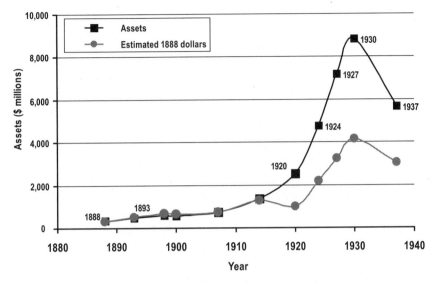

Figure 1.3. Total assets of building and loans in the United States, 1888–1937.
Source: Nominal dollar amounts from Mason (2004);
constant dollar amounts calculated by author.

the number of B&Ls ebbed over this period. After the Panic of 1907 and during the World War I era, the number of B&Ls grew at a steady pace, though the real value of their total assets remained relatively flat. In the boom period of the early 1920s, B&Ls grew quite rapidly in both number and real assets, buttressed by the social and cultural mores that favored homeownership and by the general boom in real estate and the economy.

Although the nominal assets of B&Ls grew rapidly during the 1920s, this was an inflationary period, so that the real value of B&L assets did not grow quite so fast. With the real estate problems of the late 1920s and the advent of the Great Depression, after 1930 the number of B&Ls began to decline as did their total assets. Notwithstanding this decline, at the beginning of the Great Depression savings and loans held about one-third of the outstanding home mortgages in the United States (Hoffman 2001, 155). Moreover, some financial institutions, including most commercial banks, fared even worse than B&Ls in the early 1930s, in part because bank depositors could withdraw their funds more quickly than those who held B&L shares, which exacerbated bank runs and failures.

Within the mix of suppliers of mortgage credit in the early twentieth century, there were significant differences in the structure and nature of credit provided by various types of lenders. B&Ls provided longer-term loans with higher loan-to-value ratios than banks or insurance companies. In the 1920s, the average term of mortgages was eleven years for those written by B&Ls, versus six to eight for those from insurance companies and two to three for those from commercial banks (Lea 1996). Average loan-to-value ratios were 60 percent for B&Ls and 50 percent for those from other lenders. The shorter term, interest-only loans with relatively low loan-to-value ratios made by banks and insurance companies were known as "straight" mortgages. Homeowners with these loans had to take out new loans much more frequently, and so would incur the upfront costs associated with borrowing more frequently. The limited loan-to-value ratios of these loans typically required the involvement of a substantial second mortgage, which came with very high fees and interest rates (Gries and Ford 1932, 28). They were typically offered by "marginal participants" in the financial industry and were often unregulated and operated in violation of state usury laws.

Even before Herbert Hoover and the federal government began promoting homeownership as a social and economic goal in American life, the B&L industry had attempted to spread the gospel of homeownership—with the B&L as the core of that gospel—through advocacy of its own. Some observers have suggested that the B&L movement was at least partially linked to the social reformers of the late nineteenth and early twentieth centuries (Mason 2004). B&L leaders seized upon the appalling housing conditions of urban slums and tenements of the late nineteenth and early twentieth centuries that had been revealed by reformers such as Laurence Veillor and Jacob Riis. It is not clear that these reformers viewed homeownership as a solution to the housing problems of the poor. However, the broader working classes also suffered from housing problems; the B&Ls argued they could help attain stable homeownership and better living conditions for the "classes above the lowest" (Robert Treat Paine Jr., in Mason 2004, 42). Another feature of B&Ls that was consistent with the concerns of social reformers was the assimilation of immigrants. By encouraging thrift and hard work, the logic went, immigrants would turn away from the vices that reformers had sought to discourage.

The Camel's Nose: The Federal Government and Homeownership

Up until World War I, any intentional role of the federal government in promoting homeownership was very limited. At the end of World War I, however, about the time of the Bolshevik Revolution and the Red Scare, there was a coming together of ideological and financial interests that focused first on a propagandizing and educational approach to promoting homeownership through a variety of means that fell short of direct involvement in the financing of owner-occupied homes. The National Association of Real Estate Boards (later, the National Association of Realtors) had organized its own Buy a Home campaign in 1914 only to dissolve it in 1916 due to wartime restrictions on building (Hornstein 2005). But as soon as the war ended in 1918, it seized on concerns about communism and collectivism by first reigniting its homeownership promotion efforts and then teaming up with the U.S. Department of Labor to begin the national Own-Your-Own-Home campaign. In addition to Realtors, local chambers of commerce were heavily supportive of these campaigns in part because homeownership suggested a more stable and more locally captive labor force.

In 1921, Hebert Hoover became secretary of commerce under President Warren Harding and took charge of the federal government's role in housing policy, developing within the Commerce Department a research and educational capacity with a heavy focus on promoting homeownership. The department distributed an Own-Your-Own-Home brochure to millions and organized local housing conferences in concert with local business groups (Hutchinson 2000). Hoover even argued early on for government involvement in financing homes to reduce the reliance on very high-cost second mortgages. But until the 1932 creation of the Federal Home Loan Bank system, the federal government's role in promoting homeownership did not entail any substantial role in the financing process.

Hoover and the Department of Commerce continued to promote ownership of single-family homes through a number of means, including the Better Homes in America movement and the Architect's Small House Service Bureau (Hutchinson 2000; Vale 2007). The first program was a national competition in which local committees organized and promoted competitions in which schools, chambers of commerce, and others would design and build a model home in their communities. The Architect's Small House Service Bureau was an independent organization sponsored by the Department of Commerce to promulgate higher quality plans for home construction throughout the country.

The 1930s marked the watershed of strong, direct federal involvement in U.S. mortgage markets. The massive failures of banks during the Great Depression and the collapse of the housing and construction markets provided the context for the establishment of some important agencies and programs. The policies and practices of these institutions had a tremendous impact on the long-term landscape of mortgage and financial services in the United States.

Initial federal activism in the mortgage market is often attributed to Roosevelt's New Deal. To be sure, the 1934 National Housing Act, which created the Federal Housing Administration (FHA), was one of the most important pieces of housing legislation in the twentieth century. However, it followed the Federal Home Loan Bank Act of 1932, which President Hoover proposed and signed. This bill created the Home Loan Bank system to provide liquidity to savings and loans to increase their role in the mortgage market. Hoover and others saw the longer-term, higher loan-to-value amortizing mortgage provided by savings and loans as a key tool in promoting homeownership and stimulating the housing market (Hoffman 2001, 159–62). The law gave the federal government a much larger role in promoting and standardizing the mortgage market. Government not only authorized but also invested in the creation of the new secondary-market institutions. The federal government initially capitalized the Home Loan Banks, and the member institutions were required to purchase small amounts of stock to gradually become the owners of the banks.

The Home Loan Bank system fostered a new standardization and federal endorsement of the B&L-type loan. It was also the first direct government vehicle for dealing with the long-term/short-term liquidity mismatch that faced B&Ls with short-term deposits. By allowing banks to "rediscount" their mortgage assets, the government was creating liquidity, thereby stimulating the mortgage and housing market. Beyond subsidizing and stimulating the longer-term B&L mortgage, the Home Loan Bank system responded to the credit allocation imbalances present in the B&L system. Because B&Ls were generally local institutions, imbalances could arise in terms of the supply and demand for credit across the country. Some areas, especially growing ones, might have an excess demand for mortgages, whereas older parts of the country might have an excess supply of savings and investment available to fund them. By providing for a system of routinized inter-B&L borrowing, the Home Loan Bank system allowed more money to flow around the country (Hoffman 2001, 163).

Like most government policy regarding financial markets, the Home Loan Bank bill was contested. Insurance companies and mortgage companies who viewed B&Ls as competitors and did not provide the B&L form of loan argued against the bill. They claimed that the Home Loan Banks were unnecessary and encouraged unsound lending with overly long maturities and excessive loan-to-value ratios. They argued that the nonamortizing straight mortgage—essentially a short-term (3–7 years), interest-only loan—was proper finance. By encouraging longer-term mortgages, Home Loan Bank opponents argued, the Home Loan Banks would encourage precisely the sort of overbuilding that helped cause the Depression in the first place.

When Franklin Roosevelt was elected, he pushed for more aggressive interventions in the housing market. The Home Loan Banks did little for homeowners who were losing their homes through foreclosures, which were occurring at the rate of one thousand per day. Moreover, because they were wholesale institutions, the banks were perceived as benefiting only lenders and not borrowers. In fact, they were vulnerable to this charge, in part because, although the Act did call for direct lending, the banks did not have any such capacity.

High interest rates were a particular problem during the Depression because the country was experiencing deflation. When deflation occurs, nominal interest rates should become very low or negative, yet in reality they do not, so borrowers are in effect experiencing very high interest rates. The high real interest rates and the devastated economy meant that house prices fell, while outstanding loan amounts did not, so that owners were left with very high loan-to-value ratios. And then, of course, foreclosures led to even greater effective housing supply, lower prices, and a vicious cycle of housing market decline.

Rather than merely reorganizing the Home Loan Banking system to suit the demands for more direct assistance to homeowners, Roosevelt and Congress passed the Home Owners Loan Act (HOLA) of 1933. A primary purpose of HOLA was to pull people out of foreclosure by purchasing delinquent loans from lenders and restructure them to prevent foreclosure by directly refinancing people at risk of foreclosure. Another key purpose was to stabilize B&Ls and other lenders by allowing them to essentially rid themselves of many defaulted loans.

HOLA created the Home Owners Loan Corporation (HOLC), which purchased mortgages in default from lenders using funds raised in the bond market. HOLC also made refinance loans directly to homeowners, with the intent of providing a more manageable loan (Crossney and Bartelt 2005). It was capitalized and owned by the federal government and governed by the Federal Home Loan Bank Board. To enable homeowners to remain in their homes, HOLC used long-term federal bonds to buy the loans, extend the term of loans, and lower monthly payments. Up to 80 percent of the loans were fully amortizing over fifteen years (Hoffman 2001, 168–70).

HOLC has generally been perceived as successful. It made loans from 1933 to 1936 and did not incur substantial losses over the long term. The HOLC received 1.9 million loan applications. This accounted for approximately 40 percent of homes with residential mortgages during the period (Doan 1997). The HOLC funded approximately one million loans for a total of $3.1 billion. Thus HOLC served approximately 20 percent of homeowners with existing mortgages, a remarkable number. By 1935, HOLC held 12 percent of the country's outstanding residential mortgage debt (Colton 2002). About 20 percent of HOLC borrowers ended up defaulting, but given the times and the adverse selection designed into the program, this might be considered a default rate well below what might have been expected, and more importantly it seems to be well below what would have happened to these borrowers without HOLC intervention. Green and Wachter (2007) point out that HOLC's success was due in part to "good timing" because it was able to take short-term, adjustable-rate loans with balloon payments and convert them into long-term, fixed-rate amortizing loans.

The HOLC has been accused of institutionalizing redlining practices through the use of its risk-rating maps. However, recent research suggests that the agency did not disseminate their risk-rating maps, did not cooperate with the FHA in its fairly aggressive redlining practices, and actually made many loans in areas that it rated as high risk (Crossney and Bartelt 2005).

HOLA also created the federal savings and loan (S&L) charter in large part to provide a vehicle for the establishment of what were formally called building and loans in places where none existed and is generally credited with institutionalizing the term S&L. In addition, the federal government through the Home Loan Bank Board could invest in the establishment of new federally chartered S&Ls. The establishment of the federal S&L charter increased the standardization and professionalization of S&Ls, shifting them in the direction of becoming an "industry" rather than a "movement" of community-based financial institutions (Hoffman 2001; Mason 2004). Originally, S&Ls referred to deposits as "shares," much like the credit union movement still does. Later, the terminology changed to "savings accounts."

The next major development in federal mortgage policy was the National Housing Act of 1934. The chief content of the 1934 Act was the creation of Federal Housing Administration mortgage insurance, which has had a major influence on mortgage lending practices and patterns since the 1930s. The FHA was created in large part to stimulate job creation. But the FHA was responsible for introducing a key credit enhancement that had a strong direct effect on credit availability and served as a model for modern private mortgage insurance, which became a critical tool in assisting homebuyers with less than 20 percent equity to purchase a house.

In addition to offering mortgage insurance, the FHA established the twenty- and later thirty-year, fully amortizing, fixed-rate mortgage with an 80 percent loan-to-value ratio as the dominant, standardized mortgage format for the remainder of the twentieth century. FHA loans also increased the standardization of mortgages generally, setting the stage for the eventual expansion of secondary-market activity and securitization that dominated the last quarter of the twentieth century. FHA was an innovator and leader in the standardization and commoditization of mortgage credit.

The legacy of the FHA is an excellent example of how government involvement and innovation in financial markets led so-called private-sector developments. In fact, it is hard to call almost any major, successful development in mortgage markets wholly private; most were initiated and/or encouraged in some substantial way by public policies and programs. This is the nature of housing credit. It is not that the FHA "invented" the concept of mortgage insurance, for example. In fact, mortgage insurance had been used as far back as the late nineteenth century by mortgage companies to improve the marketability of the loans that they sold to investors. Rather, it is the financial and institutionalizing power of government and government-sponsored entities that makes their involvement in mortgage markets so influential and that leads to standardization and the widespread adoption of products and practices.

FHA mortgage insurance increased the supply of mortgage credit and allowed for predictable, low-risk, long-term financing, making the true effective costs of financing lower and reducing the risks to borrowers due to uncertainties regarding the availability and pricing of credit in the future. From the 1930s to the 1940s, the average term for mortgages made by S&Ls increased from eleven years to fifteen years (Lea 1996). For insurance companies, who were larger FHA users, the average term increased from six to eight years to twenty years. Overall, the average loan-to-value for mortgages increased from less than 60 percent to 75 percent, and the bulk of loans became fully amortizing, helping homeowners to build equity over time.

The impact of the FHA on the overall housing market was very large. By 1937, FHA housing starts accounted for 45 percent of all housing starts in the United States (Jackson 1985, 326). From 1935 to 1939, FHA insured loans accounted for 23 percent of single-family lending (Vandell 1995). This share grew to 45 percent during the years 1940 to 1944, while accounting for 22 percent of outstanding residential mortgage debt by 1945 (Klaman 1961; Vandell 1995).

The end of World War II saw the advent of the Veterans Administration (VA) program. Within one year after the war, VA-guaranteed mortgages had increased from 1 percent to 9 percent of outstanding residential mortgage debt (Klaman 1961). From 1945 to 1956, during the peak of the postwar suburbanization boom, VA loans accounted for 35 percent of net new mortgage flows, with the FHA accounting for another 14 percent. Together, these two government programs accounted for approximately half of all single-family mortgages being made in the United States during the postwar decade.

Due to the VA program's attractive features, the FHA share dropped sharply. The FHA program gradually declined in significance until the late 1960s when Congress authorized a substantial expansion of FHA activity, including a major subsidized loan component. By 1970, FHA loans still accounted for almost 30 percent of single-family loans.

Although the FHA was generally initiated as a program to stimulate the construction industry, it was later modified to support various segments of the housing sector. During and after World War II, more specialized FHA programs were created to increase the supply of military housing, national defense housing, urban renewal housing, nursing homes, mobile home parks, and housing for the elderly, among others (Vandell 1995). As government-sponsored secondary markets expanded the conventional mortgage market, and S&Ls offered more long-term fixed-rate mortgages, some of the demand for FHA, particularly among middle-income borrowers, declined. The fees charged by the FHA created an adverse selection problem in which only higher-risk borrowers were targeted by FHA lenders, creating a market more segmented by income and risk. To some, this segmentation seemed appropriate, as government intervention in the market for middle-income homebuyers seemed unnecessary during the generally good economic times of the 1950s and 1960s. However, the FHA program was traditionally seen as "actuarially sound," which meant that it would be self-funding from its fees and premiums and not require outside funds from the U.S. Treasury. From the middle 1960s to 1969, the median value of FHA-financed units dropped from 14 percent below the national median home value to 24 percent below the national median.

The powerful postwar involvement of the FHA and the VA in the mortgage market was also associated with a shift—at least for a while—away from the conventional S&L circuit and toward the FHA/VA housing finance circuit, in which insurance companies and commercial banks were major deliverers of capital to the mortgage market. (S&Ls were relatively smaller players in the FHA and VA loan market.) Insurance companies, which in the past had purchased individual loans or invested in mortgage company debentures, now began to develop correspondent relationships with mortgage companies, in which they would agree to purchase pools of loans from the mortgage companies. These were not mortgage-backed securities, which came later, but literally bulk purchases of loans that the insurance company agreed to purchase once they were made by the mortgage company (Klaman 1961).

After introducing FHA insurance and before creating the VA loan, the federal government created the Federal National Mortgage Association (now known as Fannie Mae) in 1938 to create a secondary market in FHA-insured loans. Fannie Mae allowed a new form of intermediation between nondepository mortgage originators such as mortgage companies and investment capital from other sources. This meant that a new source of capital became available for the mortgage market, often benefiting from implicit guarantees from a government corporation. In 1968, Fannie Mae became a "government-sponsored enterprise" (GSE), meaning a for-profit, privately owned corporation that is subject to some—albeit limited—federal oversight and receives various forms of federal subsidy. Fannie was able to raise capital through the sale of common stock to the public. Its mission also changed to focus on providing liquidity to the non-GSE, or conventional, mortgage market.

Thus, the two major "circuits" for housing finance developed in the United States both relied heavily on federal intervention and support over the course of their development. The S&L circuit was supported by deposit insurance and the Home Loan Banks provided a critical source of liquidity, while also drawing some support from FHA and VA programs. Second, mortgage companies, commercial banks, and insurance companies made loans supported by FHA and VA programs and later by Fannie Mae and Freddie Mac (the Federal Home Loan Mortgage Corporation). Before the 1960s, the FHA/VA circuit was particularly important. Beginning in the late 1960s, as VA and FHA programs declined in their overall share of mortgages, the S&L circuit grew more dominant. This generally persisted until the 1980s and the explosion of the GSE secondary markets and securitization, which essentially superseded the old FHA/VA circuit and once again favored nonlocal lenders such as mortgage companies. In both circuits, the public sector seeded, nurtured, and was largely responsible for the size and functioning of mortgage markets, and especially for the dominance of the long-term fixed-rate mortgage.

The Rise of Securitization

Over 2007 and 2008, as the mortgage crisis gained national prominence, many readers of daily newspapers were introduced to the term "mortgage securitization" for the first time. Those more familiar with the workings of mortgage markets, however, were already well acquainted with a set of practices that went back—in one form or another—almost forty years. Put most simply and broadly, securitization is a process in which funding of—or investments in—mortgage loans is separated from the origination (and originator) of the loans. The loans stand, together in pools with many other loans, "on their own" and are no longer tied to the fate of the originating lender. A key objective of securitization is to isolate the loans that provide the cash that eventually flows to the investors from the originating lender. In general, the alternative is either for the loans to be sold as individual "whole loans" to buyers who assume these loans as individual loans that they (or their agent) then service, or for the loan to remain on the balance sheet of the lender. Debenture sales, like those used by the early mortgage companies, are still an option, but have not been widely used in the United States.

Securitization led directly to the widespread "vertical disintegration" of the lending process (Jacobides 2005). It enabled the origination process to be separated from the process of funding and servicing the loan. This process has also been called the unbundling of the mortgage process, although the term unbundling is less precise and can refer to several different mortgage market processes. Vertical disintegration meant that more contractual relationships were now required between originators, issuers of the securities, investors that purchased the securities, credit rating agencies, servicers, and other mortgage market participants. In the dominant S&L circuit, these functions were generally integrated within the local S&L that originated, funded, and serviced the loan.

Securitization, in its various forms, was spurred and fostered by a variety of deregulatory and tax policy changes over roughly a twenty-five-year period. As securitization structures became more complex and introduced greater layers of vertical disintegration between the sources and uses of credit, more highly engineered, and more complex, securitiza-tion structures enabled higher and higher levels of default risk to be tolerated at the point of origination. These greater complexities and degrees of separation between sources and uses of credit also obscured the underlying characteristics of borrowers and mortgages and increased the frictions between different parties in the chain of capital.

Mortgage securitization has often been portrayed as a private-sector financial innovation. Yet, it was the Government National Mortgage Association (Ginnie Mae), the federal agency that facilitates the purchase of FHA loans, that issued the first residential mortgage-backed securities (RMBS) in 1970, guaranteeing interest and principal payments on pools of FHA- and Veterans Administration–insured mortgages. In the middle 1970s, Ginnie Mae also spurred the use of RMBS by directly subsidizing below-market-rate RMBS so that investors would get market-rate returns (Geisst 1990, 91–93). RMBS further increased the number and types of investors in the mortgage market, as well as the number of new lenders in the market. Also in 1970, the Emergency Home Finance Act created the Federal Home Loan Mortgage Corporation, now Freddie Mac, to provide secondary-market capacity for Home Loan Bank system members and allowed Fannie Mae and Freddie Mac to perform secondary-market operations for conventional mortgages.

The first generation of RMBS was the "pass-through" security. Prior to the development of pass-through RMBS, lenders frequently sought to convert loans into cash in order to replenish their cash available for lending and to reduce a variety of risks that can come from holding a large amount of long-term mortgages on their balance sheets. But to do this, lenders would have to sell the mortgages that they had originated one at a time. This was expensive and cumbersome.

Ginnie Mae, and later Fannie Mae and Freddie Mac, reduced the transaction costs of converting loans into cash. They purchased the loans and assembled them into pools of similar types of loans. These pools also enabled the diversification of risk by including loans from many lenders and different regions. They then issued bonds or "certificates" in which the cash flow generated by the loans in the pool was passed through to the investors in a pro rata fashion. This was a fairly straightforward and trans-parent process. Again, in addition to the diversification of loans across lenders and regions, a major apparent advantage for investors of these new securities compared to the old-fashioned debenture issued by mortgage companies before the Great Depression was the fact that these bonds were not as exposed to the risk of the originating lender going bankrupt.

There are variations on the pass-through structure, including one in which the GSE or Ginnie Mae does not actually purchase the loans but guarantees the loan pool that is assembled by another issuing firm. Regardless of the details, this sort of pass-through security does not involve any complex hierarchical structuring into different layers of risk and thus such "single-class" pass-throughs are typically not classified as part of what are know as "structured finance" vehicles.

Pass-through RMBS, though assisting in geographically diversifying the underlying default risk that investors would face, did little to deal with another sort of risk facing investors: prepayment timing risk. When interest rates decline, borrowers prepay their loan by refinancing. This can hurt pass-through RMBS investors who had hoped for an ongoing, predictable income stream from the RMBS. And because interest rates are generally lower, it will be difficult for these investors to find an investment opportunity that will generate the same sort of return at similar levels of overall risk as the original investment in the security.

At least partly in order to deal with this problem, Freddie Mac issued the first collateralized mortgage obligation (CMO) in 1983 (Green and Wachter 2007). A CMO is a more complicated form of RMBS than a pass-through because it allocates prepayment risk across different investors—some of whom are more willing to accept such risks than others—by structuring the security into different segments that pay back over varying schedules. Also, CMOs offer the ability to create a vertical hierarchy of default risk by allowing some bondholders to receive their principal back before others and some more risk-tolerant bond holders to bear losses associated with defaults of the underlying loans before the holders of less risky senior bonds. These different levels of risk, which are usually accompanied by varying rates of investment return, are generally called "tranches" (French for "slices") and are generally classified according to the rating they receive from the credit rating agencies, such as AAA, AA, A, BBB, BB, B, and so forth.

Figure 1.4 illustrates the basic structure of a CMO mortgage security and indicates the roles of different parties in the mortgage funding and investment process. As is the case with a pass-through RMBS, CMO securitization allowed originating lenders to fund loans with access to only short-term debt from "warehouse lenders" rather than from a ready source of deposits on which a bank or S&L might rely. Increasingly, beginning in the 1980s, lenders used independent mortgage brokers to market and bring loan applications to them for final underwriting and origination. Some lenders use both "retail" (where they take applications

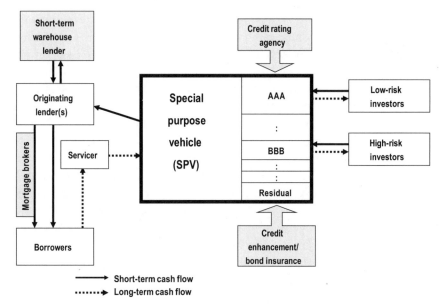

Figure 1.4. Cash flows in a collateralized mortgage obligation (CMO) securitization.

directly within the lending organization) and "wholesale" (where they accept applications via brokers) operations to make loans.

Once the lender assembled a substantial pool of loans for sale, it sold the loans to what was called a special purpose vehicle, or SPV, which effectively removed the loans from the lender's balance sheet. The SPV was typically set up by an investment bank, which then structures the RMBS. The loans were formally held by a trust. The loan repayments flowing from the pool of loans were then distributed per the securitization agreements to different investors in different ways and with varying priorities.

Within the CMO structure, the principal and interest payments from the pooled loans were allocated to the different tranches depending on the securitization structure. In one common type of CMO, the most senior tranche AAA investors received all principal payments before any principal payments were paid to more junior (e.g., AA or below) investors. In this way, the lower-level investors (with lower-rated bonds) did not receive any principal payments until the higher-level investors had been completely paid off. The CMO became the dominant form of non-GSE RMBS in the 1990s and was used to fuel the initial subprime boom described in chapter 3.

Other entities beyond the issuer of the RMBS became very important. First, the tranched bonds were rated by a credit rating agency, typically Standard & Poors, Moody's, or Fitch. These firms evaluate risks on all sorts of debt instruments and provide ratings of such risks. It was important for them to have good information on the nature of the underlying loans in a RMBS. Another party that increasingly came into play as nonagency securitization grew was the bond insurance firms. Their role was to provide insurance for investors who invest in RMBS.

A typical subprime CMO capital structure is shown in figure 1.5. It shows that the senior tranche typically constituted approximately 80 percent of a subprime CMO structure. This debt was typically rated AAA by a credit rating agency and had first claim on all cash flow and collateral related to the mortgage pool. All losses on the loan pool were typically applied to the most junior class or tranche of investors remaining until the principal of that class was completely exhausted. At the bottom of the risk hierarchy in a CMO, the originating lenders typically held all or a portion of the most junior position, or equity tranche, as a form of credit enhancement to the more senior debt. This is frequently referred to as the "residual." This residual was essentially the amount of overcollateralization in the security. That is, the cumulative dollar amount of the bonds issued was some fraction (in the case of figure 1.5, the fraction is 98.1 percent) of the principal balance of the mortgage loans backing the bonds. In this way, the RMBS issuer, which may or may not have been the same entity as the originator of the loans, should have absorbed the initial losses of the mortgage pool. Theoretically, having the originator hold the residual should have encouraged originators to underwrite loans more carefully. However, as figure 1.5 shows, this residual was often quite modest. Moreover, in the 2000s some originators were able to sell off their residuals to investors in collateralized debt obligation arrangers.

Besides overcollateralization, senior tranche investors could also be protected from losses by other forms of credit enhancement to the RMBS. These included the use of excess spread, in which the loan payment cash flow exceeded payments to servicers and all investors, so that excess profit accrued to the equity tranche investors (to reward them for incurring greater risks). Typically, no losses were distributed to any higher-level investors until the excess spread was reduced to zero. Senior tranche investors were often further protected by the practice of "shifting interest," in which all principal payments were applied to senior tranches for an initial period (e.g., the first three years), during which time more junior investors received only the agreed upon interest (or coupon rate).

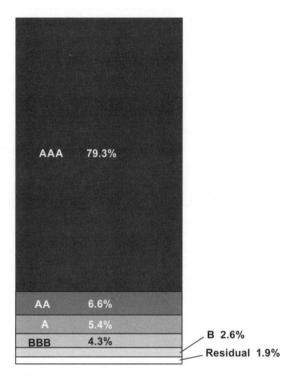

Figure 1.5. Typical subprime CMO tranche structure;
percent of principal balance of underlying mortgages.
Source: Ashcraft and Schuermann 2008; based on Bear Stearns data.

CMOs and similarly structured finance vehicles had an important impact on mortgage markets because they essentially peeled apart various types and degrees of risk and allocated these to different classes of investors depending on their appetite and tolerance for different sorts of risk. In this way, investors who would not invest in a pass-through security backed by loans exhibiting anything but the lowest default risks or were likely to prepay could invest in a bond that was designed to be highly secure. These AAA senior tranche bonds would provide relatively modest interest rates to investors, with lower-rated and riskier tranches earning higher interest rates. CMOs also served investors with different preferences for when they would receive their principal back and how much prepayment risk they would likely bear. In these ways, CMOs appealed to a broader segment of potential investors and drew more capital into mortgage markets. They also enabled the capital markets to provide credit to a wider spectrum of credit risk at the borrower end.

Thus, securitization encouraged what has been called "risk-based pricing" (although how accurately the pricing matched the risk is subject to debate) rather than the traditional system of "credit rationing," where essentially no institutional lender would lend to borrowers below certain more conservative risk thresholds. In the brave new world of securitization, the more innovation employed, and the more the mortgage cash flows were repackaged, the more risk could be tolerated in the home financing transaction. As the risk at the origination level increases, defaults and foreclosures increase, which can create substantial negative spillovers on communities and longer-term impacts on borrowers.

Through a combination of pass-through RMBS and CMOs, Fannie Mae and Freddie Mac served as buyer-holders of loans in their portfolios as well as conduits of mortgage capital from investors to lenders. Securitization via the GSEs offered several advantages to lenders. It provided greater diversification in risks in the value of the lender's assets, yielded more liquidity to lenders because these diversified assets are more marketable than whole loans, and redistributed credit supply across regions, so that regions with few local sources of credit suffered from fewer constraints on credit flows.

One consequence of the growth of securitization and the GSEs, however, was that S&Ls lost market share to mortgage companies that had gained access to inexpensive funds and were able to offer long-term, fixed-rate mortgages at competitive interest rates. The national scope of mortgage companies and their lack of branches allowed them to benefit from economies of scale and specialization. S&Ls were still both savings and lending institutions that had relied upon their local knowledge for competitive advantage. In the age of securitization, such advantages were made much less relevant by the commoditization and pooling of residential credit.

In its early forms at least, securitization promoted the standardization of mortgage terms and underwriting requirements. This standardization was accompanied by an increased supply of computer-processed and national-scale credit information systems, reducing the benefit of local information. And the scale and inherent subsidies of the secondary markets meant that they offered lenders lower-cost capital for making mortgages. Loans became more standardized and "one-size-fits-all." Mortgages increasingly resembled commodities rather than individualized products. These changes also resulted in growing economies of scale for most of the stages of the lending process, including funding and servicing. At the same time, these large new national lenders—mostly mortgage companies or bank-owned mortgage companies—developed more "wholesale" lending channels, in which they originated loans through large numbers of sometimes quite small-scale and often localized mortgage brokers.

Federal Policy in the Late Twentieth Century: Nurturing Securitization and Backdoor Deregulation

Although Fannie Mae was created in 1938 and Ginnie Mae and Freddie Mac introduced RMBS in 1970 and 1971, the eventual dominance of securitization in mortgage markets by the late twentieth century is perhaps best attributed to the federal financial deregulation of the early 1980s followed by some specific industry-supported legislation later in that decade. By explicitly favoring the securitization circuit over the traditionally dominant S&L circuit, federal policymakers provided crucial help in shifting the structure of the mortgage industry from a predominantly local to a predominantly national system and from one in which most loans were made by relatively more regulated lenders (S&Ls) to one in which predominantly unregulated mortgage companies and a growing set of essentially unregulated mortgage brokers dominated. Combined with the failure of policymakers and regulatory agencies to increase regulatory supervision of these emerging lenders, these moves meant that the path toward greater overall deregulation of the mortgage marketplace was indeed well paved by the middle to late 1980s. Moreover, legislators and regulators constructed policy that allowed for regulated depository institutions, especially commercial banks, to acquire or affiliate with these less regulated entities so that the new financial conglomerates could conduct most of their mortgage lending through less regulated and/or less supervised mortgage company subsidiaries and/or affiliates, thereby minimizing regulatory oversight.

A critical ingredient in the growth of securitization was the Depository Institutions Deregulation and Monetary Control Act (DIDMCA) of 1980, which phased in the general abolition of state usury limits on first mortgages by 1986. DIDMCA also extended the ability of national banks (those regulated by the Office of the Comptroller of the Currency, or OCC) to be governed only by the usury limits of their home state. This ability, labeled "interest rate exportation," allowed depositories to generally override state usury limits, and some form of exportation abilities were eventually given to most other types of depository institutions, including those not regulated by the OCC. The ability to export rates from low regulation states, which was given to national banks in a 1978 Supreme Court decision, made it harder to regulate from the state level and allowed large national lenders increased advantages in the marketplace, again increasing returns to scale in the industry (McCoy and Renuart 2008).

With the adoption of the Alternative Mortgage Transaction Parity Act (AMTPA) in 1982, federal policymakers continued their moves to override state consumer credit protections and make it easier to commoditize credit at a national scale, thus fueling large-scale delocalized lending sources. AMTPA overrode state laws that regulated various terms of "alternative" loans, including those with features such as adjustable interest rates and balloon payments. The law also allowed mortgage companies, which are primarily state regulated, to opt for federal regulations issued by the federal S&L regulator (now the Office of Thrift Supervision) rather than comply with the lending regulations of the state in which they were operating. Thus, AMTPA provided significant federal preemption to nondepository lenders, similar to the expanded federal preemption that DIDMCA had provided to depository institutions. And these nondepositories were precisely the sort that relied especially on securitization as a means of funding their loans. Ironically, DIDMCA and AMTPA were partly designed to help S&Ls recover from their struggles in the financial marketplace. In the long run at least, they most likely did the opposite.

The RMBS market grew during the decade, with RMBS issuance by Fannie Mae and Freddie Mac increasing from $14 billion in 1982 to $160 billion in 1986 (Chinloy 1995). Of course, in addition to the policy changes, the development of the CMO was a parallel factor in RMBS growth, but it is unlikely that this level of growth would have occurred without the deregulatory actions in DIDMCA and AMTPA.

The early 1980s were also important for laying the groundwork for later policy changes that directly supported mortgage securitization. In 1981, President Ronald Reagan created the President's Commission on Housing in part to look at housing finance problems, including unstable interest rates and the problems they caused for the mortgage market. In 1982, the Commission found that "a broader-based and more resilient system will be needed to supply the funds a strengthened housing finance system will require. . . . The nation can no longer rely so completely on a system of highly regulated and specialized mortgage investors and a single type of mortgage instrument if the strong underlying demand for housing credit is to be met" (Colton 1983, xxix and 120).

As the director of the Commission later recalled, the Commission argued that all sorts of lenders and borrowers should have "unrestricted access" to the money and capital markets. Moreover, the Commission advocated that mortgage-market participants—and by this it appears they were thinking more of investors and originators than of borrowers— should have "reliable ways of managing interest-rate risk" (Colton 2002, 11). The Commission recommended a variety of specific policy proposals to more closely and easily link broader capital markets to the "underlying demand" for housing credit. These included exempting RMBS from taxation at the issuing level and having the Securities and Exchange Commission promulgate regulations for streamlined self-registration of issuing RMBS.

At least two statutes followed directly from the recommendations of the President's Commission on Housing. First, the 1984 Secondary Mortgage Market Enhancement Act (SMMEA) facilitated non-GSE or "private-label" securitization in various ways, including exempting RMBS from state-level registration and expanding the ability of banks and thrifts to hold RMBS as assets on their balance sheets (McCoy and Renuart 2008). The CMO was also directly supported by a piece of the 1986 Tax Reform Act, which created the real estate mortgage investment conduit (REMIC), a legal structure for trusts that are used in structured RMBS, especially CMOs. REMICs eliminated any problems with potential "double" taxation of cash flows as they flow through the CMO.

By furthering securitization and enabling lenders utilizing the secondary markets to provide loans at lower cost, at greater scale, and across a larger geographic scope, DIDMCA and the pro-securitization policies put pressure on traditional, localized S&Ls. They had difficulty competing on price or terms. Larger, national-scale mortgage companies could provide loans at lower cost—in part because Fannie Mae and Freddie Mac passed on some of their explicit and implicit federal subsidies in the form of lower-cost capital.

DIDMCA also eliminated Regulation Q, which had limited the rates depositories could pay on deposits. S&Ls were under pressure to pay higher and higher returns on deposits, yet their assets were predominantly in fixed-rate loans. This created a mismatch between their cost and use of funds and drove down their profits. Finally, S&Ls were also freed to make commercial real estate loans, which would open a Pandora's box of new problems for the industry, while increasing deposit insurance from $40,000 to $100,000. Thus, lenders were given greater insurance yet allowed to enter into high-cost risky ventures. As Mayer (1998, 373), commented "How did commercial mortgages, historically a high risk form of lending, solve the maturity mismatch? . . . The question answered itself—pretty quickly too." Congress was pressured by the industry to allow them to enter riskier enterprises. These amounted to desperate attempts to dig out of a hole that had been built by earlier deregulatory moves and government-supported competition from the GSE secondary markets.

In 1982, the Garn–St. Germain Act further loosened regulations on savings and loans, again due to political pressure from the contracting S&L industry. Regulators also relaxed capital standards, so that S&Ls were allowed to have weaker balance sheets. What had been considered thrifts in need of shutting down were instantly reclassified as institutions having only manageable difficulties. A regulatory policy called Memorandum R-49 allowed S&Ls to sell their mortgages and invest in new higher-risk securities (Mayer 1998, 379). Thus, S&Ls, which had being squeezed by new government-sponsored competition and a mismatch between assets and liabilities, were encouraged to invest in high-risk commercial real estate and securities with the hope that these might pull the industry back from the brink of extinction. With increased deposit insurance and an increasingly hands-off regulatory structure, institutions were allowed to funnel depositors' money, backed by the federal government, into speculative investments. The result was the largest collapse of U.S. financial institutions since the Depression. From 1986 to 1995, 1,043 thrifts with over $500 billion in assets failed. As of 1999, the crisis had cost taxpayers an FDIC-estimated $124 billion and the industry another $29 billion (Curry and Shibut 2000). These estimates do not consider many tangible and intangible opportunity costs, however, such as the diversion of the bulk of the thrift regulatory infrastructure into the cleanup and the chilling effects that the crisis had on credit markets generally. As will be shown in chapter 5, large-scale financial crises have contagion and legacy effects that can make loans more difficult to get or more expensive, even for credit-worthy borrowers.

The Garn-St. Germain Act also allowed depositories to cross state lines to acquire failing institutions, providing the first major move toward interstate banking. At the same time, depositories capitalized on the increasing failures of thrifts and banks to argue for eliminating limitations on intrastate bank branching.

Then, in the late 1980s, more changes in bank and thrift regulation supported the growth of securitization even more. The 1989 Financial

Institutions Reform Recovery and Enforcement Act (FIRREA)—the S&L "bailout" bill—required thrifts to rid themselves of loans to improve their liquidity and lower their risks. Mortgages in portfolio received a 50 percent reserve requirement rating while RMBS received only 20 percent. This effectively increased the cost to lenders of holding loans in portfolio.

By the 1990s, Fannie Mae and Freddie Mac's loan purchases accounted for more than one half of new mortgage originations. The preemption of state consumer protections increased the market for RMBS by increasing the returns to investors (by increasing fees and rates paid by borrowers). By stoking the creation and growth of a new set of lenders, by removing deposit rate regulations favoring S&Ls, and by fostering the development of the mortgage brokerage industry, federal policy essentially constituted the death knell for S&Ls and installed a regime of both government-sponsored and private-label securitization as the dominant sources of mortgage capital.

Figure 1.6 shows that the decline of the S&L circuit (thrifts) began in the middle 1970s as RMBS issuance began. When S&L market share began dropping in the 1980s it was essentially absorbed by GSE RMBS.

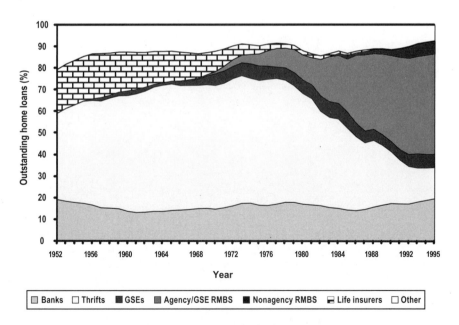

Figure 1.6. Outstanding home loans by funding source, 1952–1995.
Source: Federal Reserve Board, flow of funds accounts.

Private-label RMBS began slowly in the middle 1980s but began to grow at a faster pace in the early 1990s, as the early subprime mortgage market developed.

By 1995, the GSEs and GSE mortgage RMBS accounted for 51 percent of outstanding mortgage credit. Banks had reached a share of 19 percent, with thrifts down to 14 percent, down from a high of 58 percent in 1973 and 26 percent in 1989, the year of the savings and loan crisis bill (FIRREA). Private-label RMBS was just beginning to get started, rising from 2 percent of outstanding mortgages in 1990 to 6 percent in 1995.

Before moving into the growth of high-risk mortgage lending in the second half of the 1990s, it is important to first look back at some of the problems with mortgage markets before the emergence of major high-risk mortgage markets.

2

Mortgage Market Disparities
and the Dual Regulatory System
in the Twentieth Century

The problems in U.S. mortgage markets during the 1990s and 2000s cannot be understood without a serious discussion of the pervasive and persistent problems of lending discrimination and redlining, problems that—in various forms—persisted throughout the twentieth century and into the twenty-first century. In this chapter I outline the history of these problems and the policy responses to them from the early part of the twentieth century to the early 1990s. Chapters 3 through 6 then cover these issues in the high-risk lending eras beginning in the 1990s. Without a sober look at the problems of disparate access to home loans, one would be encouraging a naïve nostalgia for systems that, while having some advantages over those of more recent high-risk markets, frequently exhibited many significant inequities across race and space.

Discrimination and redlining in institutionalized home lending markets date back to these the earliest period of these markets. In 1917, for example, the *Cleveland Advocate*, a black newspaper, reported that banks had refused to lend to blacks attempting to develop large-scale housing for blacks on the Chicago's South Side (Cleveland Advocate 1917). In 1922, following the 1919 Chicago race riot, the Chicago Commission on Race Relations determined that blacks faced barriers in securing mortgages. Some lenders completely avoided areas where blacks lived (Hillier 2001).

Banks, S&Ls, and mortgage companies generally made very few loans in black neighborhoods during a good portion of the twentieth century. Loans to black borrowers in white neighborhoods were even rarer. Abrams (1955, 176) called local S&Ls the "watchdogs of neighborhood purity" that would rate any area where residents had resisted minority home-seekers as "out of bounds" for future loans to minorities. This left blacks seeking mortgages to build or buy homes with primarily two alternatives. They could borrow from a black financial institution, and such institutions were often scarce or poorly capitalized. Alternatively, they could borrow from an informal lender who would lend at exorbitant rates and under abusive conditions.

Because they were often unable to secure a mortgage, blacks often had to rely upon land contracts to buy homes. In a 1955–56 study of real estate agents, most considered the land contract to be a key source of financing for black buyers (Helper 1969). Land contracts are essentially rent-to-own schemes, where the "seller" of the home receives a monthly payment over a period of time. If any payments are missed, the "buyer" forfeits all rights to the property and has earned no financial equity in the house. In addition, sometimes very large "down payments" are required, which are not recoverable if the seller reclaims the property. Land contracts generally provide little to no protection for the buyers, and can be used by investors and property owners to recycle properties among different vulnerable buyers repeatedly to extract large down payments over and over again. Land contract purchases can also involve effective prices for homes that are much higher than would be obtained through traditional financing.

The use of land contracts was driven by poor access to institutional lenders. Often, however, the sellers were actually speculators—frequently real estate agents—who purchased the houses from homeowners. These speculators typically financed their activities with lines of credit from small S&Ls. In one case in the early 1960s, a small S&L was found to have 25 percent of its assets invested in two contract sellers (Bradford and Marino 1977, 64–65).

Frequently, speculators repossessed the homes and then sold them again. The limited geographic markets where blacks were allowed to buy, combined with their narrow options for financing, proved a double penalty in many cases in terms of the effective prices they paid for the homes and the financing. The speculators were able to extract very large profits from the buyers.

An important force in the history of lending discrimination and redlining in the United States was the Federal Housing Administration. Beginning in the late 1930s, the FHA promoted and helped institutionalize redlining practices. Although lending discrimination and redlining practices of private-sector lenders preceded the creation of the FHA, the agency adopted, formalized, and legitimized such practices. It used risk-rating maps and expected that its extensive collection of maps would help an appraiser "refresh his memory as to the danger points in a neighborhood" (Hillier 2001). Although earlier maps generated by the Home Ownership Loan Corporation (HOLC) may have influenced the FHA's risk-rating system, the FHA, more than the HOLC, institutionalized and supported redlining by categorizing loans according to risk levels and by directing appraisers and lenders to place considerable emphasis on racial composition and neighborhood change. In fact, Crossney and Bartelt (2005) find that, unlike the FHA, the HOLC made many loans in areas that it had classified as high risk.

FHA manuals advanced redlining by both FHA and non-FHA lenders. The agency viewed itself as a standard setter and as a developer and disseminator of good underwriting practice. The participation of the FHA in redlining was recognized fairly early on, first by Myrdal (1944) and then more fully by Abrams (1955).

The geographic biases of the FHA had direct implications for minority loan applicants. Only 2.3 percent of FHA-insured mortgages outstanding in 1950 were associated with nonwhite borrowers, even worse than the 5 percent of conventional mortgages with nonwhite borrowers (Gordon 2005).

Frederick Babcock, a researcher who had earlier argued that racial change hurt property values significantly, was involved in the earliest versions of the FHA's *Underwriting Manual* (Helper 1969, 202). He is credited with providing the FHA's risk-rating grid for neighborhood analysis that was used in the agency's manuals. The 1935 FHA *Underwriting Manual* listed among the adverse influences on a neighborhood the "infiltration of inharmonious racial or nationality groups." It also stated that a neighborhood's appeal is enhanced by the "kind and social status of its inhabitants." The 1936 version of the manual included "racial occupancy" among adverse influences (section 233 of the 1936 FHA *Underwriting Manual*, quoted in Abrams 1955, 231). The FHA also urged the use of racial covenants in home purchases to protect against racial transition (Jackson 1985).

Beyond the explicit bias of FHA neighborhood evaluation systems, FHA programs often financed newer developments on the edges of metropolitan areas (Jackson 1985). The agency and its programs favored the construction of single-family over multifamily projects. It also provided more advantageous financing for purchase rather than repair or improvement. FHA lending overwhelmingly flowed to suburban areas. Jackson (1985) found that more than 91 percent of FHA home purchase loans in the St. Louis area from 1935 to 1939 were for homes in the suburbs, and that more than half of homebuyers had lived in the city before their purchase. This is despite the fact that, in the 1930s, more single-family homes were constructed in the city than in the suburbs

(Jackson 1985, 209, 210). He found similar patterns in New Jersey and the Washington, D.C., area.

The FHA's discriminatory lending practices did not end overnight. The 1948 Supreme Court decision in *Shelley v. Kraemer* outlawed racial covenants in real estate transactions. Despite this case, it took the FHA until 1950 to explicitly halt its favoring of racially restrictive covenants in its underwriting. It was not until 1962 that President Kennedy issued Executive Order 11063, which prohibited discrimination in the use of federally funded or managed housing programs, including FHA and Veterans Administration loans.

A sometimes underappreciated actor in helping to uncover discrimination in home lending markets was the U.S. Commission on Civil Rights. Created in 1957, the Commission began by conducting research and holding hearings on discrimination in a variety of areas, including housing. In a 1961 report, the Commission concluded that "little has been done by Government or the lending community to reduce or discourage discriminatory practices" (U.S. Commission on Civil Rights 1961, 30). It described the results from a 1959 Chicago survey of the 243 S&Ls in Cook County. Only twenty-one S&Ls made loans in a "heavily Negro-populated South Side area" during a one-year period, and only one white-owned S&L made a home purchase loan to a black family in a white neighborhood. The Commission also argued that bank and S&L regulators had the ability to reduce discrimination and redlining. For example, the Commission maintained that the Office of the Comptroller of the Currency had the "legal authority and the effective power to require the elimination of discriminatory mortgage lending practices by national banks" (U.S. Commission on Civil Rights 1961, 41.)

Following growing civil rights activism and urban unrest in the 1960s and especially the assassination of Martin Luther King Jr., Congress passed the Civil Rights Act in 1968. Title VIII, known as the Fair Housing Act (FaHA), called for the prohibition of discrimination in housing markets. In a 1976 case, *Laufman v. Oakley*, the courts confirmed that the Fair Housing Act extended to redlining. However, the courts defined redlining only as the practice of "denying loans" for housing in certain neighborhoods, even if the applicants were creditworthy. Its definition did not include the exclusion of certain neighborhoods in marketing or outreach efforts. The courts also held that plaintiffs must be able to show that the lender acted with "discriminatory animus" due to the race or location of the applicant (Nier 1999). Thus, if a lender had a policy, such as a high minimum loan amount, that only had the "effect" of rejecting black applicants or applicants from lower-income neighborhoods, it was not guilty of discrimination. Of course this begged the question of whether such lending policies were merely "cover" for racial bias and whether, regardless of the motivation, such practices should be covered by the law.

There were other problems with using the FaHA as a tool for fighting lending discrimination and redlining (Dane 1993; Massey and Denton 1993). The original statute had little teeth. The Department of Housing and Urban Development (HUD), the enforcing agency, was only allowed to engage in "conference, conciliation, and persuasion" as the means of enforcing the law. It could refer a case to the Justice Department, but the attorney general was generally authorized to act only if there was evidence of a "pattern and practice" of discrimination. Only 10 percent of the cases that HUD could not conciliate were referred to the attorney general, and a very small number of these were pursued (Massey and Denton 1993).

Beyond the limitations of the FaHA statute as a tool for fighting lending discrimination and redlining, there was also the question of implementation by regulators. Lackluster implementation of the statute was the first clear indication that federal bank regulators were not very supportive of policies that attempted to address discrimination and redlining. In 1971, after seeing no signs that regulators were taking any actions to enforce FaHA, a group of civil rights and public interest groups petitioned bank regulators to develop and issue fair lending regulations (Goering and Wienk 1996, 401). By the mid-1970s, other agencies, including the Office of Management and Budget and the Department of Justice, called for action by the regulators. By 1976, only one regulator (the Federal Home Loan Bank Board) had issued final regulations, and those fell far short of what fair lending advocates had called for. The other regulators only proposed that banks be required to adopt nondiscrimination policies and display equal opportunity posters in their lobbies.

As regulators failed to aggressively enforce the Fair Housing Act, the overall issue of fair access to credit—not just in housing—was beginning to receive more attention. In October 1974, the Equal Credit Opportunity Act (ECOA) was signed into law by President Ford. In 1976, ECOA was amended to prohibit lending discrimination by race and age as well as gender. In some ways, ECOA was a stronger and more robust law than the Fair Housing Act. The legislative history of the ECOA demonstrated that Congress intended for the law to cover more than "disparate treatment" in the making of loans but also something termed "disparate impact." Disparate treatment is when lenders explicitly use race, or some other protected class, as a factor to treat potential borrowers differently. Disparate impact occurs when individuals or businesses receive equivalent treatment but a lending policy has a disparate, adverse impact on members of a minority group or another protected class. Even if a lender applies a certain policy universally, if the policy disproportionately harms minority borrowers, then it can only be justified if there is a "business necessity" for such a policy. A common example of a policy with disparate impact is the use of a minimum loan amount. If minority homebuyers, on average, tend to buy less expensive homes than white buyers, a minimum loan size can have a disparate impact on minority applicants.

In the spring of 1974, community activists, led by Gale Cincotta's National People's Action, met with the staff of Senator William Proxmire of Wisconsin, the number-two Democrat on the Senate Committee on Banking, Housing, and Urban Affairs. The next year, Proxmire became chair of the banking committee and introduced a bill calling for the collection and disclosure of data on savings account and lending patterns of banks and thrifts. The Home Mortgage Disclosure Act (HMDA) was introduced the day after the release of an OCC survey of six cities showed that minorities were rejected for loans at twice the rate of whites of similar income levels (Hallahan 1992).

HMDA was a highly contested piece of legislation. In congressional testimony, studies demonstrating uneven lending patterns were presented from Chicago, Baltimore, Milwaukee, and other cities. Industry interests were quickly represented by a coalition opposing the bill led by Senator Jake Garn (R-UT) and Representative John Rousselot (R-CA). Very early on, the bill was changed to call only for the disclosure of data aggregated at the census tract level. No information on the race or gender of borrowers was included.

Proxmire took the lead in pushing HMDA but soon ran into difficulties in his own committee. He agreed to exclude savings data to reduce concerns about the costs to industry and limited coverage to metropolitan areas, which reduced opposition from many small banks in rural areas. In exchange for giving up these items, Proxmire was able to change the reporting geography from zip code to census tract, which allowed for somewhat more precise disclosure.

Although industry interests, the Federal Reserve Board, and the Department of Housing and Urban Development opposed HMDA, the bill had a good deal of public appeal. Proxmire and his allies were successful in making a strong connection between redlining and neighborhood decline in Senate hearings (Moskowitz 1987).

After passage of HMDA in 1975, community activists and public interest groups kept up the pressure for moving beyond data reporting and disclosure. The Community Reinvestment Act (CRA) was introduced by Senator Proxmire in January 1977. It was signed by President Carter in October as Title VIII of the 1977 Housing and Community Development Act. The fight for CRA was eased in many respects by the groundwork laid by the victory on HMDA (Immergluck 2004). The HMDA congressional debate had already placed redlining and disinvestment on the federal agenda and had effectively tied redlining to neighborhood decline.

Although CRA was not as contested as HMDA, there was still significant opposition. Regulators, especially the Federal Reserve Board, publicly opposed CRA on the stated grounds that they already had the authority to assess credit flows and claimed that they already did so. Supporters generally portrayed CRA as a law aimed as much at regulators as at banks. It was a forceful command to regulators to do their jobs and pay attention to redlining issues. The regulators had been taken to task in the HMDA hearings and elsewhere for poor enforcement of the Fair Housing Act. The legislative history suggests that CRA was in large part a "congressional rebuke" to the four bank and thrift regulators and a clear message to them to emphasize urban lending obligations as an important component of the public purpose for which they were chartered. Regulators did not employ "systematic, affirmative" programs to encourage lenders to evaluate how well banks served their communities (Dennis 1978).

The basic justification used to argue for CRA was that banks and thrifts were given public charters in large part to serve the "convenience and needs" of their communities and thus the public had a right to expect them to fulfill that obligation. Regulators and congressional and financial industry opponents branded the bill "credit allocation." They argued that banks would be required to make a specific number of loans or portion of its loans in a certain community. Even when advocates for the bill pointed out that CRA would not do this, some denounced the law as a "foot in the door" toward mandatory credit allocation (McCluskey 1983).

The enforcement provisions of CRA were based largely on the existing merger and branch approval process, with the examination procedure expanded to cover CRA concerns explicitly. To the chagrin of many community reinvestment advocates, who had seen regulators move slowly on enforcing fair lending law, the final bill also relied heavily on the discretion of the regulatory agencies. It left much of the CRA regulations and process to administrative rule-making and, as a result of the rules that followed, to examiner judgment. The reliance on examiner discretion, especially in bank evaluations or examinations, was a strong tradition in bank regulation (Khademian 1996). Regulators reacted very negatively to the notion of any highly prescriptive legislation that might tell them how to evaluate the community reinvestment record of a bank or thrift (Dennis 1978).

The CRA statute directed the four federal financial institution regulators—the Federal Reserve Board (FRB), the Office of the Comptroller of the Currency (OCC), the Federal Home Loan Bank Board (later the Office of Thrift Supervision), and the Federal Deposit Insurance Corporation (FDIC)—to develop regulations and operations to carry out the purpose of the Act. In the first few years of CRA's implementation, regulators appeared to go out of their way to send a message to banks that they did not want to influence lending patterns. In examination procedures issued after the regulations, the agencies stated that banks would not be required to document that they were actually extending the types of credit they had listed as available in their CRA Statements (McCluskey 1983). Then, in January 1980, the Federal Reserve Board, the regulator most hostile to the CRA, issued a "Community Reinvestment Act Information Statement." The statement assured the industry that the Board would be very understanding of explanations when banks made few loans in low- and moderate-income segments of their community: "The Board believes that there are many reasons why a particular neighborhood may generate more deposits than loan requests, or more requests than deposits, and that disparity in a particular area . . . is not prima facie evidence of discrimination" (Federal Reserve Board 1980).

Community reinvestment advocates, banks, and others waited to see how regulators would implement the statute. The worst fears of the advocates came to pass when regulators revealed early patterns of CRA grades. The Federal Reserve showed in late 1981 that it had rated only 3 percent of banks as less than satisfactory in 1980. The Board adopted a policy of only requiring review of merger applications for those institutions with the worst of five possible grades, representing only 0.2 percent of institutions and only two banks in 1980. Little appeared to change in this pattern through the 1980s: from 1985 to 1988, of the twenty-six thousand CRA exams conducted by regulators, only 2.4 percent received less-than-satisfactory ratings (Fishbein 1993).

Another big question mark that awaited both banks and community groups after CRA was passed was what actually would happen to banks found not to be fulfilling their CRA obligations. The law called for regulators to take CRA performance into consideration before they approved applications by banks to merge with another bank, open a branch, or make other significant changes to their charter. Would regulators actually reject important applications on CRA grounds? The answer, for at least most of the 1980s, was clearly no.

Among the four regulators, the FRB was initially the most resistant to affirmatively implementing CRA. The Board had "disengaged" from the other three regulators over the use of the CRA and credit needs analysis as a regulatory tool (McCluskey 1983). Although the other regulators were also less than vigorous in their enforcement of CRA, the FDIC and the OCC did deny a few applications on CRA grounds in the early years.

Stymied Progress: CRA and Fair Lending from the late 1980s through the mid-1990s

In 1986 and 1987, community reinvestment activism was on the upswing in many large cities (Immergluck 2004). Then, on May 1, 1988, the *Atlanta Journal-Constitution* published a large front-page article, the first in a four-day series titled "The Color of Money" (Dedman 1988a). Reporter Bill Dedman demonstrated that white neighborhoods received five times as many home purchase loans from Atlanta's banks and S&Ls as black neighborhoods with similar income levels. Even lower-income white neighborhoods were better served by banks and S&Ls than higher-income black areas. Dedman went on to expose the fact that 98 percent of banks and thrifts received CRA ratings of satisfactory or better and that regulators had denied just eight applications on CRA grounds since the Act's passage (Dedman 1988b). The "Color of Money" series had an immediate national impact, and its timing was critical. Senator William Proxmire, the original sponsor of the CRA, was about to retire. The Senate Banking Committee had held hearings on the Act's implementation six weeks before the series began and he had questioned regulators' enforcement efforts then. The Committee had heard from witnesses that CRA exams had become essentially impossible to fail.

Senator Proxmire took advantage of the Dedman series to draw additional attention to regulators' weak enforcement of the law. He asked them to respond to the series and to report on their enforcement activities by the end of the summer. The increased public and congressional scrutiny of regulators had a clear effect of making weak regulator enforcement a much more prominent issue. At the time, CRA ratings were not publicly available, so the lax enforcement of CRA, while understood by those who followed the law closely, was not widely known.

During 1988, lending studies and media coverage in Atlanta, as well as in Boston and other cities, increased public and congressional scrutiny of the activities of CRA regulators. It was no coincidence that, in April 1989, regulators issued only their second CRA policy statement since the original regulations were promulgated (Garwood and Smith 1993). In it, regulators emphasized that banks would be evaluated on their actual lending performance rather than simply on promises of improvement. The statement did not make significant changes in CRA regulation, but it was a clear signal that regulators were feeling some pressure to implement the law in a more substantive way. The regulators laid out a new, or at least newly articulated, expectation that banks were to document their CRA activities. They clarified their position on banks' commitments to improve CRA performance at the time of applications. They stated that commitments for future lending or CRA activity would not be viewed as part of an institution's CRA record, but could be considered as an indicator of "potential for improvement."

While clearly a reaction to the growing criticism of lax regulation, the joint policy statement was not enough to appease Congress. In 1989, allies of the reinvestment movement were able to make a number of changes to CRA and HMDA through the passage of the savings and loan bailout bill, the Financial Institutions Reform Recovery and Enforcement Act. These changes proved much more significant than the regulators' moves. FIRREA required the public disclosure of most aspects of CRA exams. This was a major step. Now community groups and others could identify how regulators had rated a bank's CRA performance. This served at least two purposes. First, it gave the public and community groups some information on the CRA performance of different banks. Foundations, churches, local governments, and even the American Bar Association began using CRA ratings as a screen for selecting their banks. But, more important, disclosure of CRA ratings made it possible for those dealing with banks more directly, either as CRA advocates or as potential community development partners, to understand how regulators viewed the banks' performance. A community group could look to target banks that had received satisfactory ratings when the group felt the banks deserved "needs to improve" or worse ratings. Some groups began providing information about banks to regulators and arguing that banks ought to be downgraded. FIRREA also changed the five-level, numerical CRA rating system to a four-level descriptive classification of "Outstanding," "Satisfactory," "Needs to Improve," and "Substantial Noncompliance."

Arguably, the greatest impact that FIRREA had on community reinvestment and fair lending, however, was not the changes in to CRA itself but the changes it made regarding HMDA, which had been limited in its usefulness in two critical ways. First, it did not call for the collection or disclosure of information on the race or income of borrowers. Second, only originated loans were included, so no information on applications or denials was available. Under FIRREA, lenders had to report on each formal loan application, including the race, income, and gender of the applicant; the loan amount; the purpose of the loan; and whether the loan was approved, denied, or withdrawn. These changes had a large impact on the usefulness and power of the data. It was not simply the addition of racial information but the shift to application-level disclosure that made HMDA so much more crucial to the reinvestment and fair lending movements.

In November 1991, the Federal Reserve, after providing the banking industry with advanced notice, released a national analysis of the first year (1990) of the new, post-FIRREA HMDA data. It showed that minorities were two to three times more likely to be rejected for home loans than whites of similar income levels (Canner and Smith 1991). Numerous studies soon followed, and the large differences in denial rates between minority and white loan applicants drew a great deal of media attention (Immergluck 2004). The attention to race-based differentials in mortgage lending was arguably the single most important factor in improving access to home purchase loans in the early 1990s. Lending by prime lenders to minorities also increased as the attention to racial disparities detailed by the new HMDA data led to better enforcement of fair lending laws.

The effect of increased scrutiny of regulators' enforcement of CRA was significant. The proportion of banks receiving a CRA rating of less than satisfactory rose significantly during the late 1980s and early 1990s. From 1985 to 1988, only 2.4 percent of institutions examined received less than satisfactory ratings (Fishbein 1993). From July 1990 through September 1991, about a quarter of all banks and thrifts were evaluated under the new disclosure law. The percentage receiving less than satisfactory ratings increased to 11.7 percent, a substantial increase. Only 8 percent of these new exams resulted in outstanding ratings. Certainly disclosure of exams may have had an effect on the ratings. However, the later return to satisfactory or better ratings of more than 97 percent of the banks suggests that other factors were also at work, including the increased scrutiny and criticism that the regulators underwent in the late 1980s.

In the late 1980s, the "Color of Money" and other media stories and congressional hearings helped create a revived interest in CRA among community groups, the media, and policymakers. Regulators seemed to respond and the proportion of banks and thrifts receiving less-than-satisfactory CRA ratings increased. By 1993, however, the percentage of banks receiving less-than-satisfactory ratings had dropped back down to less than 5 percent, from a level of about 12 percent in 1990. Community reinvestment advocates argued first to the Clinton campaign and then to the new administration that the CRA, as it was being implemented and enforced, was not resulting in substantial amounts of community reinvestment activity. In 1993, federal banking regulators proposed major revisions to CRA rules that promised to focus more on actual lending results and less on such processes as demonstrating community contacts and advertising efforts. The Clinton administration, under its "reinventing government" efforts, also promised bankers less paperwork. "CRA reform," as it was called, was promoted as an attempt to make both sides happy.

The initial CRA reform proposal called for evaluating an institution's lending, in part, by comparing its market penetration in low- and moderate-income neighborhoods within its assessment area to its penetration in middle- and upper-income neighborhoods. The proposal did not have a highly formulaic or deterministic methodology, but did suggest this relative market penetration approach as a starting point. It did not call for any lending requirements per dollar of local deposit, the sort rejected in the original Senate CRA hearings. The "market share approach," as it was generally called, was actually quite similar to commonly accepted methods for measuring disparities in a wide variety of social science and business areas, including employment discrimination and affirmative action set-aside programs. Many bankers and some regulators, however, opposed the move, again crying "credit allocation."

After eighteen months of public comment and debate, in April 1995 the four federal banking regulators—the Federal Reserve Board, the Office of the Comptroller of the Currency, the Federal Deposit Insurance Corporation, and the Office of Thrift Supervision (OTS)—released the final version of the new CRA regulations. The new rules replaced the twelve assessment factors in the previous regulations with an outcome-based evaluation system. This system was intended to assess how well institutions served their communities on lending, investments, and financial services, rather than on how well they conducted needs assessments and documented community outreach.

Although a shift from process to outcomes was the primary goal of the regulatory changes, there was also some attention given to "easing the regulatory burden" on banks, especially for smaller institutions. As a result, a two-tiered evaluation system was established, with banks classified as "small" (less than $250 million in assets) having more limited evaluations than "large" institutions. CRA evaluations for large banks and thrifts consisted of three component tests: the lending, investment, and service tests. The lending test, which measures a bank's performance in direct lending primarily via mortgages and small business loans, accounts for 50 percent of the overall CRA rating. The investment test, which accounts for 25 percent, considers a bank's investment in community development activities such as investments in community development loan funds or minority-owned banks. The service test accounts for the remaining 25 percent of the overall score and is where banks are evaluated for branch locations and the provision of basic, affordable deposit services.

CRA reform was an improvement to CRA policy although, like most regulations, it proved only as effective as the willingness of the regulatory agencies to implement it with some vigor. Despite the improvements in the 1995 changes, the evaluation process remained heavily dependent on the political will of the agencies and staff implementing the regulations. Moreover, the new rules did very little to define acceptable performance. This was still in the hands of the agencies and the examiners.

Beginning in 1997, the first real year of CRA reform, outstanding ratings began a steady decline, although needs-to-improve and substantial noncompliance ratings remained at extremely low levels. The number of institutions receiving outstanding ratings, while usually not focused on by the media or even by some advocates, is important because an outstanding rating goes a long way toward giving a bank an effective "safe harbor" against the possible denial of an application. It is much more difficult to effectively criticize or challenge a bank with an outstanding rating. Moreover, for any grading system to be effective, the top grade should truly represent exemplary performance. Especially for the vast majority of larger banks, which typically have the greatest impact on lower-income communities, the realistic range of CRA grade is between satisfactory and outstanding. It is extremely rare for a large institution to receive a needs-to-improve or substantial noncompliance rating (Immergluck 2008).

Despite some of the positive developments in the 1990s, post-reform CRA ratings did not signal a return to the more aggressive CRA enforcement of the years immediately following FIRREA, when regulators increased less-than-satisfactory ratings to more than 10 percent of exams. Within a few years of FIRREA, regulators returned to their practice of very rarely giving needs-to-improve and substantial noncompliance ratings (Immergluck 2004). All four agencies followed this trend, and CRA reform did not have a lasting effect on this practice.

As was the case with CRA, the intensity of enforcement of fair lending laws ebbed and flowed in the 1990s. Before then, in 1988, after Democrats retook control of the Senate, several amendments to the Fair Housing Act were passed. The amendments permitted court costs to be recovered by plaintiffs if they were victorious, created a process for trying cases before an administrative law judge in HUD, and empowered these judges to compensate victims for damages as well as to levy substantial fines. The amendments also permitted the secretary of HUD to initiate fair housing investigations, rather than merely respond to complaints.

Some of the factors that led to changes in CRA and HMDA also led to better fair lending law and enforcement. The FIRREA improvements to HMDA—especially adding race and gender information on loan applicants—gave regulators and the Department of Justice a new tool to identify potential discrimination. And the 1988 changes to the Fair Housing Act increased the gravity of Justice Department actions (Walter 1995).

Fair lending law is important, not simply because it specifically addresses discrimination against individuals, but because it includes enforcement mechanisms that CRA does not. These include civil fines and the consent decrees that can compel banks to change their processes and behavior. Moreover, fair lending law covers all mortgage lenders, not just banks and thrifts. Given the growing market share of nonbank lenders, this made fair lending law an increasingly important tool for improving access to credit.

Following the 1988 amendments to the Fair Housing Act, pressure mounted on the regulators to use match-paired testing to detect discrimination by lenders. Matched-pair testing involves identifying pairs of loan applicants who are similar in most respects other than their race or ethnicity (or some other trait protected under the law) and having them inquire about obtaining a loan at a particular lender. If the minority applicants are discouraged from applying or treated worse in some way than the white applicants, then there is strong evidence of lending discrimination. In 1991, the Consumer Advisory Council of the Federal Reserve Board recommended that the Board sponsor a systematic matched-pair testing study of mortgage lenders at the preapplication stage of the lending process. The Board, however, rejected this suggestion. In the early 1990s, small amounts of federal funds began to be made available for fair lending testing through the Fair Housing Initiatives Program (FHIP), in which HUD funds nonprofit fair housing groups to enforce fair housing laws.

The Justice Department began its "fair lending initiative" in 1992 when the department and Decatur Federal Savings and Loan entered into a consent decree to settle the first suit alleging a pattern and practice of lending discrimination under ECOA and the Fair Housing Act. The Decatur suit followed directly from an investigation that used HMDA data and showed very large disparities in denial rates between minority and white borrowers of similar incomes. In this case and others like it, the Justice Department found evidence that bank employees were providing assistance to white applicants that they were not providing to black and Hispanic applicants (U.S. Department of Justice 2001). A short time later, the department announced its investigation of Shawmut Mortgage Company, an affiliate of Shawmut National Bank, for fair lending violations. Then, in the spring of 1993, the OCC issued a bulletin explaining that offering disparate levels of assistance to borrowers of different races and ethnicities was a form of discrimination. Later that year, based on the Justice Department investigation, the Federal Reserve Board denied Shawmut National Corporation's application to acquire a bank. At the end of the year, the Justice Department entered into a consent decree with Shawmut. In the fall of 1994, HUD entered into a voluntary fair lending "best practices" agreement with the Mortgage Bankers Association.

A key policy event occurred in April 1994, when a federal Interagency Task Force on Fair Lending issued a joint policy statement (Interagency Task Force on Fair Lending 1994). One of the key points of the statement was a declaration that the agencies would follow the courts in considering disparate impact discrimination a violation of the law. In this statement, the regulators said that lenders that adopt lending policies having disproportionately negative effects on a protected class will be found to be discriminating under fair lending laws, unless they can show a business necessity for doing so. This meant that lenders could not easily use lending policies such as large minimum loan sizes or compensating balance requirements (in which borrowers are required to keep minimum bank deposits at the lending institution) to steer clear of lending to minority homeowners or businesses.

The lending industry worked behind the scenes to undercut the administration's efforts on fair lending. In 1995, for example, after Republicans gained control of Congress, Representative Bill McCollum, a Republican from Florida and longtime supporter of banking causes, proposed legislation to modify ECOA and the Fair Housing Act so that they would not cover disparate impact discrimination. The bill made it out of subcommittee but not out of the full House Banking Committee.

Another key step in fair lending enforcement was the move to consider discrimination not only in the approval of loans but also in marketing and sales. In August 1994, Chevy Chase Federal Savings Bank entered into a consent decree with the Department of Justice to settle charges that the bank had failed to market its services in minority neighborhoods. The Justice Department had found that the bank made very few loans in black neighborhoods in Washington, D.C., and Prince Georges County and that it had very few branches in or near these areas. In the decree, the bank agreed to open branches in the affected neighborhoods. By 1995, 60 percent of the loans made by the bank were in black neighborhoods (U.S. Department of Justice 2001). The Chevy Chase case was a critical statement against not only discrimination but also against redlining, and it considered disparate marketing and branch presences as a form of redlining.

In the late 1980s and early 1990s, some observers began arguing that Fannie Mae and Freddie Mac underwriting policies, and the perception of those policies by lenders, created impediments to lending in lower-income and minority neighborhoods (Immergluck 2004). Critics argued that GSE underwriting policies encouraged lending in middle- and upper-income areas. Reminiscent of criticisms of the FHA, the complaints focused on how the growing secondary market firms had created an unlevel playing field that worked to the detriment of more diverse, mixed-use urban neighborhoods.

Fannie Mae and Freddie Mac's charters required them to pay attention to the extent that their activities benefited low- and moderate-income families. Since the 1970s, HUD had established a nonbinding goal that 30 percent of the mortgages purchased by the GSEs be for families with incomes below the metropolitan median income and that 30 percent be for homes located in central cities. However, Senate hearings had established that HUD had not monitored the agencies' progress toward these goals. In 1991, some consumer groups argued that Fannie and Freddie should be required to devote a portion of their earnings to low-income housing, similar to the approach used with the Federal Home Loan Bank system (Fishbein 2003). Others argued that that somewhat stronger lending goals for lower-income households ought to be codified in a statute. A coalition of national consumer and housing groups met to develop a proposal and decided on the second approach. Their proposal called for a new, more targeted affordable housing goal in addition to the "30/30" goal that HUD had developed. This new goal was to count only housing for borrowers under 80 percent of the local area median income, with a portion directed at those with incomes below 60 percent of the median income. The GSEs supported a special affordable housing goal in legislative debate but opposed codifying the 30/30 goals. According to Fishbein (2003), the "compelling evidence of the GSEs' weak performance in serving low income housing needs proved out." The 30/30 provision as well as the special affordable housing provision were enacted in the Federal Housing Enterprises Financial Safety and Soundness Act of 1992 (GSE Act). The Act gave HUD "mission" regulatory authority over the GSEs, directing it to set annual affordable housing purchase levels, collect data, and monitor compliance with fair lending laws.

Following the 1992 GSE Act, Fannie and Freddie penetration in lower-income lending markets improved somewhat. The percentage of loans benefiting modest-income and minority tracts increased. The GSEs generally improved their lending performance through developing marginal and cautious modifications to their regular conforming loan purchases. They allowed somewhat lower down payments, generally requiring borrowers to go through homeownership counseling with qualified counseling agencies. They lowered credit score requirements modestly and were somewhat more flexible with debt-to-income ratios.

However, in the 1990s, the GSEs did not relax their credit standards dramatically and, at least in their direct lending activities, did not appear to engage in the sort of high-risk lending practices in which the emerging subprime lenders were engaging, such as debt-to-income ratios above 50 percentage points to borrowers with very weak credit scores. At the same time, consumer groups and others began to become concerned in the late 1990s that the GSEs were—through a variety of financing activities— becoming more actively involved in the subprime industry, especially by investing in mortgage-backed securities or by providing guarantees for such securities (Immergluck 2004).

Mortgage-Market Consolidation, the Dominance of Securitization-Enabled Lenders, and the Dual Regulatory System

The increasing dominance of securitization in mortgage market funding and the concurrent decline of the traditional S&L mortgage circuit meant that larger lenders were able to gain advantages from economies of scale and the advantages of vertical disintegration—especially through the use of broker networks and large-scale servicing operations. The rising importance of GSE secondary markets facilitated the consolidation of the lending industry and the shift toward origination through mortgage companies, both independently owned and bank-affiliated mortgage companies such as Citifinancial. Even between 1989 and 1995 there was substantial consolidation in the mortgage market, with the share of the top twenty-five lenders increasing from 26 percent to 39 percent over this brief period (Apgar and Fishbein 2004). The consolidation trend accelerated in the late 1990s and early 2000s, with the share of the top twenty-five reaching 79 percent by 2002.

Beyond consolidation, the shift of funding sources from deposits and related sources to securitization was accompanied by a shift in who originated mortgage loans. In the late 1960s through the late 1970s, when most consumer protection, fair lending, and community reinvestment laws were being designed, banks and especially thrifts (including S&Ls) dominated mortgage lending markets throughout the United States.

When CRA was being formulated, the locally based S&L, drawing significantly on local deposits, was the dominant source of mortgage loans, with commercial banks being the second largest lender type. Figure 2.1 shows the changes in market share among the major different types of mortgage originators. In 1976, the year before CRA was adopted, the share of all mortgage originations occurring in regulated depositories (other than credit unions) reached its peak at 82 percent, which was actually substantially higher than the 70 percent share in 1970. The share of originations made by S&Ls alone had reached a postwar peak of 55 percent. Mortgage companies (with funding largely from life insurance companies) had been major actors in previous decades, especially in the 1950s, but were less important by the mid-1970s, and the decline of S&Ls, at least in the mortgage market, did not hit its stride until the 1980s.

In this context, many of the early architects of CRA, including Gale Cincotta and National People's Action, began their community reinvestment organizing by arguing that banks and S&Ls that accepted deposits from residents of local communities had an obligation to "reinvest" those deposits, in the form of mortgages, back into those same communities. This "closed-loop" model of how lending works might have made some sense for S&Ls and local banks (although even depository institutions had access to secondary markets that enabled funds to be moved around

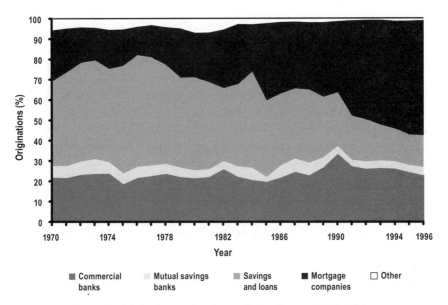

Figure 2.1. Origination market shares of by lender type, 1970–1996.
Source: United States Housing Market Conditions, U.S. Department of Housing and Urban Development, Winter, 1997.

the country from places with excess capital to places with capital short-ages). However, it did not apply well to mortgage companies that did not accept deposits.

The dominance of S&Ls and banks in the mortgage market in the 1970s helped shape the design of CRA so that it was largely crafted around a mortgage market dominated by depository institutions. This facet of the design, in turn, meant that the justifications for CRA articulated by policymakers depended partly on a social contract between communities and the depositories active in those communities, and not between communities and the broader set of suppliers of mortgage credit such as mortgage companies and credit unions.

The laws governing the chartering of depository institutions, especially for national banks and thrifts, also provided a precedent for community obligations, because these institutions were under some obligation to serve the "convenience and needs" of the communities in which they were chartered. Because depositories were generally beneficiaries of federal deposit insurance programs, CRA designers quickly latched onto these benefits as the primary basis for a sort of quid quo pro logic used to justify the law. But this logic meant that lenders that were not *direct* beneficiaries of deposit insurance should not be subject to CRA. Yet, in many ways, nondepository lenders depended on commercial banks (e.g., through wholesale financing vehicles and short-term borrowing) and on a much broader set of government-provided or sponsored financing infrastructures including the FHA and the GSEs.

When CRA was designed around covering depository institutions only, it may have appeared to be a reasonable approach. Few observers anticipated the steep decline in S&L activity that was to occur over the following twenty years and the ascendance of the mortgage company as the dominant source of mortgage originations. The decline in the S&L share of the mortgage market was very steep during the 1980s and early 1990s, and most of that lost share went to mortgage companies. By 1986, the S&L share of originations was down to 35 percent from its high of 55 percent in 1976. By 1993 the share was down to 18 percent and the mortgage company share had increased to 52 percent. The mortgage company had become the originator of most mortgage loans.

The shift of lending from S&Ls to mortgage companies, the depository-oriented design of the Community Reinvestment Act, and the architecture of financial regulatory supervision meant that increasingly over the 1980s and into the 1990s there effectively developed a dual regulatory system in which both segments were very sizable (Apgar, Calder, and Fauth 2004). There was one system for depositories and one for nondepositories. Depositories were covered by CRA and nondepositories were not, although banks or thrifts that owned mortgage companies increasingly could opt to have their mortgage company activity considered in their CRA examinations.

All mortgage lenders are subject to the federal Truth in Lending Act (TILA) and fair lending laws. However, banks and thrifts are subject to regular examination for compliance with not just CRA but also fair lending laws (the Fair Housing Act and the Equal Credit Opportunity Act) and the Truth in Lending Act. Mortgage companies have generally not been subject to routine examination for compliance with any of these laws on a regular basis. Federal regulatory agencies have large cadres of well-trained examiners to conduct these regular examinations. Meanwhile, mortgage companies are typically regulated by state mortgage banking agencies in the states in which they conduct business. Suffice it to say that, in most states, the capacity of state mortgage regulators is generally not as great as that of the federal regulatory agencies.

The result of this dual regulatory system is that, as capital flows into credit markets, there is an incentive for the capital funding the higher-cost and higher-risk loans—loans with more potential for containing abusive terms and exhibiting high foreclosure rates—to flow to mortgage companies. Investors in higher-risk and higher-cost mortgages will naturally seek less-regulated channels. So the dual regulatory system established in the latter decades of the twentieth century formed a regulatory springboard for the segmentation of lending markets and the concentration of high-cost and high-risk products in the most vulnerable communities.

3

The High-Risk Revolution

As late as 2006 or even early 2007, the typical reader of a daily U.S. newspaper was unlikely to be familiar with the term "subprime mortgage." If asked what this term meant, it is likely that she would have responded something like "a low interest-rate loan." Yet, by the summer of 2007, the term "subprime loan" had worked its way into the everyday lexicon of many Americans. By 2008, the American Dialect Society (2008) had named "subprime" its "word of the year" for 2007, and many, if not most, Americans had acquired a substantial—if sometimes somewhat vague or only partially correct—understanding of what the term meant. The subprime crisis, as it was soon called, became one of the hot topics of blogs and Internet conversation as well as the subject of daily stories in print media.

However, with the weekly if not daily headlines on the "subprime crisis" during 2007 came the common perception that the development of the subprime loan market was a very recent phenomenon dating back no earlier than 2000 or even 2002 or 2003. Not well recognized by much of the media, yet alone the general public, was the fact that the growth of high-risk—including, but not limited to subprime—home lending did not arrive in a single explosion, but rather over two periods of rapid growth, one beginning in middle 1990s and the other beginning in approximately 2002. The first boom was marked by a surge in primarily subprime refinance lending—loans made to existing homeowners with substantial equity in their homes—with somewhat slower growth in subprime home purchase loans. Most of these loans were what are called "cash-out" refinances, in which the outstanding debt on the home increases after the loan is made, and the loan is not intended primarily for the purpose of reducing the interest rate but for extracting cash for some other purpose. In the prime market, a much larger share of refinancings is done in order to obtain a lower interest rate.

Subprime cash-out refinance loans in the 1990s were often made to borrowers with substantial financial equity in their homes, so that, even after the loans were made, they exhibited relatively moderate loan-to-value ratios. This meant that lenders and investors took on mostly loans with moderate levels of collateral risk due to the low loan-to-value ratios. The substantial equity available in refinance loans also meant that mortgage brokers and lenders often had ample opportunities to "strip" owners' equity away by charging excessive fees that would be added onto the loan amount. Thus, a borrower who had only $50,000 in outstanding debt on their $150,000 house could easily be refinanced into a new, $120,000 loan. This meant that $70,000 of new money was available, a substantial portion of which might go to paying fees to the broker and lender and related or unrelated parties, such as providers of lump-sum credit insurance. In fact, the loan might be structured in such a way as to precipitate the need for a quick refinancing, giving the broker another opportunity to strip out more equity.

Although subprime home purchase loans were being made in substantial numbers before 2001, it was during the second boom in high-risk credit, beginning in 2002, that subprime home purchase loans took off more rapidly, together with the new class of "exotic" or alternative mortgages aimed at prime borrowers. During this second boom, both purchase and refinance loans from subprime lenders increased quite rapidly, although the rate of increase for purchase loans was greater, especially after 2003. Layered on top of the second boom in subprime and exotic mortgages was the growth of very low- or zero-down-payment home-purchase loan products. And, while subprime mortgages made during the first boom did not perform well compared either to conventional prime loans or to Federal Housing Administration loans, the loans made during the second boom, especially during the peak of that boom in 2005 and 2006, performed even more poorly. Some of these loans were caught in a cycle of upward-spiraling housing costs, which were, in fact, fed by subprime and exotic loans that provided for much larger loan amounts per dollar of borrower income. Especially in markets such as California, Florida, and parts of New England, where land supply was relatively constrained, much of the increased "affordability" enabled by these products was merely capitalized into the prices of homes, so that an additional dollar of affordability enabled by increasing effective debt-to-income ratios largely benefited housing developers and sellers, thus not improving market affordability for buyers.

Figure 3.1 shows the increases in home purchase and refinance loans made by subprime lenders from 1993 to 2004. Although subprime lenders made some prime loans, most of their loans were priced and structured as subprime mortgages. Moreover, some "prime lenders," those not classified by the U.S. Department of Housing and Urban Development as specializing in subprime loans, made subprime loans, and the number of subprime loans made by prime lenders likely increased over time, suggesting that the steepness of the curves in figure 3.1 likely understates the overall rate of increase in the number of subprime loans. Nonetheless, figure 3.1 provides a good picture of the relative increases in subprime purchase and refinance lending over a substantial period. It also shows the share of subprime lending that was used for home purchase over this period. Although interest rate and other market fluctuations—in part following the 1997–98 Asian and Russian financial crises—caused the number of subprime refinance loans to drop and the number of purchase loans to plateau, from 2002 on the subprime market entered a new, second boom. Again, the rate of increase for subprime purchase loans in this second surge of high-risk lending exceeded the rate of growth of subprime refinance loans.

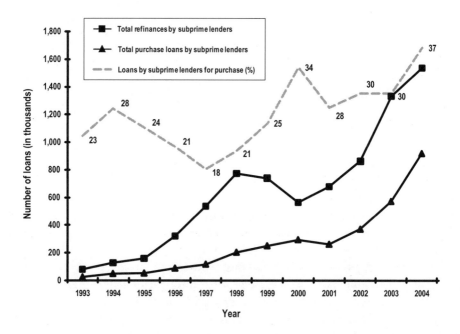

Figure 3.1. Refinancing and home purchase loans by subprime lenders, 1993–2004, United States.
Source: Home Mortgage Disclosure Act; U.S. H.U.D. list of subprime lenders.

The very strong growth in subprime refinance loans in the 1990s meant that, by 1997 and 1998, essentially the peak of the first boom, only about 20 percent of subprime originations were for home purchase. Due to a substantial drop in refinance loans in 1999 and 2000, this share increased to 34 percent in 2000, but then dropped to 28 percent in 2001. But as the new subprime boom occurred, both purchase and refinance loans grew, but purchase loans grew faster, so that the share of subprime lender loans for home purchase hit 37 percent by 2004.

Figure 3.2 extends this analysis with related data through 2006. From 2004 on, Home Mortgage Disclosure Act data disaggregates loans by first-lien status as well as by whether the annual percentage rate (APR) on the loan is above a certain threshold, which is set at 3 percentage points above the interest rate on comparable U.S. Treasury bonds. Unfortunately, this definition makes it somewhat problematic to maintain a consistent definition of high-cost or subprime loans over time, because interest rate dynamics affect the portion of loans falling above the threshold from year to year. That is, in some years, 3 percentage points above comparable Treasury rates may be a relatively higher rate compared

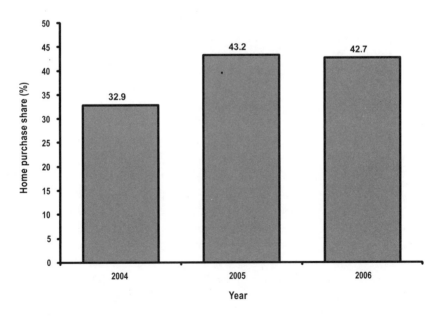

Figure 3.2. Share of first-lien high-rate home purchase and refinance loans that were home purchase (includes only loans for 1–4 unit homes; excludes manufactured homes). *Source:* Federal Financial Institutions Examination Council, 2005, 2006.

to other years. Nonetheless, the high-APR threshold does allow us to compare the distribution of subprime loans (which we approximate here by high-APR loans, as has been done commonly) between purchase and refinance purposes. Figure 3.2 shows that, using the HMDA high-APR threshold, the share of first-lien subprime purchase and refinance loans that were for home purchase was approximately 33 percent in 2004 but rose to approximately 43 percent in 2005 and 2006.

The First Boom in High-Risk Lending: 1992–1999

In the early to middle 1990s, while prime lenders were being encouraged to do more lending to lower-income and minority borrowers by somewhat stronger enforcement of the Community Reinvestment Act and fair lending laws and the new lending goals for the government sponsored enterprises (GSEs) Fannie Mae and Freddie Mac, a new set of lenders were gaining a strong toehold in many of the same markets that advocates had argued were underserved for years by conventional banks and thrifts and by Fannie Mae and Freddie Mac. Researchers and community groups began to notice that, increasingly, more nonbank mortgage lenders were making substantial numbers of conventional (i.e., non-government-insured) loans in minority neighborhoods.

High-cost and abusive lending were not unknown phenomena in the early 1990s. Consumer advocates, such as the National Consumer Law Center, had managed to get the Homeownership and Equity Protection Act passed by 1994. It was aimed at protecting consumers against extremely high-cost loans and related abuses, although industry lobby-ists had managed to get the law watered down so that it primarily added disclosure requirements and was focused on only extremely high-cost loans, missing most of the new subprime market. And mortgage lenders had been implicated in house-flipping fraud schemes, where Federal Housing Administration (FHA) loans were used in schemes in which investor-buyers would do minor cosmetic repair to homes—some of which had previously been FHA foreclosures—and then sell them to naïve owner-occupants who often were overpaying for unsound homes.

The rapid growth of the new specialized subprime lenders in the 1990s was largely happening in parallel with developments in the prime sector, in which community-reinvestment-oriented lenders had, often in part-nership with nonprofit organizations and the GSEs—and encouraged by invigorated enforcement of fair lending laws and the Community

Reinvestment Act—developed new, more responsive loan products for underserved markets. During this first era of subprime growth, there was a key difference between the lending strategies of prime, community-reinvestment-oriented lenders aiming to serve underserved markets and those of subprime firms. The community reinvestment lenders focused primarily on making home purchase loans, as this was seen as the key unmet need in the mortgage arena for lower-income and minority borrowers. Housing groups, community development corporations, national nonprofit community development intermediaries, and some federal agencies had been advocating for the expansion of homeownership. Less attention was paid to lending and borrowing in the home equity and refinance arenas—lending to people who already owned their own homes.

In the meantime, the rapidly emerging subprime sector, while making some home purchase loans, was initially focused on exploiting the market for refinance and home equity loans. The Tax Reform Act of 1986 and the demographic maturation of the surge in postwar homeownership meant that aggregate U.S. home equity—and thus the latent demand for cash-out refinance and home equity loans—had grown dramatically in the latter decades of the twentieth century. Moreover, because many of the potential borrowers of such loans had large amounts of net equity in their homes, loans could be made with moderate loan-to-value ratios, which would compensate for other risks such as weaker credit histories. This allowed the loans to be pooled as backing for securities that would then provide ample capital for higher lending volume. Because early subprime loan pools and the resulting securities were not highly engineered and were primarily undergirded by loans with substantial excess collateral (the loan-to-value ratios of the underlying loans were relatively low, often well under 75 to 80 percent), bond rating agencies such as Standard & Poors could rate the risk of these bonds relatively accurately.

The low loan-to-value ratios also meant that, even if property values stagnated or declined, borrowers would still have substantial equity in their homes. This would not only minimize the collateral risk faced by lenders but would give borrowers a stronger financial incentive to maintain their on-time payments. A number of studies have shown that very low levels of equity in a home, especially when loan-to-value ratios exceed 97 percent, lead to higher foreclosure rates (Austin 2007; Government Accountability Office 2005).

At the same time, while subprime refinance loans defaulted at much higher rates than prime refinance loans in the late 1990s and early 2000s, the higher fees and rates charged on such loans enabled lenders to pay investors higher returns to compensate for higher investment risk. Moreover, the national diversification of risks through large-scale mortgage-backed securities allowed lenders to spread risks, thereby limiting the risks of a particular mortgage-back security. Thus, although on the West Side of Chicago, the foreclosure rates of a subprime lender might approach 10 or 15 percent of outstanding loans going into foreclosure over the course of a year, nationally the lender might only have a 3 to 5 percent foreclosure rate. Such a foreclosure rate would still be far higher than a prime lender, but as long as the losses were no greater than predicted by the lender and its investors, this was acceptable. Of course, the concentrated and high foreclosure rates in particular submarkets, especially when the lender might have a high overall market share in these areas, could mean a high number of foreclosures in such places, with attendant social costs to neighbors and the broader community.

Explaining the First Boom

The explanation for the growth and spatial concentration of subprime lending in the mid to late 1990s involves the confluence and interaction of a number of economic and social conditions with a set of policy developments, some of which had been initiated more than a decade earlier. Overall, if one is forced to point to a particular development as the single greatest factor in the growth of the subprime market in the 1990s, it would have to be the vertical disintegration of the lending industry—in turn made possible primarily by the growth of securitization and the decline of the competitive advantage of the traditional depository institution model within mortgage markets (Jacobides 2005). However, the growth of securitization and vertical disintegration did not appear out of thin air. They were enabled by a set of national and international economic and demographic conditions and, especially, by a series of deregulatory public policy moves in the financial services arena dating back to at least the early 1980s. What is also critical to understand about the initial subprime boom is its reliance upon and exploitation of the geographies of social disadvantage and isolation and the private efficiencies that were enabled by such geographies for the benefit of mortgage brokers, lenders, and investors (Apgar, Calder and Fauth 2004; Squires 2003; Wyly et al. 2007). Moreover, the failure of policymakers to address this geographical divide—even when given the statutory ability to do so—helped enable this exploitation.

Chapter 2 explained the basic process of securitization and how this process was developed by government and government-sponsored secondary market agencies. As Lea (1996) explains, the growth of government-sponsored securitization created a circuit of capital flowing into mortgage markets that was an alternative to, and competitive with, the savings-and-loan-based system that was largely built up through the ability of savings and loans to borrow through the Federal Home Loan Bank system. The standardization of lending practices, especially as promoted by the FHA, fed the development of a national secondary market for mortgages. As states placed limits on interest rates, up-front fees, and loan terms, lenders maintained that such laws restrained the continued growth of more nationally uniform lending markets. They argued that these markets would bring the benefits of economies of scale to homebuyers, thus reducing the costs of a typical homeowners' mortgage. Thus, although government was crucial to the standardization of mortgage markets in the 1930s, by the 1970s industry lobbyists were arguing that government—in this case, state government—was a barrier to financial innovation. This was because, they argued, different states were restricting the ability of lenders to offer uniform "alternative" or higher-cost loan products, inhibiting the ability of secondary markets to create pools of uniform products that would not have to respond to differing state consumer protection laws.

Securitization had made a major impact on the mortgage industry by the mid to late 1980s, following the deregulatory moves of the early 1980s. By 1993, the GSE share of conventional mortgage originations hit a historical peak of 59 percent, up from only 35 percent of conventional originations in 1985 (Van Order 2000). As recently as 1980, the GSE share of *outstanding* single-family loans had only been 10 percent, but by 1993 it had risen to 42 percent. Thus, the 1980s federal policy of disabling or overriding state-level lending regulations, many of which were aimed at consumer protection, was a fundamental, proactive move to support and grow the secondary market for mortgages, including the market for mortgages with "alternative" features including adjustable rates, prepayment penalties, and balloon payments. Of course, part of the reason lenders wanted more freedom to offer such products was to be able to shift interest rate and other risks off their balance sheets and onto borrowers and, in some cases, investors. Lenders using secondary markets for capital also saw such deregulation as another way to gain further competitive advantage over lenders that had to rely on their own capital or on that of the Federal Home Loan Bank system.

Lenders utilizing secondary markets argued that a large portion of the savings provided by large, more robust secondary markets would be passed on to homebuyers and homeowners in the form of lower interest rates and fees. Although this may have been true to some extent, the deregulation of mortgage lending meant that the regulatory groundwork had been laid for an entirely new range of mortgage products, some of which would shift substantially greater risks onto borrowers than was the case with the standard thirty-year fixed-rate prime loan.

The result of the new deregulated landscape was that non-GSE (or "private-label") subprime securitizations grew rapidly, from just $35 billion in 1993 to $150 billion in 1998 (U.S. Department of Treasury and Department of Housing and Urban Development 2000). Private-label securitization was not a new phenomenon in the 1990s, and had been used for "jumbo" loans that exceeded the loan limits of the GSEs, but by the early 1990s it had paved the way for expanded subprime securitization. In addition to providing the deregulatory groundwork for the expansion of the securitization of higher-risk mortgage products, GSEs had fueled the market for the computational technologies needed for the growth of structured finance. In the world of high-risk lending, with the complex carving apart of different risk segments (tranches) and the allocation of these to different investors, such technologies were even more necessary in the second high-risk boom.

While federal policymakers were overriding states' ability to regulate abusive lending practices and products in the 1980s, they were doing nothing to create a new system of financial regulation—or even expanding existing regulatory resources—for what was to become an rapidly growing set of new, essentially unregulated mortgage lenders. They were also driving a stake in the heart of already struggling savings and loans, by providing their competitors with cheaper secondary-market capital and free rein from a more extensive regulatory regime.

Banks and thrifts—which had traditionally utilized the Home Loan Bank circuit for accessing lending capital—were subject to the Community Reinvestment Act, fair lending laws, and consumer compliance regulation. Moreover, for these depository institutions, lending laws were implemented by a cadre of thousands of bank examiners across the four federal bank regulators. These examiners would conduct regular, proactive exams of the depositories for their compliance with these laws. Granted, such exams were hardly considered rigorous, especially during the 1980s, but there was at least a regulatory infrastructure set up to police lender activities and respond to consumer complaints.

At the same time, the new mortgage companies that came to dominate the subprime market were subject to no substantive regulatory infrastructure. These firms were not regularly examined by any federal agency, and state regulatory enforcement, if any, was very weak. The only federal agency with authority over enforcing consumer protection laws regarding the fast-growing set of subprime mortgage companies was the Federal Trade Commission, an agency not at all equipped for such levels of activity. And, with the undoing of state consumer protection laws, there were few laws on the books that state regulators or the FTC could enforce, even if they did have sufficient staff and enforcement capacity.

To this day, independent and even bank-owned mortgage companies generally undergo no regular examinations by federal regulators, and state regulators generally have much less capacity than their federal counterparts. Federal regulators have some ability to evaluate the lending patterns of the subsidiaries of banks and thrifts, but it is unclear how systematically this is done. Moreover, the Federal Reserve, which had the power to examine the mortgage company subsidiaries of bank holding companies, chose not to do so even as concerns over the steering of minority borrowers to subprime bank affiliates was being raised (Ip 2007; Andrews 2007). The Federal Trade Commission had some authority to address lending abuses, but it was not been given sufficient resources or direction to do so. States were seen as the principal source of regulatory oversight.

The rise of securitization via both the GSEs and through Wall Street and the lack of any meaningful regulatory restraint meant that the geographic scope and scale of mortgage lenders increased. Interstate banking restrictions, which had begun to fall well before the 1990s, were essentially phased out by the mid-1990s. From 1992 to 1997, the share of mortgage loans originated by the top twenty-five lenders in the United States rose from just over 30 percent to over 50 percent, reaching 78 percent by 2002 (Apgar, Calder, and Fauth 2004; Apgar and Fishbein 2004). Many of these lenders made many of their loans through wholesale operations, using independent mortgage brokers to market to and qualify potential borrowers. The increased scale and dominance of large lenders also occurred in the subprime market. The market share of the top five subprime lenders increased from 20 percent in 1996 to 40 percent by 2002. The top twenty-five subprime lenders accounted for 88 percent of the subprime market in 2002, up from 47 percent in 1996.

The rapid growth of large lenders with access to larger, more robust capital markets and serving national lending markets meant that lenders relied increasingly on a rapidly growing industry of mortgage brokers.

The use of brokers provided these large lenders with the ability to quickly ramp up the scale of their lending operations, which was critical in their quest for all-important market share. From 1991 to 1998, the number of brokers grew at an annual rate of 14 percent (Kim-Sung and Hermanson 2003). In 2000, thirty thousand mortgage brokerage firms employed an estimated 240,000 workers and accounted for approximately 55 percent of all mortgage originations.

Lenders and investors benefited from the use of mortgage brokers in several ways. The most obvious is the fact that brokers relieved lenders of the need to reduce and expand staffing as lending markets ebbed and flowed. However, the advantages of wholesale lending, with brokers serving as the retail network, extend beyond this. If violations of consumer protection or fair lending laws occur in the origination process, lenders and investors could claim that they lacked knowledge of or input into any illegal or harmful actions that were proximately carried out by the broker. Moreover, wholesale lenders who did not scrutinize brokers closely for improper or illegal practices could gain market share by reducing compliance costs passed on to brokers and by appealing to brokers that engage in predatory or abusive lending practices or discrimination. A wholesale lender with strict oversight of its broker network may lose brokers and thus market share, especially in a market segment that engaged in substantial abusive practices.

Race and the Emergence of the New Dual Loan Market

As described earlier, refinance loans accounted for the bulk of the first subprime boom. However, this boom was disproportionately concentrated in increases to minority borrowers and in minority neighborhoods. Figure 3.3 shows the rates of growth in subprime lender refinances from 1993 to 1998 by the race and ethnicity of the borrowers. The first thing to note is the very large increase in HMDA loans where race is not reported. The number of such loans was not at all insignificant, especially by 1998, accounting for more than 240,000 loans and over 30 percent of subprime lender refinances. There have been significant reporting loopholes in HMDA—many of which have since been tightened—allowing lenders to avoid comprehensive reporting. Loans with no racial information increased more than twenty-five times from 1993 to 1998. In 2000, 35 percent of refinance loans by subprime lenders had missing racial data compared to 19 percent of loans by prime lenders (Bradford 2002). In twenty-one metropolitan areas in the United States, subprime lenders failed to report race on more than 50 percent of their refinance loans, and this rate went as high as 67 percent. Wyly and Holloway (2002) found that cities with higher subprime activity had higher nonreporting rates. In examining Atlanta data more closely, they also found that nonreporting rates for refinance applications were much higher in black neighborhoods than in white ones. They estimated that African Americans were overrepresented among missing-race loans, constituting over one-third of all 2000 HMDA unreported records. Thus, the very large numbers of race-missing loans were almost certainly disproportionately loans to African Americans and other minorities.

The poor reporting of the race of borrowers in HMDA data initially obscured the disproportionate growth of subprime lending in minority communities. Fortunately, the location of the loans was reported at much higher levels, and this helped analysts document the disproportionate surge of subprime lending in minority and, especially, in African American neighborhoods.

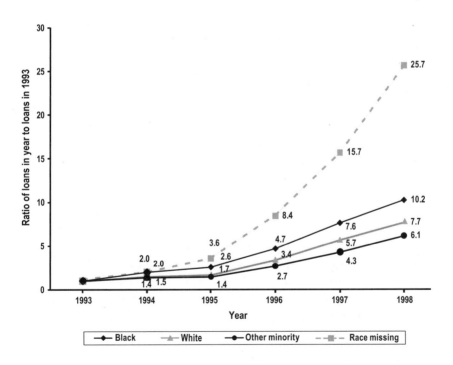

Figure 3.3. Rates of growth in subprime refinance lending by race of borrower, 1993–1998, United States.
Source: Home Mortgage Disclosure Act data.

Looking at the racial composition of neighborhoods shows that refinance lending grew much faster in predominantly black neighborhoods than in white neighborhoods. Some of the earliest work documenting these trends took place in Chicago, where it was shown that the number of refinance loans made in predominantly black (75 to 100 percent black) census tracts grew by twenty-nine times from 1993 to 1998, while subprime lending in predominantly white (90 to 100 percent white) tracts grew by only 2.3 times (Immergluck and Wiles 1999). In 2000, the U.S. Department of Housing and Urban Development analyzed lending patterns in the United States and more closely in five large cities (U.S. Department of Housing and Urban Development 2000). By 1998, subprime lenders dominated lending in black neighborhoods across the country. In predominantly black neighborhoods, those where 75 percent or more of residents were black, subprime lenders made 51 percent of the refinance loans compared to only 9 percent in predominantly white neighborhoods. Moreover, the same study found that homeowners in predominantly black neighborhoods were more than twice as likely as homeowners in low-income white neighborhood to receive subprime loans. In upper-income black census tracts, 39 percent of refinance borrowers received their loans from subprime lenders versus only 18 percent in low-income white neighborhoods. Refinance borrowers in upper-income black neighborhoods were six times more likely than borrowers in upper-income white neighborhoods to receive subprime loans. These same basic patterns were found in HUD's studies of Atlanta, Philadelphia, New York, Chicago, and Baltimore. Later analyses have documented similarly hypersegmented markets in cities throughout the country (Bradford 2002).

The racial composition of a neighborhood can be confounded with lower education levels and differences in credit history, as well as other factors, so a number of researchers have conducted studies with broader data sets to identify the factors accounting for the concentration of subprime loans in minority neighborhoods. Calem, Gillen, and Wachter (2004) found that, after controlling for education, income, and housing-stock characteristics, black neighborhoods still had much higher levels of subprime lending than white neighborhoods. For refinance loans, an all-black neighborhood was expected to have a subprime share that was 24 percentage points higher than an otherwise equivalent white neighborhood, even after controlling for the credit history of neighborhood residents. Silver (2003) analyzed the lending in six additional cities—Baltimore, Detroit, Houston, Atlanta, Milwaukee, and Cleveland—and again found similar results. Even after controlling for housing turnover, age of housing stock, median income, percentage of residents aged sixty-five and older, and the percentage of residents with high-risk credit scores, the percentage of residents who were black was a consistently strong determinant of subprime lending activity. In all six cities, the percentage of residents in a census tract who were black had a highly significant effect on the proportion of refinance loans made by subprime lenders. In every city, going from an all-white neighborhood to an otherwise equivalent all-black neighborhood resulted in the proportion of subprime lending increasing by at least 11 percentage points (in Baltimore). The effect was typically closer to 20 to 25 percentage points and exceeded 40 percentage points in Houston. Moreover, in four of the six cities the percentage of residents over age sixty-five had a significant and positive effect on subprime refinance lending.

Calem, Hershaff, and Wachter (2004) later expanded the earlier research by Calem, Gillen, and Wachter (2004) to seven cities and analyzed data for two years. They found that individual race, ethnicity, and income are significantly and positively related to the likelihood of receiving a loan from a subprime lender. They also find that lower educational levels have a positive effect on the likelihood of receiving a subprime loan.

Two important studies were able to bring in individual credit history information and control for it as well as numerous other characteristics in investigating the likelihood of receiving a subprime loan. A study of home purchase loans conducted by an affiliate of the Mortgage Bankers Association of America found that the probability of a home purchase borrower receiving a subprime loan, after controlling for credit history, location, and other variables, increased by approximately one-third, from 0.8 percent to 2.5 percent, if the borrower was black (Pennington-Cross, Yezer, and Nichols 2000). The loan sample in this study had relatively few subprime loans in it, but the increase was relatively substantial and statistically significant. A later study with a large set of refinance and purchase loans also found similar results. In studying a large national set of loans, Gruenstein-Bocian, Ernst, and Li (2008) found that African American homebuyers were 31 percent more likely than a similarly situated white borrower to receive a high-rate (versus low-rate), fixed-rate mortgage with a prepayment penalty.

As the home loan market became increasingly segmented by race, so that minority communities were served primarily by subprime lenders, homeowners in such communities were—either deliberately or systematically—steered toward higher-cost products, some of which contained more restrictive terms. Because minority communities were targets of high-risk lenders and received little attention from prime lenders, the odds of minority borrowers with good credit receiving higher-cost loans were higher than that of white borrowers with good credit.

The dual mortgage market, including the resistance of prime lenders to market and make loans in minority communities, can create a sense of futility among minority homeowners in considering banks and other prime lenders as potential lenders. In Fannie Mae's 2001 National Housing Survey, only 34 percent of credit-impaired respondents were confident that they got the lowest cost mortgage available, compared to 68 percent of all homeowners surveyed (Fannie Mae 2001). Thirty-two percent of credit-impaired homeowners did not care whether they got the lowest cost mortgage, they were "just happy to be approved," compared to only 10 percent of all respondents. Moreover, more subprime respondents reported not knowing anything about their credit rating.

The proportion of loans made by subprime lenders that contained abusive practices has been the subject of considerable debate, but it was rare to find a case of a predatory lending that did not involve a subprime lender. A couple of local studies have surveyed recipients of subprime loans to understand the incidence of various predatory lending practices (Stock 2001; Stein and Libby 2001). In a study of 255 very high-cost loans in Dayton, Ohio, 75 percent were found to have prepayment penalties and 24 percent had balloon payments. The researchers also interviewed subprime borrowers who were in the process of foreclosure as well as those who were not. Thirty-nine percent of respondents in foreclosure and 33 percent of respondents not in foreclosure stated that the initial contact with the lender was initiated by the lender via phone or mail. Forty-five percent of foreclosure respondents and 24 percent of other respondents said that their loans' terms at closing were different than what had been discussed. Eighty-six percent of foreclosure respondents and 68 percent of the respondents who noted a difference in terms accepted the difference, perhaps due to pressure at the closing from the lender. And finally, 19 percent of nonforeclosure respondents and 42 percent of foreclosure respondents were encouraged to borrow more than they had intended. In California, Stein and Libby (2001) interviewed 125 subprime borrowers and found that 39 percent of subprime respondents said that the idea of taking out a home-secured loan came from the lender-broker. They also found that 64 percent of respondents had refinanced their homes six times. Forty percent of the refinances had taken place within two years of the prior loan, a strong indicator of flipping.

The researchers found that 38 percent of the subprime borrowers fit a "worst case scenario" characterized by a combination of onerous loan terms, high costs, and aggressive sales tactics.

Technology, Subprime Lending, and Racial and Geographic Market Segmentation

At least four technological innovations were key in the development of the subprime market in the 1990s and beyond: (1) geodemographic marketing tools; (2) data warehousing and mining; (3) Internet usage between wholesale lenders and brokers; and (4) credit scoring and automated underwriting (Gale 2001). These innovations worked, both individually and in combination with each other, to increase economies of scale and thus further the consolodation and geographic scales of the lending industry, but also to provide a new set of tools for those seeking to segment mortgage customers in all sorts of ways.

Geodemographic marketing technologies allowed lenders to identify clusters of potential borrowers by income, age, home value, and race and ethnicity (proxied sometimes by neighborhood location). For example, Claritas, Inc., a marketing technology firm, developed neighborhood classification systems such as "Upper Crust" and "Trying Rural Times" (Gale 2001). These firms' segmentation models served to legitimize neighborhood stereotypes, which were then likely to result in the segmented marketing of high- and low-cost financial products.

Data mining and warehousing involves the creation of elaborate data sets on current and potential customers. It was principally enabled by faster computers and the ability to store large amounts of data, as well as advances in data mining algorithms and programming (Gale 2001). Lenders were able to extract highly detailed data and utilize statistical models to sort "good" and "bad" prospects. In 1999, a bank research firm estimated that about half of banks with more than $1 billion in deposits used profit data to make customer decisions. According to industry analysts, banks spent an estimated $500 million in the late 1990s on software and consultants, with spending projected grow to at least $500 million per year in the near future, according to one 1999 estimate (Brooks 1999). Banks began using these systems to charge less-lucrative customers more for specific services, and then waive fees for more affluent customers.

During the 1990s, a variety of more specialized real estate data firms developed targeted marketing data systems specifically for the mortgage industry and made them accessible via the Internet to even the smallest mortgage brokers. The Internet also assisted brokers in gaining access to highly sophisticated data mining and warehouse operations maintained and sold by such firms as First American Real Estate Solutions and DataQuick. By 2001, industry data repositories captured an estimated 85 percent of real estate transactions (Livermore 2001). Some firms began providing Internet-based subscription services that allowed brokers and lenders to gain access to highly customized and targeted prospect lists, using searches based on five- or nine-digit zip codes, the age of the borrower, recent property transactions and mortgage activity, the identity and type (subprime/prime) of the current lender, whether the loan was an FHA or VA loan, current cumulative loan-to-value ratio, an estimate of "available equity," other property details (e.g., current estimated market value, presence of swimming pool), as well as address and phone number. At least one firm marketed its services on the Internet explicitly stating that it could provide data on the "ethnicity" of homeowners (Immergluck 2004).

Many firms began offering data on pre-foreclosure filings that could be easily downloaded over the Internet for a relatively affordable monthly subscription. Homeowners in the pre-foreclosure stage are particularly susceptible to predatory lenders who may flip them into a new loan, preventing foreclosure in the short run, but often not for very long.

The Internet also facilitated the broker's "backroom" operations—its connections to its pool of lenders. The Internet has often been portrayed as providing more direct access to mortgages to savvy, intensive rate-shoppers, and that no doubt happened to some degree. But what has generally been ignored is the important boon that the Internet provided to mortgage brokers. Brokers were able to obtain approvals from a variety of lenders in a matter of hours or even minutes via Internet connectivity. The broker became the "Internet-enabled" link between the borrower and the lender (Gale 2001).

The Second High-Risk Boom: Expanding to the Home Purchase Market and the Emergence of Exotic Products

With the 1997–1998 Asian and Russian financial crises and the recession of 2000–2001, subprime lending stalled during the 1999 to 2001 period (see figure 3.1). However, by 2002 the second boom in subprime lending was under way, this time accompanied by the dominance of a set of alternative loan structures that were applied to both prime and subprime loans. Although many of these loan structures had been employed before, they were generally used in boutique or niche loan markets, often aimed at high-net-worth real estate investors and the affluent self-employed. In this new boom, however, many of these new features were applied to a broad spectrum of borrowers in both the prime and subprime markets.

Subprime mortgages in the first boom were most often structured as thirty-year fixed-rate mortgages. Although fees and rates were substantially higher than those for prime loans, and many of the loans included prepayment penalties or balloon payments, they were structured somewhat similarly to the traditional thirty–year fixed-rate loan that had come to dominate U.S. homeownership throughout most of the twentieth century. Due to the higher risks involved, loan-to-value ratios were generally lower than for comparable prime loans.

However, in the second high-risk boom, subprime loans were often structured so that they had adjustable rates, with initial rates fixed for only two or three years and the likelihood of substantial increases in rates after that. These adjustable rate mortgages (ARMs) were called "2/28" or "3/27" hybrids, with the first number referring to the initial, fixed-rate period and the second number to the remaining adjustable-rate period.

In addition to the hybrid adjustable-rate structure, subprime loans in the second boom tended to exhibit features that increased their default risk compared to the loans of the first boom. First, as described earlier, home purchase loans constituted a substantially larger portion of the second boom. Another development in the second boom was the rapid growth of no- or low-documentation loans (sometimes also called "stated-income" loans). With these loans, lenders were not required to document the incomes of the homebuyers. Before the late 1990s, low-doc loans had been restricted primarily to self-employed borrowers or wealthy investors with high levels of net worth. Figure 3.4 shows that the share of subprime loans that had low or no documentation rose from less than 30 percent in 2001 to more than 50 percent by 2005.

Another area of continued deterioration in lending standards in the high-risk lending boom was the tolerance of even greater maximum debt-to-income ratios than in the first boom. Figure 3.5 shows that the average debt-to-income ratio for subprime home purchase loans increased from just under 40 percent in 2001—already a fairly high number given the growing dominance of adjustable-rate loan structures—to over 42 percent by 2006. Because these figures are means, an increase of 2 percentage points can mask substantial increases in the proportion of loans with very high ratios.

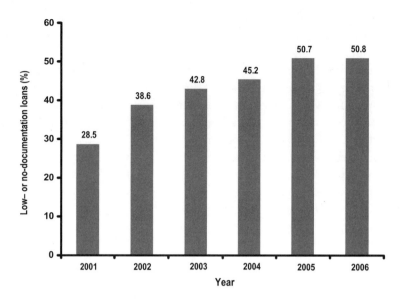

Figure 3.4. Share of subprime loans that are no– or low-documentation.
Source: Freddie Mac data compiled in U.S. Senate Joint Economic Committee (2007).

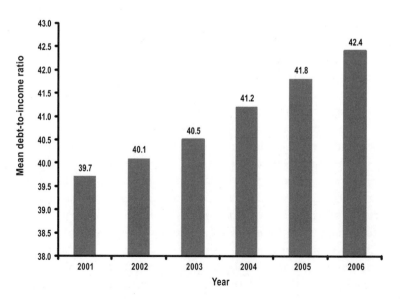

Figure 3.5. Mean debt-to-income ratios for subprime home purchase loans.
Source: Freddie Mac data compiled in U.S. Senate Joint Economic Committee (2007).

Exotic Mortgage Structures in Prime and Subprime Markets

The growth of nontraditional or "exotic" mortgage products, which were marketed to both prime and subprime borrowers, gained considerable momentum after 2001. Exotic loans include those in which payments were large enough only to pay interest accrued (interest-only), those in which payments are less than even the accrued interest (negative amortization), and payment-option mortgages, in which the borrower had the option of payments that are negative amortization, interest only, or interest plus some principal. Many of these loans were also structured as hybrids, with initial periods of fixed interest-rates (often for a four- or five-year period), then becoming an adjustable-rate loan.

Before 2002, many of these products and loan features either did not exist or were marketed quite selectively to wealthy homebuyers and real estate investors. The available indicators show strong growth in exotic mortgages, especially from 2001 to 2005. Loan Performance, Inc., tracks loans sold to third parties other than Fannie Mae and Freddie Mac. Although this leaves out a sizeable segment of the overall mortgage market, it likely includes a large portion of the growth in exotic loans. These data show that among tracked loans, those that were interest-only rose from under 5 percent in 2001 to approximately 35 percent in 2005 (Loan Performance 2006). Negative amortization loans rose from less than 1 percent in 2003 to more than 7 percent by 2005. In California, this figure topped 17 percent in 2005. Loan Performance also listed twelve metropolitan areas in California and ten in other states where interest-only loans accounted for more than 50 percent of the loans that they tracked.

Most exotic mortgages in the second boom involved adjustable interest rates. In the first half of 2005, an estimated nine out of ten interest-only loans had adjustable-rate components (Fishbein and Woodall 2006). Initially low interest rates—sometimes called "teaser" rates—made these adjustable rate mortgages appear more affordable, contributing to their popularity.

Much of the increase in ARM activity in recent years has been attributed to exotic products. The Federal Housing Finance Board's Monthly Interest Rate Survey (MIRS) of major lenders tracks the prevalence of ARMs (both traditional and exotic) among home purchase loans (Federal Housing Finance Board 2006). Because large loans that exceeded GSE purchasing limits (called jumbo mortgages) were more likely to be ARMs, the survey distinguishes between jumbo and nonjumbo loans. The share of mortgages that are ARMs fluctuates widely. Traditionally, as rates for fixed-rate loans fall, the short-term savings that ARMs can provide decline, and fixed-rate loans increase. However, from 2001 to 2003 interest rates generally fell, but ARMs increased for nonjumbo mortgages. Then, although rates remained relatively flat, ARMs increased dramatically in 2004, making up 71 percent of jumbo loans and 31 percent of nonjumbo loans in the MIRS data. Even so, these data likely understate ARM growth in later years, especially in the subprime market and for loans with teaser introductory rates.

Rising property values are likely to increase demand for exotic mortgages. However, such products also enable buyers to afford higher-cost homes, fueling demand, thus becoming a cause as well as an effect of higher home prices. Many lenders promoted such products as means for buyers to afford larger homes. In highly competitive home loan markets, originators, including brokers and retail loan officers paid on commission, competed less by helping the borrower find the loan with the lowest interest rate or fees and more by finding the loan—no matter how poorly structured—that would deliver the largest amount of principal per dollar of income. This often meant a loan with one or more exotic features, including an adjustable rate, a payment-option feature, a teaser rate, and/or stated-income status (which allowed for exaggerating income). These "layered" risks can interact in a multiplicative, and not simply additive, fashion, thereby greatly increasing the default risks of the loan.

Very Low and Zero Down-Payment Loans

During much of the twentieth century, the standard down payment requirement for a conventional home purchase loan was 20 percent. Until the 1990s, down payments below 20 percent typically required either private mortgage insurance or the use of a government-insured or government-guaranteed loan. Figure 3.6 illustrates the introduction of low and zero-down-payment loan products in the United States. The Veterans Administration introduced a zero-down-payment loan program as early as 1944. The FHA followed with a program permitting down payments of 5 percent in 1948 and then 3 percent in 1957. In the 1970s, the GSEs began purchasing loans on which the homeowner had put as little as 5 percent down. In 1994, Fannie Mae introduced a 3 percent down product, and Freddie Mac followed with a similar product in 1998. In 2000, both GSEs began offering products that required no down payment through programs that generally required mandatory prepurchase homeownership counseling aimed at preparing buyers for homeownership.

Notwithstanding the increased growth of programs aimed at increasing the number of conventional home purchase loans with very low down payments, the FHA remained a major provider of such loans through 2000. Almost 90 percent of FHA loans had loan-to-value ratios above 95 percent in 2000, while the figures for Fannie Mae and Freddie Mac were 4.4 percent and 6.1 percent, respectively (Government Accountability Office 2005).

In figure 3.6, the innovations shown in light gray indicate the relatively incremental approaches employed during much of the twentieth century to broaden access to homeownership for those with modest assets. Most of these innovations were the result of deliberate public policy and were closely scrutinized for their loan performance. The zero-down programs of the GSEs in the 1990s, for example, were generally carefully designed to include prepurchase counseling and cautious requirements regarding credit score and history. There were some poorly designed initiatives before 2000, of course. For example, when the FHA introduced more aggressive, essentially zero down-payment loans (that also had subsidized interest rates) in the late 1960s, increased loss rates and concentrated foreclosure rates led to the program eventually being curtailed.

The very low and zero down-payment innovations introduced more broadly after 2000 and shown in dark gray in figure 3.6 were designed and implemented less carefully than most of the earlier innovations. The first

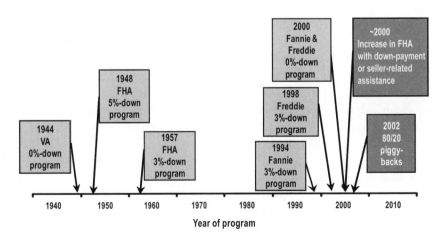

Figure 3.6. The historical progression of low and zero down-payment programs.

major "second-boom" innovation that spurred very low or zero down-payment home buying was a much greater use of second-lien home purchase loans, commonly called "piggyback" mortgages, which enabled home buyers to buy loans with less—often much less—than a 20 percent down payment. These loans were often called "80/20" or "90/10" mortgages, where the first number stood for the first mortgage's portion of the home price and the second number stood for the second mortgage lender's share of the purchase price. In such schemes, borrowers would put no money down to buy the home.

The traditional scheme to reduce down payments below 20 percent involved conventional lenders requiring borrowers with less than 20 percent down payments to purchase monthly private mortgage insurance (PMI), which insured the lender against an insufficiency of collateral in the event of foreclosure. The PMI pays the lender for any shortfall between the proceeds from the sale of the foreclosed home and the loan balance. However, PMI insurers, because they would bear a large portion of the costs of loan losses in the event of defaults, were generally more prudent underwriters than second mortgage lenders. With the advent of aggressive piggyback lending, where the second mortgage lender would take on this risk and make PMI uneccessary, many borrowers no longer required PMI. As subprime lenders began offering piggyback mortgages, enabling home buyers to make very small or even zero down payments, the constraining effects of PMI underwriting was eliminated.

Home Mortgage Disclosure Act data showed that 22 percent of first-lien home purchase loans originated in 2005 and 2006 involved a piggyback loan (Avery, Breevort, and Canner 2007). Moreover, the HMDA data show that more than 45 percent of 2006 second-lien home purchase loans were high-rate loans, that is, essentially subprime loans, as compared to only 25 percent of fist-lien purchase loans. Data from Loan Performance, Inc., show that the proportion of first mortgage loans with "silent seconds," in which a second mortgage was not disclosed to the first mortgage lender, increased from 1.3 percent in 2000 to 15.8 percent by 2004 and 27.5 percent by 2006 (Ashcraft and Schuermann 2008).

Although some piggyback loans involved substantial down payments (e.g., an 80–10–10 structure, where the borrower makes a 10 percent down payment), many involved very high cumulative loan-to-value ratios. SMR Research found that, in 2005, over 50 percent of piggyback loans had cumulative loan-to-value ratios of over 95 percent, which includes the 80/20 and 90/10 structures that became very common, especially among subprime lenders (SMR Research Corporation 2005).

The second area of post-2000 innovation in the area of very low down payments was a much greater use of down-payment assistance in FHA programs and GSE programs, and some variations on down-payment assistance proved to be problematic. Some down-payment-assistance programs allowed buyers with essentially no equity of their own to purchase a home. This may be a feasible approach for some segment of borrowers, but the risks are higher than with low down-payment programs and are best implemented with a required prepurchase counseling requirement. GSE programs followed this approach.

From 2000 to 2005, the proportion of FHA-insured loans that had loan-to-value ratios (LTVs) greater than 95 percent and involved down-payment assistance grew from 35 to nearly 50 percent (U.S. Government Accountability Office 2006). From 2000 to 2004, the proportion of FHA loans involving down-payment assistance from a nonprofit organization grew from 6 to 30 percent. Many lenders permitted down-payment assistance from third parties, especially for first-time homebuyers. Both the FHA and the GSEs stipulated that such assistance cannot come from anyone with an interest in the sale of the property.

The FHA, however, also allowed another option, permitting seller-funded down-payment assistance via a nonprofit intermediary. This scheme allowed residential developers to make donations to nonprofit organizations, which would then turn around and provide down-payment assistance to families that would buy homes from the developer. The developer then could, and sometimes did, essentially recoup the donation by increasing the price of the home. The net result is that the FHA would provide 100 percent financing of the market value of the home, that is, the value in the absence of the seller-funded assistance.

Partly as the result of aggressive, seller-funded down-payment assistance programs and increased 80/20 or 90/10 piggyback loans, the proportion of homebuyers buying homes with zero down payments increased significantly after 2000. Moreover, many of these loans were also layered with additional nonstandard terms, including hybrid adjustable loans with teaser rates, low or no documentation, and interest-only or payment-option structures. Data from the 1999 American Housing Survey (AHS) showed that only 5 percent of owner-occupiers who purchased single-family homes in metropolitan areas in 1998 and 1999 indicated "no down payment" when asked what their main source of the down payment was for their house. By 2005 the AHS data showed that this figure had reached 13.3 percent for 2004 and 2005 nationally (American Housing Survey 1999, 2005). Given that many zero-down-payment programs were aimed at lower-income borrowers or were more common in high-cost metropolitan areas, these products are likely to be substantially more prevalent in some areas than in others.

Explaining the Second Boom in High-Risk Mortgage Lending

Together with the forces propelling the initial high-risk surge of the late 1990s, two key factors played a role in propelling the second boom in high-risk lending, one of which was both a cause and an effect of high-risk lending. This factor was the strong appreciation of home values in many metropolitan markets, especially those on the West Coast, in Florida, and in many parts of the East Coast. Even some inland markets, such as Chicago, Las Vegas, and Phoenix, experienced relatively strong housing appreciation from 2000 to 2005. Figure 3.7 illustrates what some call the "virtuous cycle" of housing appreciation and its linkage to the development and expanded use of "innovative" or "affordability" loan products.

As figure 3.7 suggests, affordability problems among homebuyers meant that lenders responded by developing new "affordability products," using layers of exotic features, both for prime and subprime borrowers. As home prices increased, lenders increasingly competed for home loan customers by attempting to offer customers larger loans, so that borrowers could purchase larger homes or homes in more desirable areas. These loans often involve the exotic products described above—including payment-option or interest-only loans, zero-down piggyback loans, stated-income loans (again, allowing for the exaggeration of incomes)—as well as generally higher debt-to-income ratios. In an era in which securitization dominated, originators' profits were driven by loan volume and associated fees. This meant that the drive for market share dominated the design and underwriting of loans. Among retail lenders, loan "officers" increasingly became mere salesmen paid mostly on commission and, of course, for wholesale originators, brokers could go elsewhere if a lender was not "flexible" enough.

The exotic loan products increased the effective purchasing power of homebuyers in most markets, thereby shifting the demand curve for homes upward. Especially in areas where the supply of land is relatively fixed, at least in the short run the higher home-purchasing power of households was largely absorbed into higher home values (Green and Wachter 2007).

Figure 3.7. The "virtuous" cycle of high-risk lending and housing prices.

Therefore, in many tight real estate markets, homebuyers, as a group at least, did not benefit in the long run from the "affordability" of the new loan products. Instead, home sellers—as well as the Realtors and lenders—benefited from higher home values. The fragility of this credit-dependent appreciation cycle is fairly obvious. The underlying repayment performance of many of the high-risk loans was essentially buttressed by strong growth in housing values in many of the larger housing markets across the country. In such regions, if a borrower experiences difficulty in repaying a loan, rising values enable him or her to either refinance the loan or sell the house and pay off the loan relatively easily. If values do not increase enough, however, or markets stagnate and make selling or refinancing difficult, these options become scarce, and defaults and foreclosures will increase, thus putting further downward pressure on housing markets.

Even in regions that did not suffer from large appreciation bubbles, even moderate growth became dependent on lax lending standards and excess lending. These markets often had weaker constraints on the aggregate supply of land. Thus, as credit-induced demand increased, the metropolitan area simply expanded and prices did not increase as dramatically. However, even these markets were vulnerable because, as credit markets seized in 2007, and the pendulum swung back in the direction of excessively restricted credit, the supplies of credit that these markets depended on for their sprawling growth were no longer available, and demand for housing declined, leading to downward price pressures as well. Thus, while the virtuous cycles were most evident, and most egregious, in tighter housing markets, the vicious cycle downward had national impacts on credit availability, causing a "contagion effect."

The non-localness of modern lending markets meant that rapid regional housing price declines were less isolated. Through downward effects on national credit availability, the bubbles bursting in large regional housing markets caused national credit markets to pull back, thus causing downward pressure on regions where house prices had not grown so aggressively.

The second principal cause of the second boom in high-risk-mortgage lending was the increased supply of higher-risk capital and the resulting decrease in interest-rate risk premiums in mortgage-related capital markets. This increased supply of capital came principally from large institutional investors looking for marginally higher returns on their investment portfolios. The continuing globalization of financial markets also meant that capital was pouring in from other continents as well as the from the traditional U.S. sources (Bernanke 2005).

This increased capital availability meant that the cost of high-risk-mortgage credit became relatively cheaper, compared to lower risk credit, so that "risk premiums" contracted. The excess supply of higher-risk capital was at least proximately located in the increased complexity of structured finance instruments designed to diversify the risk of an individual mortgage transaction ever more broadly across ever more investors and more highly complex investment products.

As discussed in chapter 2, mortgage-backed securities were well established before the end of the 1990s. However, many of the RMBS structures—including the collateralized mortgage obligations (CMOs) that had become increasingly popular in the 1980s and 1990s—were relatively straightforward in their structure, especially compared to the mortgage securities that were developed after 2000. More important, these earlier RMBS structures were relatively transparent and so less difficult for investors or credit rating agencies to evaluate for risk.

The Role of Complex Financial Innovations in the Second High-Risk Boom

As was the case in the first boom in high-risk lending, securitization markets played an important role in the second boom and interacted with the "virtuous" cycle of housing appreciation to greatly expand the flow of capital into high-risk markets. Figure 3.8 shows that the issuance of mortgage-backed securities in the subprime market increased from $87 billion in 2001 to almost $450 billion by 2006. In the Alt-A market, which includes many stated-income and alternative mortgages—mostly to borrowers with strong credit scores—issuance of RMBS increased from approximately $11 billion in 2001 to more than $365 billion by 2006. The combination of this explosive growth of securitization since 2001, as well as the decline of GSE issuance from 2003 to 2006, meant that the securitization of subprime and Alt-A loans together almost equaled GSE issuance by 2006 ($814 billion versus $905 billion). Adding in the nonagency securitization of jumbo mortgages meant that nonagency securitization exceeded GSE securitization ($1,033 billion to $905 billion) in 2006.

The simple growth of nonagency CMO-type RMBS was not the entire story of why so much capital flowed into high-risk mortgage markets starting in 2002 and 2003. There were fundamental shifts in the financial engineering of mortgage securities, including most notably the vertical layering of securities, which would themselves be made up not only of underlying mortgages but also of RMBS—in other words, the creation of securities that were themselves generated by cash flows from

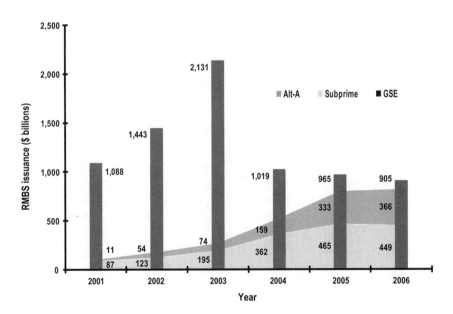

Figure 3.8. Issuance of mortgage-backed securities in the Alt-A, subprime, and GSE markets. *Source:* Inside Mortgage Finance from Ashcraft and Schuermann (2008).

other securities. Thus, the borrowers were now even further removed from the eventual funders of their loans. In the first wave of nonagency securitization, pension funds and other institutional investors would invest in RMBS, which were composed of thousands of individual mortgages. They may be super senior investors or higher-risk AA or BBB investors, and they relied on the credit rating agencies to correctly evaluate the risks of the underlying loans and the tranches (based on available enhancements and the level of subordination beneath their particular tranche).

Enterprising financial engineers devised a way to add liquidity to (that is, increase the demand for) even the lower (that is, higher risk) RMBS tranches. A new form of supposedly diversified, but also highly complex, security was applied heavily to the subprime and Alt-A mortgage markets—the collateralized debt obligation, or CDO. The CDO involved the additional layering or intermediation between the institutional investor and the borrowers. Figure 3.9 provides a somewhat simplified description of how CDOs work. The traditional RMBS structure is indicated in the upper left portion of the diagram, in which a pool of typically thousands of loans is sold to a special purpose vehicle, and the loans are assembled into a trust. The cash flows from these loans are allocated to different RMBS bonds issued by the RMBS issuer.

However, with more highly structured CDOs, the resulting RMBS bonds—particularly those with less than AAA ratings—are themselves pooled with RMBS bonds derived from other loan pools, and these other RMBS bonds may also be of varying quality or ratings. The cash flows from these bonds are then pooled in the CDO special purpose vehicle and a new set of CDO bonds are produced, with senior and subordinate tranches. By this tranching of the cash flow coming from a pool of RMBS (and potentially other CDO bonds), the "sow's ear" of lower grade bonds produced what were thought to be "silk purses," in the form of higher-rated CDO bonds. The CDO is generated from a spectrum of RMBS and sometimes other kinds of bonds, some of which may be other CDO bonds. Of course this all presumes a great deal of knowledge of the risk of the underlying mortgages or other assets, because now investors are essentially betting that the arrangement of cash flows from a large number of lower or mixed-grade investments will yield some amount of higher-grade investments.

The true value of these highly structured investments depended on investors' expectations of how well they will pay back and that, in turn, depended on the credit rating agencies evaluation of the risks within the

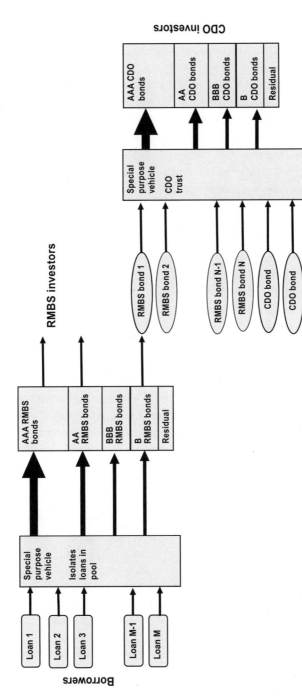

Figure 3.9. Highly structured mortgage finance: The organization of collateralized debt obligations.

CDOs. What became painfully clear by mid-2007 was that the rating agencies did not have a good handle on the risks—especially in the event of a downturn in housing prices—of many fairly traditional CMO-type bonds, yet alone most CDOs.

Moreover, the CDO increased the value of higher-risk, lower-rated CMO bonds, thus increasing the markets' overall appetite for higher-risk lending. In order to provide credit enhancement to the higher rated, senior tranches of CMOs, originators were often required to purchase lowest-rated, highest-risk "residual" tranches from the CMOs derived from their loans. Beyond reducing risk to higher-tranche investors, the assumption of the residual should theoretically encourage the lender to be more risk averse in its lending because it will absorb the first losses emanating from the loan pool. However, the CDO market enabled some lenders to sell off their residual interests to CDO arrangers, thereby reducing its "skin in the game," or exposure to losses from its own lending practices (Engel and McCoy 2007).

Another innovation employed in the second high-risk lending boom was the structured investment vehicle (SIV). An SIV was a specialized investment company set up solely to purchase long-term, fixed-income investment assets, such as mortgage-backed securities, by using less expensive, shorter-term commercial paper. SIVs required that the company was able to borrow frequently and inexpensively, both to remain liquid and to earn a profit. Commercial and investment banks set up SIVs as off-balance-sheet investments, to reduce their risk. However, many banks essentially guaranteed the liquidity of SIVs, ensuring that they would refinance the commercial paper debt if needed. Thus, when the credit crisis hit in 2007, many banks were forced to essentially bail out the SIVs that they had set up and managed, sometimes actually acquiring their assets and putting them on the banks' balance sheet.

What came to be known as "structured finance," the engineering of CMOs, CDOs, SIVs, and other complex mortgage-related investment vehicles, turned out to suffer from a broad array of perverse incentives and transactional failures. In the next chapter, we turn to systemic problems in these securitization structures that, without sufficient regulatory oversight or interventions, produced large amounts of default risk in the origination of home loans.

4

Mortgage Market Breakdown

The Contributions of Transactional Failures, Conflicts of Interest, and Global Capital Surpluses

The growing dominance of private-label and increasingly complex securitization in the late 1990s and early 2000s together with a largely hands-off regulatory response combined to create the national mortgage crisis of 2007 and 2008. This chapter explains how hypercomplex, vertically disintegrated mortgage markets led to substantial market failures in limiting lending risks at the point of origination as well as to attendant losses to investors, borrowers, and communities. These increasingly complex securitization schemes created many "transactional failures" in the relationships between different parties in the mortgage credit supply chain, such as loan originators, credit rating agencies, issuers of securities, and investors in those securities. Many parties involved in supplying mortgage credit had little capital at stake in the lending process and were rewarded merely for processing more and more loans through their systems.

The increased complexity of mortgage-related securities made them less transparent to investors, who did not understand their underlying risks well. Structured finance also created investor subgroups that had conflicting interests; thus, in the event of a specific loan modification or workout, different types of investors would suffer or benefit differently. This created a threat of litigation against servicers and trusts, which might have been more aggressive in modifying loans but for these conflicts.

On the capital markets side, a variety of forces created an excess of global savings that, in turn, led to an excess supply of capital looking for higher returns than had been available in more traditional, secure investments. This meant that investors in mortgage-related securities were increasingly willing to pay a premium to invest in bonds backed by higher-risk loans. The resulting "capital-push" nature of higher-risk-lending markets meant that loan originators were given an incentive to meet the appetite of the Wall Street securitizers rather than respond to the authentic demand for credit by homebuyers and homeowners. Mortgage originators and brokers were given higher commissions to originate inherently high-risk mortgages of various stripes. Meanwhile, the credit ratings agencies that were tasked with assessing the risk of the mortgage pools and securities derived from the pools relied on models that had not been tested in adverse housing market and interest rate conditions.

This chapter, by itself, does not explain the 2007–08 mortgage crisis. To grasp the crisis in full, it is important to also understand the policy response—and lack of response—to the changes that had occurred in mortgage markets since the early 1990s, as well as the pre-1990s policy developments. Chapters 2 and 3 describe the history of key mortgage policy development before the mid-1990s, while chapter 6 details recent policy debates in more detail.

Transactional Failures in Financially Complex, Vertically Disintegrated Mortgage Markets

The vertical disintegration of mortgage markets described in the previous chapter, together with a lack of regulatory oversight, created transactional failures between different parties in the securitization and affiliated lending processes.[1] These failures were of various types and included what economists tend to call problems of asymmetric information and adverse selection. The concern here is not with a typology of the transactional failures and where they fall in the theoretical economics literature, but with their substantive nature and how they contributed to overall failures in the mortgage marketplace.

A simplified schematic of some of the key actors in the mortgage funding process as well as some of the transactional failures that arose in the supply chain for mortgage credit is provided in figure 4.1. In the vertically integrated lending of the traditional deposit-funded lending process, such failures were mitigated through organizational management and the internal alignment of missions. Figure 4.1 is not exhaustive;

---

1. Ashcraft and Schuermann (2008) refer to what I term transactional failures as "frictions." Given the hyperliquid connections that securitization enabled between the capital markets and borrowers, I find this term less appropriate and so use "transactional failures" instead. They also offer a somewhat longer list of intraparty problems, some of which I do not cover here.

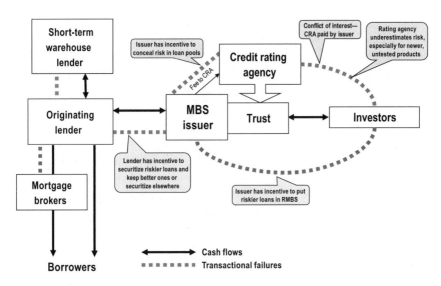

Figure 4.1. Key transactional failures and perverse incentives in the origination
and funding of securitized home loans.
Source: Adapted from Ashcraft and Schuermann (2008); also based on Mason and Rosen
(2007) and Keys, Mukherjee, Seru, and Vig (2008).

additional transactional failures have been identified in the literature (Ashcraft and Schuermann 2008). However, it describes the key failures that contributed to poor and excessively risky lending practices.

Broker-Originator Failures

The first source of transactional failures in the securitized mortgage lending process occurs between the mortgage broker and the originating lender. The broker, especially given the compensation structures common in the subprime and high-risk sectors, had little incentive to identify the least risky and most cost-effective loan product for the borrower. Brokers were compensated through a combination of up-front fees (some percentage of the loan amount) and something called a yield-spread premium (YSP). The YSP is equivalent to some portion of the capitalized value of the difference between the interest payments that the borrower pays and a minimum base rate at which the lender will originate the loan. This arrangement rewards brokers for placing people in higher-cost loans. Less savvy borrowers especially are unlikely to understand that they may be entitled to a lower interest rate. These same borrowers may be relatively higher risk borrowers and more negatively affected by higher rates and fees. The YSP effectively rewards brokers for placing what are likely to be relatively higher-risk borrowers in higher-cost loans, thereby exacerbating their chances of default. YSPs are often combined with prepayment penalties because originators/investors want to recoup the YSP. If the borrower pays off the loan early, the lender hopes to recoup the YSP through the prepayment penalty.

The incentives that brokers have had to place borrowers—especially less savvy borrowers—in higher-cost loans have had two sorts of effects. First, Kim-Sung and Hermanson (2003) found that, among elderly borrowers, brokered loans were twice as likely to be subprime rather than nonbrokered loans. Brokers were also more likely to lend to divorced, female, and nonwhite borrowers. Sixty-two percent of older nonwhite borrowers received loans via brokers, while only 38 percent of older white borrowers did. Brokers have been heavily associated with aggressive "push marketing." Fifty-six percent of older borrowers with brokered loans reported that contact was initiated by the broker, while other older borrowers reported that lenders initiated contact only 24 percent of the time. Borrowers with brokered loans were generally less satisfied with their loans and were less likely to feel that they had received honest information.

More generally, for subprime borrowers of any age, brokered loans have been found to have consistently higher interest rates than retail loans, even after controlling for differences in borrower and other loan characteristics. For a typical subprime borrower with a $166,000 mortgage, the higher costs of a brokered loan are estimated to amount to more than $5,200 during the first four years and more than $35,000 over thirty years (Ernst, Bocian, and Li 2008). This is equivalent to approximately 1.3 percentage points more in annual interest compared to a retail loan.

The second major problem in the structure of broker compensation was that it did not reward brokers for better performing loans or penalize them for excessive defaults. Brokers' income essentially depended on getting as many loans approved as possible, creating a clear incentive for falsifying incomes or assets, steering borrowers to no-documentation loans, obtaining high appraisals, and generally minimizing any risk factors in applications. During the first subprime boom of the 1990s, some lenders withheld a portion of the YSP until a loan had seasoned for a while to guard against early defaults and to prevent brokers from "churning" their borrowers through different loans.[2]

As the appetite among mortgage securitizers and originators for loans increased, mortgage brokers found themselves in increasingly strong positions to "shop" loan applications among many different lenders. Golding, Green, and McManus (2008) cite an industry statistic that more than 70 percent of brokers shopped identical Alt-A and subprime applications to two or more originators. An originator maintaining high credit standards in a loose, capital-rich market risked losing substantial market share, which was critical to overall profitability in an increasingly transaction-based industry.

The strong appetite for higher-risk loans from Wall Street issuers and the failure of brokers to be monitored for the reliability of loan applications and loan performance also gave brokers significant incentives to engage in fraudulent activities, including falsifying or inflating income and employment information and documentation. There is evidence that many subprime loans included falsified or inflated incomes or assets. A good deal of the mass media coverage of the role of fraud's contribution to the mortgage crisis suggested—with little substantive evidence—that most fraudulent loan applications were solely the work of the borrower (e.g., see Will 2008). However, there is substantial evidence that a large amount of fraudulent loan application activity was facilitated by mortgage brokers.

First, brokers were much more likely than retail lenders to make low- or no-documentation loans, which increased substantially after 2002 and among which rates of fraud and foreclosure have proven much higher. In 2005, 41 percent of brokered loans were no- or low-documentation compared to 22 percent of nonbrokered loans (Golding, Green, and McManus 2008). More directly, BasePoint Analytics (2006a, 2006b), a firm that markets antifraud software, examined a pool of three million mortgages and found that "the most serious fraud in mortgage lending today appears to be broker-facilitated."

BasePoint also found that loan fraud was heavily concentrated in a significant, but minority, share of the brokerage industry, suggesting that lenders should have been able to identify the brokers that commonly engaged in fraud. Again, because originators' liabilities for fraudulent loans were limited by claims of ignorance and because originators often had little of their own capital at risk, they had few incentives to identify

---

2. Based on comments of Kevin Byers, Parkside Associates, Atlanta, Georgia.

problematic brokers. If they applied more rigorous screening to their brokered loans, they risked losing market share in the brokered-loan market. The word that an originator was screening applications more carefully would spread fast, and some brokers would migrate away from the lender, something that lenders focused on market share and volume over credit quality would likely fear.

Fitch Ratings examined a set of forty-five loan files from early defaulting subprime mortgages that had features indicating signals indicating likely fraud (Fitch Ratings 2007). Fitch found that many of the loan files included substantial evidence of fraud that should have been easily detected by brokers or originators. For example, in some cases the borrowers' balance sheets did not correspond well to their stated income. Debt-to-income ratios often did not include obvious debts, property taxes, or other items that are usually included in these calculations. They also found frequent instances in which the box on the loan application indicating owner-occupancy was checked yet the file did not include a form indicating owner-occupancy. Finally, there were cases where the final versions of closing documents were missing. The nature of many of the discrepancies in the loan files suggests that the brokers or lenders were at least complicit in the fraud—or, in fact, the primary perpetrators of it.

The bottom line on falsified or inflated incomes and assets, however, is that originators had the ability and the responsibility to detect such behavior (and policymakers and regulators should have required them to implement such systems). If originators had been more concerned about falsified or inflated incomes, for example, they would likely have relied more heavily on antifraud systems. The most obvious of these was the ability to verify incomes through services that compared incomes on applications to those from the Internal Revenue Service. The vast majority of mortgage applicants were required to sign a document giving lenders permission to verify their incomes with the IRS. One vendor, Veri-Tax, provided this service to lenders beginning in 1999 but found them relatively uninterested in using its services. Veri-Tax estimated that only 3 to 5 percent of all the loans funded in 2006 involved an executed verification of income with the IRS (Morgenson 2008). Moreover, Fitch reported, at least as early as 2005, that it had observed a "trend of modification of internal policy to discontinue verifying self-employed income through the use of Internal Revenue Service form 4506/8821" (Fitch Ratings 2005).

The result of more aggressive, lax, and sometimes fraudulent lending practices occurring disproportionately in brokered versus nonbrokered loans has a direct impact on loan performance. Alexander et al. (2002) found that, after controlling for a wide variety of borrower and other loan characteristics, brokered loans default at significantly higher rates than nonbrokered loans.

Appraiser-Originator and Appraiser-Investor Failures

A critical actor in the mortgage origination process—and especially in high-risk lending—is the appraiser, who establishes the value of the house at the time of the origination. The importance of the accuracy of the appraisal becomes more important as property values become more volatile and when down payments or owner equity become very small. Both of these conditions were on the increase during the second high-risk boom starting in 2002.

Appraisers are typically selected by the originating lender. Originators looking to close as many loans as possible and increase market share have strong incentives to approve loans. Since the appraisal business is a highly competitive one, with low barriers to entry, as the origination business became more and more concentrated, appraisers became more dependent on business from fewer, larger lenders. This created some significant disincentives to resist originator pressure to deliver "adequate" appraised values.

An online petition of professional appraisers was initiated in 2002 and addressed to the Appraisal Subcommittee of the Federal Financial Institutions Examination Council (FFIEC), the interagency group of federal bank, thrift, and credit union regulators. The petition called upon the FFIEC to address the problem of lenders and brokers pressuring appraisers to inflate appraised values in order to get loans approved. By 2005, more than eight thousand appraisers had signed the petition, and by 2008 the number of signatures exceeded ten thousand (Callahan 2005; Appraisers' Petition 2002). The petition stated that "lenders . . . apply pressure on appraisers to hit or exceed a predetermined value" (Appraisers' Petition 2002). Moreover, the petition argued that this pressure was applied through withholding business if values are not inflated; withholding business if predetermined values are not guaranteed; refusing to pay for appraisals that do not meet target values; and "blacklisting" honest appraisers in order to use "rubber-stamp" appraisers.

Industry surveys have found that many appraisers report having experienced significant pressure from lenders to overestimate property values. A 2003 survey by October Research of five hundred appraisers in forty-four states found that 55 percent of appraisers reported such pressures (Callahan 2005). Moreover, a quarter of the respondents reported feeling such pressures in half of all the appraisals they handled.

In late 2007, New York attorney general Andrew Cuomo filed suit against First American Corporation, a large real estate data firm, and its subsidiary appraisal management company, which had been retained by Washington Mutual, the nation's largest thrift, to handle the thrift's appraisal work (Cuomo 2007). Appraisal management companies are sometimes hired by large lenders to arrange for home appraisals on behalf of the originating lender. Because there had already been concerns in the early part of the decade about lenders pressuring appraisers, state and federal regulators had begun to push lenders to work to assure that loan officers and others with vested interests in getting loans approved were not involved in selecting appraisers. By hiring an appraisal management company, one supposedly substantial enough to be sensitive to reputational risk, lenders could set up some structural distance between their own operations and the selection of appraisals.

Cuomo argued that Washington Mutual hired the appraisal management firm to shield itself from claims of favoring appraisers that would deliver high appraisals, but then attempted to influence—essentially micromanage—the selection of particular appraisers anyway, by putting pressure on the appraisal management firms themselves. Washington Mutual's size gave it substantial market power; it was one of the firm's largest customers in this line of business (Cuomo 2007). The complaint also alleged that, after apparently not receiving sufficiently high appraisals from the appraisers chosen by the appraisal management firm, the lender directed the appraisal management firm to choose individual appraisers from its "Proven Panel" of appraisers.

Cuomo's investigation essentially documented the sort of problems that had been alleged in the appraisers' petition. The documentation of correspondence between Washington Mutual and the appraisal management firm, and within the appraisal management firm, provides substantial evidence that appraisers were subject to widespread and systematic pressure to appraise properties at levels higher than they would have without such pressure.

Originator–Warehouse Lender Failures

Another opportunity for transactional failures identified in figure 5.1 was between the originating lender and the warehouse lender. Because originating lenders were often thinly capitalized mortgage companies, they often required access to a source of short-term funds that they could borrow to fund loans as the need arose. Warehouse lenders, typically commercial or investment banks, provided such short-term credit. Access to a warehouse lender allowed the originator to accumulate sufficient numbers of loans to generate pools large enough to sell to the RMBS issuer.

The warehouse lender relied on the assets of the originating lender as collateral for its short-term line of credit. Therefore, if it underestimated the quality of the originator's new loans substantially, it would have advanced funds on insufficient collateral. A number of subprime lenders that went out of business during the turbulence of 2007 did so because they lost access to their source of warehouse credit (Ashcraft and Schuermann 2008).

In order to increase their lending volumes and market share, originators had incentives to understate the risks of the loans they were making when negotiating with warehouse lenders. If it perceived that the credit quality of the originator's loans had weakened, the warehouse lender would advance a smaller amount of funds for every dollar of originations.

Originator-Issuer Failures

An important point of transactional failure occurred between the originating lender and the arranger/issuer of the securities. The lender had more information about the true quality of the loans that it sold than did the issuer that purchased the loans. Given this "asymmetric information," the lender—especially if it held loans as well as sold them—had an incentive to pass off its lower quality loans to the issuer and keep the better loans. This problem, sometimes referred to as "adverse selection," meant that, because the issuer (and eventually the credit rating agency and investors) did not have complete information on the loans, it would underestimate the downside risk of the loans that were securitized. The information that these parties had about the loans may lack some crucial details that the originator knew about but had an incentive to conceal from them. Revealing these features could lower the profit the lender would earn in selling the loans.

Keys et al. (2008) analyzed more than two million home purchase loans originated during the 2001–06 period. They found that low-documentation loans that were more likely to be securitized tended to default at a 20 percent higher rate than loans less likely to be securitized. This result held even after controlling for a wide variety of loan, lender, and borrower characteristics. Thus, even after considering credit score and a wide variety of other risk factors, securitized low-documentation loans were still more likely to be riskier than low-documentation loans held by originators.

A contributing factor to why issuers and investors did not scrutinize the characteristics of loans as much as they might is the "holder in due course" doctrine, which shields purchasers of loans and investors from being liable for most aspects of illegal activity on the part of mortgage brokers or originators. In essence, the more information the issuer and investors demand, the more liability they may incur. Therefore, issuers and investors had an incentive to not demand "too much" information from loan originators. They balanced seeking information that would help them and the credit rating agencies estimate loan performance against the problems caused by asking for too much detail—in particular, the possibility of becoming legally culpable for the illegal or deceptive lending practices of the originator or broker. This system worked against the transparency of the lending process through the credit supply chain, a transparency without which it was difficult to maintain a well-functioning mortgage market.

The key policy tool for rectifying this problem is to impose "assignee liability" provisions in mortgage lending regulations, which can override the holder-in-due-course doctrine. These provisions explicitly make purchasers and investors in loans liable for violations of law in the origination process. Assignee liability imposes substantial levels of accountability up and down the chain of capital in the securitization process. It is not a silver bullet for solving all mortgage market problems, but it is a fundamental ingredient needed for accountability and it can reduce many transactional failures in the securitization process. Assignee liability would do more than perhaps any other single policy provision to increase transparency throughout the securitization process. As we shall see in chapter 6, it is also a policy proposal that has been tirelessly opposed by the mortgage and securities industry.

Issuer-Investor and Issuer–Credit Rating Agency Failures

As in the case of the originator-issuer relationship, the interaction between the issuer and the credit rating agency and the investors also suffered from problems of asymmetric information. Although the issuer knew less about the underlying mortgages than the originator, it was likely to know more about them than the credit rating agencies or the investors (or the investor's agents). Like the originator, it had some incentive to conceal or understate flaws or downside risks in the underlying loans. An issuer may have known, for example, that the loans backing the securities issued were made disproportionately with the assistance of high-pressure brokers who had developed a reputation for encouraging borrowers to exaggerate their incomes. As loans flowed through the credit supply chain, such information often became increasingly hidden from purchasers or investors.

Investors relied on credit rating agencies too much and were not sufficiently skeptical of the agencies' ratings, especially knowing that the ratings process exhibited some significant conflicts of interest.

Credit Rating Agency–Investor Failures

The role of the credit rating agencies in the mortgage crisis of 2007 and 2008 has been fairly well established (Mason and Rosen 2007; Lowenstein 2008). The rating agencies had a clear incentive to underestimate the risk of mortgage-related securities because of how they were compensated. They were paid for their work by the issuers of securities and not by investors. Moreover, they often received compensation only for securities that received adequate ratings. Finally, the concentration and dominance of the larger issuers meant that, to stay in their good graces, the agencies were under pressure to deliver strong ratings to structured finance products. These and other problems in the rating industry of mortgage-related securities will be examined more closely in a separate section below.

Investor–Secondary Investor (CDO Investors) Failures

A primary contributor to the second boom in high-risk lending was the development of hypercomplex and higher-order mortgage securities, especially collateralized debt obligations (CDOs). CDO arrangers are essentially the lower-tranche investors in a conventional CMO-type RMBS. In fact, Adelson and Jacob (2008) argued that CDO investors were so dominant after 2004 that they "drove out" other, more judicious investors in lower-tranche RMBS. Mason and Rosen (2007) estimate that CDOs invested in $140 billion in lower-tranche (rated below AAA) RMBS in 2005, even more than the $133 billion of lower-tranche RMBS issued in that year. Therefore, CDOs accounted for essentially all the lower-tranche, first-order RMBS issued in 2005. Moreover, CDOs, which were originally intended to include a diverse set of bonds, became increasingly made up of subprime RMBS. One of the primary credit rating agencies reported to the SEC that the proportion of CDO collateral pools made up of subprime RMBS grew from 43 percent in 2003 to 71 percent in 2006.

CDO arrangers were much less discriminating in their assessment of lower-tranche RMBS bonds, increasing the overall risk tolerance of the market and feeding the appetite of RMBS issuers for riskier loans from originators (Adelson and Jacob 2008). CDOs were able to obtain higher ratings from the rating agencies than they were probably due, thereby satisfying the institutional investment criteria of CDO investors (Mason and Rosen 2007).

No "Skin in the Game" Leads to "Finding the Greater Fool"

The process of securitization connected global capital markets to home-buyers and homeowners. In private-label securitization—as opposed to GSE securitization—capital flowed through a large number of parties and was assessed, insured, and leveraged by additional parties, such as credit rating agencies, bond insurers, and credit default swap investors. What was generally consistent throughout the private-label securitization process up until the mortgage crisis was that most of the intervening parties had very little downside risk in the transactions other than the borrower and the eventual investor in the RMBS or CDO products. The brokers, originators, issuers, and CDO arrangers all essentially passed on risk to the next party while benefiting from large volumes of transactions made in a short period of time. Credit rating agencies and others played key ancillary roles and also assumed little downside risk.

Even when originating lenders did assume some risk by making "representations and warranties" about the loans they sold to issuers, in which they often agreed to take back certain types of nonperforming loans (especially those going into default early on), the balance sheets of many subprime lenders were relatively thin, so that the originator capital that was put at risk was usually quite limited (Green and Wachter 2007).[3]

---

3. According to Fitch Ratings (2007), RMBS securities typically included representations and warranties of the originator regarding the legality and lien status of the loan and the condition of the property. Some representations and warranties had specific language covering mortgage fraud, but these were somewhat ambiguous in how they would play out. If a lender's guidelines did not explicitly call for one or more means of verifying

Mishkin (2008) has argued that many subprime originators, unlike depository institutions, for example, often saw little value in their corporate charters because the principals had relatively little capital invested in these firms. Many originators went out of business, but if the investors in these firms made large earnings for many years but then the thinly capitalized firms eventually folded due to issuer or investor claims on early defaults (which they may not have been able to pay), these losses might have paled in comparison to earlier cumulative earnings.

The transactional nature of securitized lending meant that the focus of most players in the mortgage industry was on maximizing scale and market share. Scrutinizing loans or assets too closely could mean losing market presence and thus compromise overall returns.

The Credit Rating Agency Role: Challenged Models and Conflicts of Interest

Perhaps no other party in the securitization process has received more scrutiny since the collapse of the subprime mortgage market than the three primary credit rating agencies: Standard & Poors, Moody's, and Fitch. The credit rating agencies were essentially given the role of industry regulator of the securitization process, a role that the Securities and Exchange Commission (SEC) and bank regulators delegated to these firms—labeled nationally recognized statistical rating organizations (NRSROs)—through a variety of measures. After the collapse of Penn Central in 1970, the SEC began penalizing firms holding bonds (including mortgage-backed securities) with ratings below a certain level from the big three agencies (Lowenstein 2008). Later, through bank and S&L regulations such as FIRREA, bank regulators did essentially the same thing by favoring mortgage-backed securities with higher ratings from these firms in calculating a bank's reserve requirements. Despite the special status given NRSROs, they are subject to very little substantive regulation. Rather, their activities are largely subject to constraints about disclosure of activities and processes to their customers. In fact, as late as 2006 policymakers were shielding these agencies from regulation. The 2006 Rating Agency Reform Act expressly prohibited the SEC from regulating the "substance of the credit ratings or the procedures or methodologies" used to determine ratings (Securities and Exchange

---

stated incomes (such as IRS verification), then not implementing such logical protections would be unlikely to violate the representations and warranties.

Commission 2008). Although new rules were proposed by the SEC in June 2008, they were prompted by the mortgage crisis itself and are unlikely to be substantive enough to solve the fundamental problems with the rating agency system, especially because they do not call for an end of the issuer-pays model of agency compensation.

The rating agencies have been faulted for inaccurately assessing the risks of mortgage securities of different sorts, for doling out overly generous ratings to stay in the good graces of the large Wall Street RMBS issuers, and for aggressively promoting their role in providing the regulatory infrastructure for securitized lending markets. In addition, the credit rating agencies played an active role in pushing back consumer regulatory initiatives by states and localities.

The Limits of Statistical Models: Underestimating and Concealing Credit Risk

The credit rating agencies repeatedly understated and underestimated the underlying risk of subprime and other high-risk lending and the risk to investors in structured finance vehicles backed by these loans. Moreover, the agencies provided ratings that were inconsistent across different types of securities and across geography, which exacerbated the underassessment of risk by investors (Golding, Green, and McManus 2008; Mason and Rosen 2007).

The first problem the rating agencies faced was simply too little loan-level information. The complexity of the securitization processes, which increased when moving from RMBS to CDOs, made it difficult to assess the nature of the collateral backing different investments. The FDIC reviewed a set of twenty-four CDOs that had received a rating from one of the three major rating agencies (Bean 2008). It found that, for nine of them, none of the major credit rating agencies had provided a publicly available presale report. Even more alarming, for only three of the twenty-four had the agencies included "robust" performance data in their presale reports.

In addition to the lack of loan-level detail, the ability to predict the loan performance and prepayment rates of subprime loans had not been well tested during different phases of the housing cycle. In particular, the 2/28 and 3/27 hybrid adjustable rate mortgages, with initial low fixed rates, were rolled out just as the housing market was hitting its strongest appreciation. Moreover, these products helped feed housing market appreciation.

Up until 2006, the national diversification of most loan pools meant that the growing default and foreclosure problems in weaker or moderate appreciation housing markets were compensated for by the very strong loan performance in hot housing markets in California, the East Coast, and in Florida. The large size of the typical loans in these strong markets also helped compensate for higher loss rates on smaller loans in slower-market regions.

Depending on the region, by 2005 or 2006 the innovations in mortgage "affordability," including reducing effective down payments close to zero through the use of piggyback mortgages, the use of interest-only and negative amortization products, and underwriting based on initial teaser fixed interest rates, had effectively been tapped out. The "virtuous cycle" of appreciation outlined in the previous chapter (see figure 3.7) had depended on continuing "innovations" in "affordability" loan products to keep the appreciation cycle intact. As financial markets could no longer deliver increasingly affordable products (that is, products that lowered the monthly-payment-to-original-principal amount), and as interest rates began creeping up, the unsustainable bubbles were pricked, and the vicious cycles of decline set in. This led to higher defaults and foreclosures, and national credit market pullbacks, which in turn caused housing price declines in more and more regions. By late 2007, most major metropolitan housing markets were in a relatively substantial decline and defaults increased at an even faster rate than earlier in that year. By mid-2008, essentially all major metropolitan housing markets were in decline.

Models predicting defaults also had relatively minimal previous exposure to high levels of investor and second-home properties, which behave differently in the event of falling or stalling property values. Investors or owners of second homes are much more likely to let a property go into foreclosure than are owner-occupiers (Green and Wachter 2007). And the levels of investor properties and second homes were starting to reach very high levels by 2004 and 2005.

Some suggest that investors and others may have simply misunderstood the limits to diversifying risk through the pooling of loans (Mason and Rosen 2007; Green and Wachter 2007). Traditional finance theory categorizes risk into two fundamental types: systematic and unsystematic. Systematic risk is risk that affects all or most individual investments (individual mortgages, in the case of RMBS) at the same time. In the case of mortgage markets, systematic risks are derived from those phenomena that affect most or many loans, and not just small subsets of loans or particular regions of the country. Changes in interest rates, risk premiums, lending practices, federal regulations, or overall housing market trends are examples of forces that pose systematic risk in the performance of nationally diversified mortgage pools. Some of these forces may affect some regions or types of borrowers more than others, but if there is a general direction in performance, that effect is essentially the systematic portion of the overall risk of the loan pool.

Unsystematic risk is that risk that differentially occurs in one segment of the national loan pool but not in others. For example, regional variations in housing price trends represent unsystematic risk. If housing prices rise uniformly across regional housing markets, a national pool of loans would not experience systematic risk due to housing prices. But, there will always be some regional differences in housing prices, and in any particular region prices may fall or rise while national prices remain flat. This is a type of unsystematic risk that can be addressed through diversification.

A local lender in a declining region may wish to hold a more geographically diversified RMBS rather than the equivalent dollar amount of locally originated loans, for fear that the local loans exhibit too much unsystematic risk. But if the national real estate sector weakens overall, and prices fall in most places, there will be systematic risk that diversification will not reduce.

In the case of structured finance, because the high-risk loan features, increasingly lax underwriting, and a general deterioration in housing prices were all occurring on a national scale, diversification could not overcome these fundamental problems. Moreover, given the weight of the overall securitized loan market in places such as California and Florida, pooling was only able to do so much to reduce even exposure to regional housing market risk, which had essentially become, because of the size of the regions, systematic risk in the structured finance markets.

A number of observers have pointed to the lack of robustness and consistency of the credit rating agencies' risk classifications (AAA, AA, A, BBB, BB, B, and so forth). Golding, Green, and McManus (2008) argue that a rating system works best when a given symbol corresponds to the same measure of credit risk for a "German corporate bond in 1985, a U.S. municipal bond in 1996, and a Korean mortgage-backed security in 2005." Yet Mason and Rosen (2007) found that Standard & Poors gave a higher default probability to a CDO rated AA than to an asset-backed security that it gave a lower rating of A.

CDO bonds with the same letter ratings as other types of bonds have been found to default generally at higher rates (Lowenstein 2008). This is especially the case in comparing instruments below the AAA class, in which CDO bonds had much higher loss rates than similarly rated mortgage-backed bonds and, especially, than similarly rated corporate bonds. The gross discrepancy between the performance of CDO bonds versus similarly rated corporate or other types of bonds was well known to the credit rating agencies at least by 2005. Figure 4.2 is generated directly from data contained in Moody's reports. It shows that for three below-AAA rating classes, A, Baa and Ba, the five-year loss rates for CDOs were many orders of magnitude higher than for other sorts of mortgage-backed or corporate bonds. These reports were both completed by July 2005 and were repeated in 2006. Yet, it became clear that investors had not distinguished the very large differences in the risks of a Baa corporate bond and a Baa CDO investment, for example, despite CDOs having five-year default rates that were fifteen times greater than similarly rated corporate bonds.

Because credit rating models were largely developed for corporate bonds, they were fundamentally unsuitable for rating mortgage-backed securities and related vehicles (Mason and Rosen 2007). While corporate bonds are investments in a dynamic organization that can and will adjust its investment decisions as contexts change, the pools of loans from which mortgage-backed securities are derived are not dynamic. RMBS are derived from the cash flows from a fixed, predetermined set of loans. Compared to the corporation, which can adjust its internal portfolio as

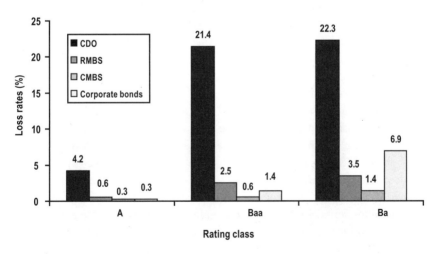

Figure 4.2. Five-year cumulative loss rates for CDOs vs. other security types for three below-AAA rating classes.
Source: Moody's Investor Service, 2005a; Moody's Investor Service, 2005b; based on securities issued 1993–2004.

interest rates fluctuate, for example, the pool of loans remains the same pool regardless of how macroeconomic conditions change. This means, Mason and Rosen argue, that bond ratings came to be used for something for which they were not initially intended and sold "on the basis of a fundamental misunderstanding of diversification."

Conflicts of Interest and Related Problems

In addition to the numerous problems the rating agencies had in accessing good loan-level data and in maintaining a more consistent ratings system across security type and time, an even more fundamental set of problems involved conflicts of interest and perverse incentives that encouraged and fed inaccurate and overly optimistic evaluations and ratings. Because the ratings agency was paid by the issuer of the securities, and not by the investors, there was a clear conflict of interest in the ratings of RMBS and CDOs. Moreover, the issuer did not pay for the rating until the rating was obtained (Golding, Green, and McManus 2008).

Besides the perverse incentive created by the issuer-pays model of compensation, there were also other problems. Before the growth of private-label securitization, the credit ratings agencies derived their revenues from a much wider set of corporations and governmental bodies, because corporate and municipal bonds were a larger part of their overall business. In the mortgage market, the issuers of securities were much more concentrated, with the largest investment and commercial banks dominating the market. This meant that the typical issuer of mortgage-backed securities or CDOs was a large client with substantial market power. If a large securities issuer was not pleased with the ratings that one of the agencies provided it could "shop" for a better rating at one of the other two agencies (Lowenstein 2008; Mason and Rosen 2007).

As securitization accelerated in the early to mid-2000s, the agencies were under even greater pressure to turn around successful ratings very quickly. Lowenstein (2008) reports how, in a 2006 securitization, the Moody's analyst had only one day to process the credit data from the bank and provide a rating. As the structured finance industry grew at a feverish pace, the agencies relied increasingly on high throughput in rating structured finance products to increase their corporate earnings and stock prices. Figure 4.3 shows the close relationship, for example, between total issuance of nonagency mortgage-backed securities and the stock price of Moody's. The company's profitability and stock appreciation depended largely on the growth of the mortgage-backed securities market, which was related to the

growth of CDOs and other complex products that RMBS fed into. Structured finance, which mostly consisted of rating mortgage-related securities,
became a larger and larger driver of revenues, accounting for 54 percent of
Moody's Investment Service revenue in 2006, up from 36 percent in 2001
(Moody's Corporation 2008; Moody's Corporation 2004).

In July 2008 the Securities and Exchange Commission issued a report
criticizing the rating agencies for their overly generous ratings of mortgage-related securities (Securities and Exchange Commission 2008). The
report uncovered many e-mails that expressed the conflicts and looseness
of the ratings process and identified many problems in the process. One
problem was that agencies made "out of model" adjustments—without
documenting the rationale for such adjustments. This means that the loss
levels predicted by the agency models were not used and some other loss
level was assumed instead. Two of the three primary agencies frequently
used such out-of-model adjustments. One "regularly" reduced the loss
expectations on subprime second-lien mortgages—one of the highest-risk

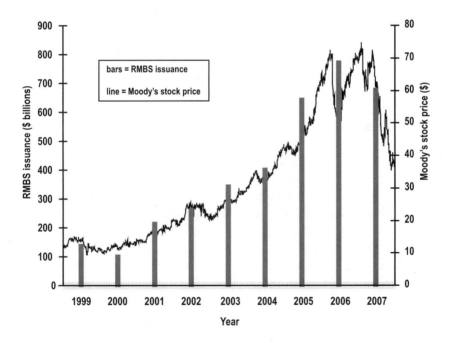

Figure 4.3. Annual U.S. nonagency RMBS issuance and Moody's stock price, 1999–2007.
Source: Moody's 2008; Securities Industry and Financial Markets Association, 2008.

forms of collateral in structured finance. Moreover the firm did not publicly disclose its practice of overriding the model data.

The SEC investigation relied, in part, on combing through internal e-mails and instant messages of the three agencies. One analyst's April 2007 e-mail complained that "it could be structured by cows and we would rate it" (Securities and Exchange Commission 2008). Another analyst's message from 2004 expressed concern that a poor rating might result in the rating agency losing the business of the issuer: "I am trying to ascertain whether we can determine at this point if we will suffer any loss of business because of our decision [on assigning separate ratings to principal and interest] and if so, how much?" (Securities and Exchange Commission 2008).

Another source of conflicting interests arose in the fact that analysts at ratings agencies could often move to higher-paying positions at the investment banks issuing structured finance products (Golding, Green, and McManus 2008). This revolving door—or rather one-way door—from rating agency to investment bank meant that rating analysts had another reason to curry favor with the issuer. Analysts and executives at Moody's, for example, were singled out for meeting regularly with Wall Street issuers to discuss market developments and for attending "closing dinners" to commemorate the completion of large deals (Lucchetti 2008).

These conflicts of interest affected the very nature of the credit rating process. The agencies provided issuers with software that allowed them to structure securities to maximize the RMBS's or CDO's ratings. One product offered by one of the major rating agencies was explicitly described as a tool that would enable issuers to maximize the amount of a securitization that would receive a AAA rating: "To help you achieve your best possible execution, SPIRE incorporates an automatic optimization feature designed to create the RMBS capital structure that maximizes the percentage of senior bonds while minimizing subordinate bonds and overcollateralization" (Standard & Poors, undated).

Rutherford (2007) confirmed a similar, if less automated, process whereby the rating agencies iteratively assisted issuers in the design of their securities, explaining to the SEC that "sponsors of structured products seek to achieve specified ratings levels. . . . They engage in iterative discussions with a ratings agency. The sponsors propose specified assets and structures of seniority within the tranches to achieve the desired rating levels, and the rating agency indicates whether or not the specified assets and structures achieve those rating levels."

Lowenstein (2008) also found that the rating agencies had iterative exchanges with issuers, allowing issuers to modify securities to fit the agencies' models and obtain sufficiently high ratings. He quoted an analyst at J.P. Morgan Chase as saying that such "gaming is the whole thing."

The conflicts of interest that plagued the rating of mortgage-related securities are best exhibited in the disconnect between the continued high ratings that RMBS and CDOs received compared to much of the information coming out in 2004 and 2005 that clearly warned about problems in RMBS and CDO securities, the subprime market, and housing prices more generally. Here are some examples of warnings about excessive risk in mortgage markets and mortgage-related securities from a variety of publications issued by the rating agencies themselves:

The market is on a continuing quest to help keep the loan originations flowing. Originations of interest-only, negative amortizations, and 40-year amortizations have proliferated in the market recently. While there have been interest-only and negative amortization loans in the prime sector for years, the presence of these types of loans in the subprime realm is largely the market's response to increasing borrower affordability and to maintain origination volume. (Standard & Poors, April 2005)

There is growing concern around the increased usage of these mortgages in new RMBS securitization, which may pose significant credit risk. (Standard & Poors, April 2005)

Some of the inherent risks that may arise include payment shock due to interest rate increases, coupled with the addition of principal repayment, undercollateralization with regard to negative amortization, and home price depreciation. (Standard & Poors, April 2005)

Due to the time lag associated with delinquencies and losses in RMBS pools, and the nature of these risks, it will be several years before the product performance is tested. (Standard & Poors, April 2005)

As with the new product types, new or expanded credit guidelines do not have the benefit of historical data to determine the effect of the associated risk layering on loan performance. Although many of these features may have been present in prior offerings, the combination or extent of such features is considerably different. It is widely believed that using the performance results of previous programs having one or more of these risk factors in most instances will not provide the full impact of these risks used in combination. (Fitch Ratings, September 2005)

The precise impact of the differences in hybrid features on loan performance, however, has yet to be measured in stressed environments. . . . If mortgage rates continue to climb and property appreciation slows down, then the interest rates at the time of reset will be higher than the current interest rates and there will be fewer refinance opportunities for borrowers. . . . Thus, Moody's expects the differences in key product features of hybrid ARMS, and the resulting differences in potential payment shock, will lead to meaningful performance distinctions. (Moody's Investor Service 2005b, May)

It is quite clear that the ratings agencies had a pretty clear picture by no later than early 2005 that default risks in the subprime market had increased a great deal, in large part due to the hazards of the layered financing structures that were being employed so frequently. They also had strong signals that housing prices in many key and important regional markets that accounted for a large proportion of the loans backing RMBS and CDO securities were stumbling or worse and that such problems were likely to grow. Thus, despite their inability to predict securities performance very precisely and their inconsistencies in classifying and rating different bonds across time and sector, they had a great deal of knowledge about the very large amounts of risk that had been financed via the securitization market. Their major responsibility at this point should have been to rerate many outstanding securities and to be much more conservative in their ongoing ratings. That, however, would have slowed down the securitization market, which had by now become a primary source of earnings and stock price growth for these companies.

Capital Push: From Bubble to Bubble, the Global Saving Glut, and an Appetite for Risk

It became clear as early as 2003–04 that the second high-risk lending boom was being fed by the increase in the appetite of investors for mortgage-related securities of different sorts. One key factor was the bursting of the dot-com stock market bubble over the 2000–2002 period. Real estate seemed to be the obvious place to put funds that were exiting stocks.

Starting in 2000, all three major U.S. stock market indices began a two-year decline. By October 9, 2002, the Dow Jones had fallen by 38 percent from its peak and the S&P by 49 percent. The technology-heavy NASDAQ had fallen even further, by 78 percent (Downs 2007).

But the collapse of U.S. stock market was not the only source of the rush of capital into mortgage markets. There is perhaps some irony in the fact that, approximately six months before he succeeded Alan Greenspan as chairman of the Federal Reserve Board of Governors, Ben Bernanke gave a speech in St. Louis in which he described the effect of a "global saving glut" on capital flows into the United States (Bernanke 2005). In the past, more developed, industrialized countries were generally net lenders to less developed countries. However, more recently, less developed countries, including some in Asia and South America as well as oil-exporting countries, had become net lenders to the United States and global capital flows increased the supply and liquidity of capital in the United States (Rodrik and Subramanian 2008; Warsh 2007; and Bernanke 2005). Moreover, some developed countries saw significant demographic shifts that led to higher savings rates. Rising oil prices also played a key role, leaving oil-exporting countries with large amounts of cash reserves that were then plowed back into international capital markets. In total, the net international lending to U.S. citizens, businesses, and governments increased from $120 billion in 1996 to $414 billion in 2000 and then to $666 billion in 2004 (Bernanke 2005). This constituted a sizeable increase in net U.S. borrowing from 1.5 percent of gross domestic product in 1996 to 5.75 percent by 2004.

As global and domestic financial markets poured dollars into mortgage-backed securities and CDOs, the issuers of these products were hungry for more and more loans and increasingly less scrupulous about the quality of such loans. The result was that aggregate activity in mortgage markets increasingly was driven more by the "demand" of investors for structured finance investments than by the authentic demand of homebuyers and homeowners for credit. Issuers and lenders pushed mortgage originators and brokers to serve the interests of Wall Street rather than the needs of homebuyers and homeowners. In his written testimony before Congress, Harry Dinham, the president of the National Association of Mortgage Brokers, argued that "in the end, Wall Street creates a demand for particular mortgages; underwriting criteria for these mortgages is set to meet this demand and this underwriting criteria, not the mortgage originator, dictates whether a consumer qualifies for a particular loan product" (Dinham 2007).

Financial Complexity and Impediments to Loan Restructuring

When complex mortgage securities were designed, little thought was given to the difficulties that these new structures would create in the event that large numbers of mortgages went into default and needed to be restructured. In the traditional originate-to-hold lending model, a borrower in distress was able to seek a loan modification from the originating lender that still owned the loan. If there was a high probability that the borrower could not continue to make regular payments on the loan, the lender would have a pretty clear choice between foreclosing and restructuring the loan or doing some other more temporary loss-mitigation work. The lender could do a relatively simple cost-benefit analysis, given some limited uncertainties, and make a decision about whether to modify a loan. Given the transactional costs of foreclosure, the portfolio lender was often more likely to work with borrowers to restructure a loan rather than foreclose, especially if the collateral value of the house was in some doubt.

In the complex world of structured finance, such a simple calculus was not as relevant. Even if it made sense for an originate-to-hold lender to do a loan modification in the case of a particular loan in default, there was no such simple process for the loan that was held in a complex trust containing thousands of loans governed by complex interparty agreements. The securities derived from the loan pool were structured in such a way that a specific type of loan modification might be expected to benefit some investors but hurt others.

Recall that different tranches of investors in a CMO-type RMBS received their payments from different parts of the loan cash flow and they were secured in different fashions. The servicer of the loan, and the trustee holding the trust in which the loan is held, must follow the prescribed procedures from the initial securitization (Eggert 2007). The rules in such agreements can be quite vague in terms of how much discretion is given to modify loans. The result is that efforts to modify loans may be seen as instigating interparty litigation. This can lead servicers to avoid exercising even small amounts of discretion to avoid such problems. Eggert (2007) calls these problems "tranche warfare," because restructuring loans can lead to removing some part of an income stream (or increasing downside risk) from one tranche while enhancing the income (or reducing downside risk) to another tranche.

Securitization can pose other impediments to loan modifications

(Eggert 2007). Some securitization agreements and tax law governing the REMIC structure can limit the number of loans that can be modified. Servicers may have an incentive to move slowly with distressed borrowers, as they generally receive the late fees that such borrowers generate. Also, because many subprime borrowers received piggyback loans, in which there was a subordinate second-lien loan involved, many borrowers had loans held in two separate trusts, which in turn required two sets of complex negotiations, with more competing interests. These problems are often not mutually exclusive, so that a particular borrower needing a loan modification may face two or more of these obstacles simultaneously.

Another problem with the structure of mortgage markets that inhibited loan modifications and was driven by the vertical specialization of the marketplace was the way that servicing was structured and priced. Servicers competed almost entirely on minimizing the costs to the investors holding interests in the loans. The entire servicing model was based on mass standardization of process and cookie-cutter procedures that would not be flexible or accommodate substantial iterative interaction with borrowers. Unfortunately, loan modifications typically require such interaction and servicers' agreements tend not to compensate servicers well for such procedures. Servicers are, in effect, sometimes rewarded for allowing borrowers to accrue late fees and penalties, which gives them less incentive for entering into modifications in a timely fashion.

Lessons from a Subprime Lender: A Brief Look at New Century Financial

In order to illustrate some of the problems that fed and exacerbated the problems with high-risk lending in the second high-risk boom, it is helpful to look at the operations of one lender in detail. The firm highlighted here, New Century Financial, has been called the "poster child" for lenders that rode the subprime boom in a big way and then rode the market collapse down at an even faster pace (Creswell and Bajaj 2007). Different lenders exhibited various sorts of transactional failures and perverse incentives to greater or lesser degrees, and no one case study will adequately describe the extent of the entire industry's problems. Nonetheless, the details described in the New Century case paint a useful picture for just how pervasive some of these problems were within the structure and operations of a major lender. Although New Century, at least until 2007, was certainly not a well-known firm to most outside the lending industry, it was a major subprime lender, especially during most of the second high-risk lending boom.[4]

New Century Financial was founded in 1995 by three executives from a mortgage company named Plaza Home Mortgage Bank after it was sold to Fleet Mortgage Group, which in turn became part of Washington Mutual (Creswell and Bajaj 2007). In the late 1990s, after the problems in the bond market following the Asian and Russian financial crises, New Century, like many other subprime lenders, had difficulty accessing its regular capital markets, but a large bank, U.S. Bank, invested in the firm to help it survive that period.

The firm came roaring back, so that by 2005 and 2006 it ranked among the top three subprime originators in the United States. Figure 4.4 shows that the firm grew significantly during the first high-risk boom in the late 1990s, but grew more rapidly from 2001 to 2005. The firm's growth during this latter period exceeded even the substantial growth of the subprime industry as a whole. New Century originations and purchases grew from just over $6 billion in 2001 to over $56 billion by 2005, for more than a ninefold increase, while the industry grew from $173 billion to $620 billion over this period, for an increase of 3.6 times. New Century was predominantly a "wholesale lender," with roughly 85 percent of its loans made through a network of over fifty thousand mortgage brokers and correspondent lenders nationwide. While mortgage brokers marketed loans and processed applications, which were then sent to New Century, correspondent lenders actually funded the loans, based on specifications from New Century, and sold them soon after they were originated to New Century. The wholesale business operated through thirty-three regional operating centers in nineteen states. New Century's smaller retail division operated under a different name, Home123. It operated through the firm's 235 sales offices in thirty-six states and also relied on a telemarketing operation and a website.

---

4. Most of the details used in this case study of New Century Financial were based on Missal (2008), which is an in-depth review of the firm's operations and finances by the U.S. bankruptcy court where New Century sought bankruptcy protection. The review involved interviewing principals of the firm and a substantial amount of analysis of firm financials and regulatory filings.

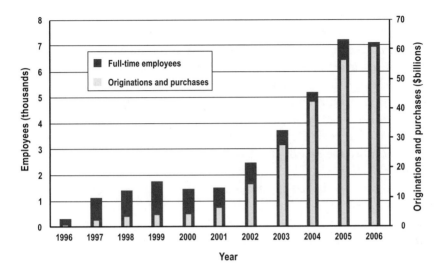

Figure 4.4. Growth of New Century Financial, 1996–2006.
Source: Missal, 2008; amount for 2006 originations and purchases was extrapolated from the third quarter figure.

Loans Characterized by Multiple and Layered Risks

Data from New Century's last three years of operation show that it originated large numbers of both home purchase and refinance loans. Most of its loans—more than 70 percent generally—were adjustable rate loans, with a substantial percentage of those structured as interest-only loans. The proportion of all mortgages that were interest-only reached almost 30 percent by 2005. Although the majority of New Century's loans were refinance loans, an increasing percentage were home purchase loans, with the home purchase share reaching 44 percent for the last nine months of 2006, which was fairly on par with the industry as a whole by that time. Moreover, the volume of home purchase loans increased from under $15 billion in 2004 to over $23 billion in 2005 and was on track to reach $27 billion in 2006. This was a deliberate strategy on the part of the company: in a Securities and Exchange filing in late 2006, the company stated, "we have made a concerted effort to increase our home purchase business" (Missal 2008).

The bulk of refinance loans were "cash-out" refinances, where borrowers received some cash from the transaction, which in turn might have been used to pay off other debt. Cash-out refinances constituted 59 percent of the firm's loans in 2004, but this share fell to approximately 45 percent by the first nine months of 2006, corresponding to the increased proportion of loans for home purchase.

Stated-income and limited-documentation loans constituted approximately half of New Century's business, at least in its last few years of operation. By the end of 2006, stated-income loans constituted over 47 percent of all New Century's loans (Missal 2008). As recently as the end of 2002, such loans had constituted less than 35 percent of all loans. An especially risky type of stated-income loan was the stated-wage-earner loan, in which the borrower received a W-2 from an employer, and so should have been able to document income, but still received a stated-income loan. Stated-income loans were originally designed primarily for self-employed borrowers who did not receive W-2s, and it was not clear why borrowers with W-2s should need stated-income loans, especially when rates on such loans were higher.

New Century also made many so-called 80/20, or piggyback, loans, where an 80 percent first mortgage was combined with a 20 percent second mortgage to provide for a zero down payment or zero equity requirement. The share of the firm's loans that were structured as 80/20 loans rose from less than 10 percent in late 2003 to more than 35 percent by the end of 2005 (Missal 2008).

New Century's use of these high-risk loan structures and terms—interest-only, stated-income, and 80/20—were not mutually exclusive. Frequently, two or more of these features were combined so that risk-inducing terms were "layered," which effectively worked to increase loan risk in a multiplicative, and not just additive, fashion. In fact, an official of the company claimed that, in 2004 at least, the company was the only lender to offer an "interest-only, 80/20, stated wage earner loan." This product actually constituted over 3 percent of the firm's originations in October 2004 (Missal 2008).

In order to fund its loans, the company utilized more than a dozen warehouse lenders, which included both commercial and investment banks. The master repurchase agreements with these lenders required the company to maintain certain levels of liquidity and meet various other financial targets. If one of these agreements was violated, it typically triggered default in the repurchase agreements with other warehouse lenders. In particular, the warehouse lenders were allowed to initiate, under various conditions, a "margin call," in which New Century would have to provide additional collateral for its loans or repay a certain amount of outstanding debt to the lender. In early 2007, some of the warehouse lenders initiated margin calls, which led to the firm filing bankruptcy.

Although New Century securitized some of its loans itself, it sold most of its loans to firms typically referred to as "investors," but these companies were not the same as the ultimate investors in the mortgage-related securities. The investors would then aggregate and securitize the loans. In selling its loans, New Century would provide a sample of loan files to the investor, which would then review the files. If the loans did not meet the investor's standards they were repackaged into new pools and remarketed to different investors. Under the terms of the "representations and warranties" that governed these sales, if there were misrepresentations about loans that were purchased or an "early payment default" in the first few months, New Century might have been required to repurchase these loans from the investor.

Problems Became Increasingly Evident, but Lending Standards Were Not Improved

At least as early as 2003, there were several signs that the performance of loans originated by New Century was degrading sharply and that the layering of high-risk loan features, especially combinations of interest-only, stated-income, and 80/20 characteristics, was causing particular problems. In 2003 and 2004, investors began to reject an increasing number of loans in pools they were inspecting for purchase (Missal 2008). Reasons cited for such "kickouts" included bad appraisals, missing documentation, or incorrect credit reports. Problems with appraisals were the largest single factor, accounting for approximately 30 percent of kickouts. Although increasing kickouts should have been a clear signal of increasing problems over the 2003–06 period, it does not appear that New Century monitored these patterns before 2006 (Missal 2008).

The firm did have internal procedures to monitor early payment defaults and other indicators. In April 2004, the firm's chief credit officer reported that the firm's internal quality assurance results were at "unacceptable levels." Internally, quality assurance staff found in an audit of loans in November and December 2003 that almost 25 percent of loans had "severe underwriting errors."

A key indicator that is frequently used to monitor loan performance for problems is the early payment default (EPD) rate. The EPD rate is the proportion of loans in which borrowers miss payments in one or more of the first three months after origination. If a loan became delinquent this quickly, there was a substantial likelihood that the loan was somehow not well suited for the borrower. Figure 4.5 shows that, by the third quarter of 2004, the EPD rate increased to nearly 10 percent, essentially twice the level of early 2004. After dipping back down in early 2005, the EPD rate began to increase again; by the spring of 2006 it was over 10 percent and continued to climb until ending in the 14–16 percent range by the end of the year.

The Response to Defaults: More Risk Please

Despite the ample warning signs that default and foreclosure rates were excessively high, especially in loans with multiple layers of risk, New Century continued to approve riskier and riskier loans well into 2006. Figures 4.6 and 4.7 show the growth in two of the riskiest loan structures—stated-income and 80/20 loans—which are closely associated with

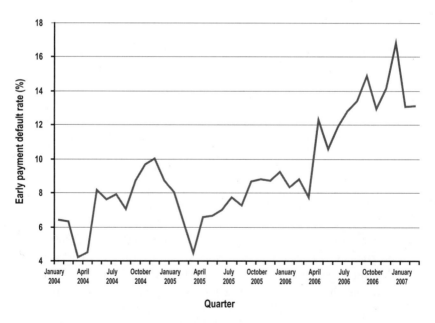

Figure 4.5. Early payment defaults for New Century loans, 2004 to early 2007.
Source: Missal, 2008.

higher EPDs and longer-term defaults. Comparing these charts with figure 4.5 shows that, rather than curtailing these products as EPDs grew—products that were known to exacerbate EPDs—New Century continued either to increase originating these sorts of loans or at least did not decrease their already high levels of production in these lines. Finally, in late 2006 the share of loans that were 80/20s began to decline some. The lender had seen its share of interest-only loans—another risky loan structure—decline in late 2005, but this was attributed less to internal controls than to a decreased appetite among investors for such products.

Why didn't New Century respond to its worsening loan performance, which it clearly knew about? The federal bankruptcy court examiner found a variety of problems, but the overarching one was that key executives at the firm were convinced that origination volume and market share were of paramount concern and that improving lending standards would harm both. Although New Century's audit committee was aware of loan performance problems, the company did little to rectify these problems (Missal 2008). In fact, leadership in the production department of the firm, which was responsible, and rewarded, for high origination volumes, reacted hostilely to such audit and quality assurance results.

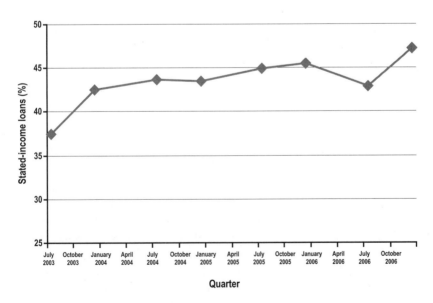

Figure 4.6. Percent of New Century mortgages that were stated-income loans.
Source: Missal, 2008.

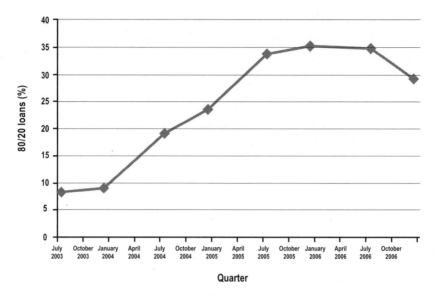

Figure 4.7. Percent of New Century loans that were 80/20s.
Source: Missall, 2008.

The production department viewed the audit unit as "an entity that increased the average cost to originate new loans" (Missal 2008). In mid-2005, the company estimated its total per loan funding cost at $505, but a few months later, despite the growing credit quality problems, the head of production set a goal of $400 per loan for total funding costs. In particular, there was an explicit goal of reducing the contribution of the audit function to per loan costs from $26 per loan to no more than $15 per loan. Then, in September 2005, the head of the production department wrote an e-mail stating that "if recollection is correct, every single audit completed has been unsatisfactory, which to me sounds like we need to amend policy as much as clean up our act. The financial results that have been accomplished over the past few years are inconsistent with audit results" (quoted in Missal 2008, 140).

In this executive's view, the short-term financial benefits of reducing per loan costs and maximizing volume should dictate policy regardless of the signals suggesting that loan performance was breaking down. And there were plenty of such signals. In this same month, September 2005, New Century's 2004 80/20 loans had a default rate that was four times higher than that of its other loans and had grown to a level of approximately 35 percent of all loans (Missal 2008). Despite continual concerns raised by the company's audit committee about deteriorating loan quality, and even after the production department stated that it would implement bonuses based partly on loan quality, the bankruptcy examiner found no evidence that loan quality concerns were ever factored into the bonus structures of regional managers. In fact, the 2006 bonus for regional managers was based on volume (30 percent), the number of brokers used (30 percent), deviations from rate sheets (30 percent), and the discretion of senior management (10 percent). The bankruptcy examiner summed up senior management's position as follows: "Senior management appears to have been mindful that such products [stated income and 80/20] exposed New Century to risks beyond those presented in earlier years, but the Examiner could discern no efforts made to address such risks in any concerted manner" (Missal 2008, 148). As long as investors were purchasing New Century's loans, the senior management apparently made the decision that short-term revenue maximization was more important than strengthening lending standards to a more sustainable level. There was clearly an element of focusing almost exclusively on short-term revenues and profits at the expense of thinking about such longer-term issues as financial sustainability and loan performance. This fed, and was fed by, a corporate culture that valued short-term excess. Journalists covering the collapse of New Century referred to the culture of the company as a "work-hard, party-hard culture" and a "culture of excess" (Hagerty et al. 2007). Former staff members have been quoted as saying that "we made so much money, you couldn't believe it" (Creswell and Bajaj 2007). There were staff events held on Caribbean cruises and in Spain, and some top producing employees were even sent to a Porsche-driving school by the company (Hagerty et al. 2007).

The focus on market share and short-term profits led executives to turn a blind eye to the deterioration in loan quality and performance. In late 2006, however, these problems eventually caught up with the company. The bankruptcy examiner found that, although there were ample data to address deteriorating loan quality and performance, the company made little effort to do so until late 2006. At that point, as the decline of the housing market became much more evident, the company did become significantly more active in reducing poor loans and defaults. Unfortunately, according to the bankruptcy examiner, this was "too little, too late" (Missal 2008).

From the perspective of New Century's original principals and key directors, it is not clear that they made many financially irrational decisions. Although they had executed representation and warranty statements committing them to repurchase some EPD loans or loans involving fraud, the volume of such loans was still quite modest compared to the loans that did not have to be repurchased. Moreover, the firm often let the repurchase requests from investors pile up, effectively discouraging such claims in order to minimize losses. Most important, however, is the fact that the firm, despite its massive volume of lending, generally managed to keep its balance sheet relatively thin in terms of capital and liquidity.

As the lender boomed from 2002 to 2005, and as the principals became increasingly aware of the loan performance problems and high incidences of fraudulent or misrepresented loan documents and appraisals, these same principals extracted their profits from the firm by exercising stock options. From 2004 to 2006, the firm's three founders together made more than $40 million in profits from selling shares in the company (Creswell and Bajaj 2007). The firm's stock price peaked at $66 per share in December 2004, just as increasing information on poorly performing loans was becoming more evident inside the firm. Even for most of 2006, the firm's stock prices were in the $40s. From August to November of 2006, at a time when EPDs had become very bad—in the 14–16 percent range—the founders sold shares at approximately $40 per share for a total profit of more than $21 million. A few months later, in early March 2007, after the company had ceased lending, its price had fallen to less than $4 per share (Simon, Hagerty, and Zuckerman 2007). Despite the rapid fall of the company, a great deal of money had been made and distributed to key executives and shareholders over the firm's twelve-year history.

5

The Economic and Social Costs
of High-Risk Mortgage Lending

High-risk mortgage lending imposes a wide array of costs—both financial and nonfinancial—on a variety of individuals, organizations, and
communities. The bulk of the initial press coverage of the 2007–08 U.S.
mortgage crisis revolved around financial losses suffered by parties that
were involved in the lending process, especially investors and lenders and
borrowers. But increasingly, as the scale and depth of the crisis became
more widely understood, there was an increasing recognition that the
costs of excessively risky lending are spread much more widely, across
entire neighborhoods and communities where foreclosures are concentrated. Even more broadly, the 2007–08 credit crisis has had global
impacts—delivered via the capital markets—including losses to naïve
individual and institutional investors in mortgage instruments and to
those who found that credit markets had seized up and that lenders were
pulling back in the provision of various types of finance.

In this chapter I will examine different types of costs imposed by high-
risk mortgage lending. Some of these are easier to quantify or monetize,
while others, such as the long-term impact of damaged credit histories,
are more difficult to measure. Because a cost is more difficult to measure
or put in dollar terms, does not make it less important, however.

I begin by looking at the sizeable increases in foreclosures that have
accompanied subprime and high-risk lending booms and their particular
impact on lower-income and minority neighborhoods. I then examine
some of the most obvious costs of high-risk lending, including impacts
on borrowers, investors, and local communities. Following the discussion of these more visible consequences, the chapter addresses the
broader negative by-products of volatile boom-bust lending cycles, their
ripple effects through credit markets of different sorts, and their potential impacts on the spatial development of metropolitan areas and
neighborhood change.

I also consider the broader regional and macroeconomic consequences of high-risk lending. These include a reliance on home equity to finance significant amounts of consumption and, thus, a reliance on increasingly lax and liquid credit markets to prop up rates of consumer spending and economic growth regionally and nationally.

The problems of widespread and historically unprecedented increases in mortgage delinquencies and foreclosures in 2007 were, by themselves, not the sole or perhaps even primary reason for the consternation of the financial markets and major players such as the Federal Reserve Board. Rather, it was the spillover of these problems into broader credit and financial markets, first in the securitization of jumbo prime mortgages, but then quickly into all sorts of financial markets. Some of these markets were heavily relied upon for the financing of essential services such as local government, as well as the broader corporate and small business sectors. Mortgage investment losses also led to major investment banks having difficulty remaining liquid or solvent, as many of them were highly leveraged and depended on fast-moving exchanges and conversions of their assets to make good on their commitments. These problems reached their crescendo with the collapse of Bear Stearns in early 2008 and the Federal Reserve's unprecedented involvement in rescuing the firm's bondholders and arranging for the firm's takeover by J. P. Morgan Chase.

In the media, concerns over losses to investors and financial institutions consistently received a higher profile than the problems of homeowners and neighborhoods. Daily newspapers and broadcast media were busier covering the insolvency of lenders and the massive write-downs of RMBS and CDOs at large banks and investment houses than the apparently less interesting—or at least less startling—story of homeowners going into foreclosure. This was partly because the eventual scope and scale of these broader systemic problems were very difficult to assess and because the highly leveraged nature of many of the institutions suffering losses meant that fundamental confidence in the financial system was threatened. Of course, there is some argument that the higher profile media coverage may also have been due to the fact that these investment losses had a material impact on the balance sheets of financial institutions and the stock and bond portfolios of middle- and upper-income households, rather than the losses of homes of what tended to be relatively modest-income households.

Finally, I consider the potential legacies of unsustainable, high-risk lending, and the 2007–08 mortgage crisis in particular, on the policy environment for addressing problems of inequities in mortgage markets, housing finance, and credit markets more broadly. The very high profile failure of the subprime market, and its concentration in lower-income and minority communities, may leave some legacy of skepticism among the public, the media, and policymakers concerning ongoing and future efforts to provide access to reasonably priced credit to modest-income households, even if such programs are well designed and pose limited risks. One might call this a "backlash" effect of unregulated, high-risk lending and its large-scale, highly visible failures.

Up until the early to mid-1990s, significant net gains had been made in reducing disparities in access to credit for minority borrowers and communities in mostly sound and equitable ways (Immergluck 2004). Many efforts of prime lenders—often encouraged by fair lending regulations and the Community Reinvestment Act—were relatively incremental and generally developed through moderate pilot programs and partnerships with nonprofit counseling agencies. Reductions in down-payment requirements to allow more households to access homeownership were, initially at least, incremental and often tied to homeownership counseling requirements. Many efforts were subjected to significant evaluative research, where loan performance was scrutinized carefully to determine what, if any, trade-offs there may have been between increasing access to credit and any increases in defaults or foreclosures. Because community reinvestment lenders are banks and thrifts, they are significantly regulated for safety and soundness, while mortgage companies are not. The rapid and essentially unsupervised growth of subprime mortgage lending contrasted sharply with—and dwarfed in scale—the affordable and generally sound approaches that prime community reinvestment lenders employed in the late 1980s and early 1990s.

Increasing and Spatially Concentrated Defaults and Foreclosures

The increases in high-risk mortgage lending—especially subprime loans—in the late 1990s and from 2002 to 2007 resulted in corresponding increases in mortgage delinquencies, defaults, and foreclosures. Although foreclosure rates—that is, the number of loans entering foreclosure per total outstanding loans—increased due to the greater risk of subprime and other high-risk products, the total numbers of foreclosures increased even more, especially in the second boom period, because the total volume of high-risk lending increased so sharply. Although high levels of defaults and foreclosures are not the only problems caused by excessively risky lending, they are among the most obvious and have the most direct impacts on borrowers, lender/investors, neighborhoods, and local governments.

Figure 5.1 illustrates changes in U.S. foreclosure rates over the 1998–2008 period, measured as the percent of outstanding loans entering foreclosure over a one-year period. Rates are broken down by prime, subprime, and FHA loans, per the Mortgage Bankers Association National Delinquency Survey. Again, when looking at foreclosure rates, it is important to understand that such measures may understate increases in the levels of mortgage distress per property or household because, as lending volume increases, the denominator in the rate also increases. That is, the total number of outstanding loans increases, so even if foreclosure rates remain constant, more homes may end up in foreclosure.

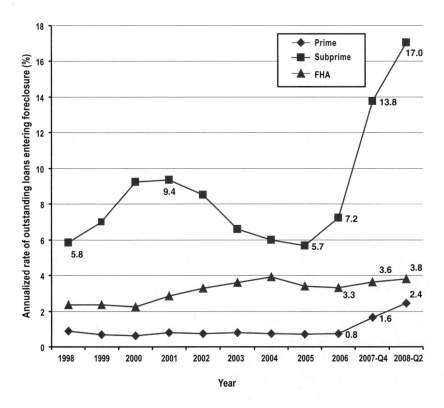

Figure 5.1. Mortgage foreclosure rates, 1998–2008.
Source: Mortgage Bankers Association, National Delinquency Survey.

Nonetheless, figure 5.1 shows that subprime foreclosure rates rose sharply from 1998 to 2000, preceding the 2000–2001 recession. Moreover, while foreclosure rates for subprime loans varied widely across the period, foreclosure rates for FHA loans—which generally are intended for borrowers unable to qualify for prime loans—remained essentially flat, with only modest increases during the 2000–2004 period, a substantial portion of which was affected by the 2000–2001 recession.

Figure 5.1 also shows that subprime foreclosure rates rose particularly steeply in 2007, reaching an annualized rate of 13.8 percent by the end of 2007, compared to a rate of 5.7 percent for 2005, which itself was much higher than historic foreclosure rates for prime loans. By the second quarter of 2008, the annualized rate of foreclosure starts (the percentage of outstanding loans entering the foreclosure process) had reached 17 percent. The chart also shows that in late 2007 and into 2008 the foreclosure rate of prime mortgages also began to increase significantly, suggesting that the breakdown in credit markets and associated declines in housing prices were beginning to cause spillovers into more conventional lending markets. Prime adjustable rate mortgages were the source of much of this increase.

Figures 5.2 and 5.3 focus on the type of loan that was the source of many of the problems in the foreclosure crisis that began in late 2006 and early 2007. These charts shows the share of outstanding loans in the first quarters of 2005 (figure 5.2) and 2007 (figure 5.3) that were entering foreclosure on an annualized basis. Thus, in the first quarter of 2005 only three states were seeing more than 10 percent of outstanding subprime ARM loans enter foreclosure per year. No states during this time saw annualized foreclosure rates above 12.5 percent. (In fact, no state rates were above 12 percent during this period.) By the first quarter of 2007, twenty-two states had annualized foreclosure rates of over 12.5 percent and another twelve had rates above 10 percent. Moreover, the volume of such loans had increased dramatically since 2003, so that the raw volume of such foreclosures was very high. Things only worsened over the course of 2007 and into 2008.

Any notion that the foreclosure crisis was limited to a few states was sorely misplaced. Of course, large numbers of foreclosures were occurring in populous states such as California and Florida, but these were by no means the only regions affected by the crisis.

Nor was the problem confined to states with weak economies. Certainly, overheated (and then cooling) housing markets and weak economies can and do aggravate foreclosure problems, in part because

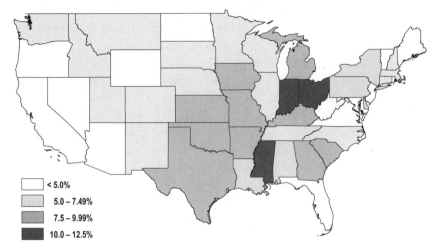

Figure 5.2. Percent of subprime adjustable rate loans entering foreclosure,
annualized rate, first quarter 2005.
Source: Mortgage Bankers Association, National Delinquency Survey.

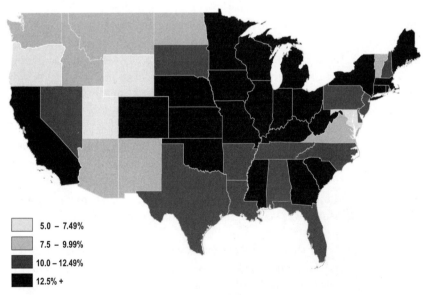

Figure 5.3. Percent of subprime adjustable rate loans entering foreclosure,
annualized rate, first quarter 2007.
Source: Mortgage Bankers Association, National Delinquency Survey.

subprime and other high-risk loans are particularly sensitive to housing market conditions and job losses. But even in states with relatively strong economies and modestly appreciating housing markets, such as Georgia, Wisconsin, Kentucky, South Dakota, and Kansas, foreclosure rates increased markedly.

Within most metropolitan areas, the increases in the rates and volumes of subprime foreclosures in the late 1990s and the middle 2000s were severely aggravated for many communities and neighborhoods because these loans were often disproportionately concentrated in lower-income and minority neighborhoods within metropolitan regions. In the Chicago area, for example, Smith (2008) found that census tracts with populations that were 80 percent or more minority had 41.6 foreclosures per 1,000 mortgageable properties in 2007, while the rate in tracts with minority populations of less than 10 percent had only 8 foreclosures per 1,000 mortgageable properties in the same year. Moreover, while increases in foreclosures stemming from the mid- 2000s high-risk boom affected a wide variety of neighborhoods, the raw volume of the increase was greater in lower-income and minority neighborhoods.

To examine these patterns in more detail, we can look at foreclosure patterns within the city of Chicago from 2005 to 2007. Chicago is a good example because the city as a whole is generally considered to have a fairly strong housing market (albeit with some slowdown in 2006 and 2007). The city is also large and has a wide variety of neighborhood types with varying income and racial demographics. Figure 5.4 includes three maps of the city broken into what are called "community areas," semiformal neighborhood groupings that have been studied dating back to the first half of the twentieth century. These community areas are groups of census tracts and are well recognized by residents of the city.

The left-hand map in figure 5.4 simply plots the share of residents in each community area who are minority group members. The next (middle) map plots the number of foreclosures filed by lenders in 2005 divided by the number of mortgageable properties in the community area. The third map plots this same ratio, but it does so for foreclosures filed in 2007. Comparing the figures shows that foreclosures per property increased the most in raw terms in neighborhoods with large minority populations, especially those on the city's South Side and West Side. At the same time, some community areas with smaller minority populations actually saw a larger percentage growth in foreclosures, in part because these communities had relatively modest foreclosure levels in 2005.

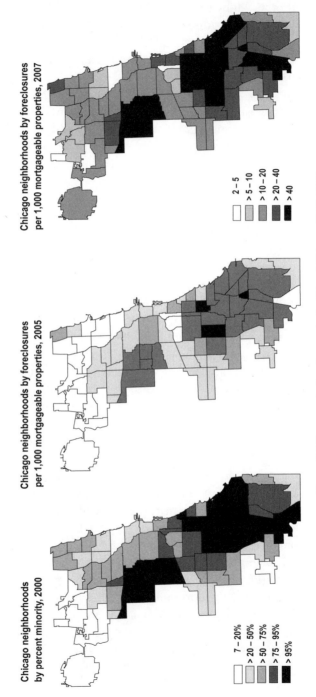

Chicago neighborhoods by percent minority, 2000

7 – 20%
> 20 – 50%
> 50 – 75%
> 75 – 95%
> 95%

Chicago neighborhoods by foreclosures per 1,000 mortgageable properties, 2005

Chicago neighborhoods by foreclosures per 1,000 mortgageable properties, 2007

2 – 5
> 5 – 10
> 10 – 20
> 20 – 40
> 40

Figure 5.4. Increases in foreclosures in the City of Chicago, 2005–2007.
Source: Author's calculations using data from Woodstock Institute (2008) and U.S. Census 2000.

Costs of Subprime and High-Risk Lending to Borrowers

High-risk mortgage lending has imposed a number of costs on homebuyers and homeowners. Although such loans may have created opportunities for some renter households to enter homeownership that could not have done so with less risky loans, it is less clear whether very many of these loans provided access to sustainable, moderate-risk homeownership or financially beneficial homeownership.

Even before considering the impact of high-cost, high-risk loans on the financial benefits, costs, and risks of homeownership, it is important to first question a common proposition that has been frequently asserted: that all subprime home purchase loans enabled home buying among households that would otherwise not have been able to purchase a home.[1]

This was clearly not the case. Many borrowers using subprime loans may not have received the same type of loan (in terms of loan size, income documentation requirements, and amortization structure), but that is not the same thing as asserting that they could not have received any home purchase loan at all. Moreover, homeownership is not an all-or nothing proposition. If a household is not able to purchase a loan at a specific point in time, it may, after saving a bit more for a down payment, achieving a slightly higher income, or improving its credit score(s), be able to attain homeownership in the not too distant future—and perhaps obtain financing at a much lower cost at the same time.

It turns out, in fact, that many subprime loans—especially in the latter years of the second high-risk boom—were made to borrowers with quite good credit. Using data from Loan Performance, Inc. on securitized subprime loans, a *Wall Street Journal* analysis found that 37 percent of subprime borrowers in the first quarter of 2007 had credit scores above 660—a relatively solid threshold for prime borrowers—up from 24 percent in the first quarter of 2000 (Brooks and Simon 2007). Another 25 percent of subprime loan borrowers had scores from 659 to 620 in the first quarter of 2007, a range that would still have qualified many for prime loans, up from 17 percent in 2000.

These borrowers were either given subprime loans when they could have qualified for the same basic loan at lower costs from a prime lender, or something about the loan—low- or no-documentation, high debt-to-income ratios, very .low down payments, and/or some other

---

1. See Goolsbee (2007), for example.

feature—increased the risk of the loan, causing it to be priced at a subprime rate. Researchers at the Boston Federal Reserve Bank found that, at the height of the second subprime boom, approximately 70 percent of subprime loan borrowers had credit scores above 620, but also found that most of the corresponding loans had features such as no- or low-documentation, high debt-to-income ratios, or high loan-to-value ratios that caused them to be priced and structured as subprime loans (Foote et al. 2008). This does not show, however, that these borrowers could not have accessed a prime loan—just that they would have had to access it under different terms, including possibly smaller loan amounts, the avoidance of layered junior, piggyback loans, or more complete documentation of their incomes.

Subprime lenders made many loans to prime-credit borrowers with substantially higher debt-to-income ratios—often significantly greater than 45 to 50 percent—than prime lenders allowed and often did not require documentation of income, while still permitting very low or zero owner equity, which gave borrowers less cushion in the event of a housing market downturn or a drop in income due to a layoff or other problem. Subprime lenders were also likely to have weaker checks on mortgage brokers, who had significant incentives to falsify incomes or encourage borrowers to inflate stated incomes.

Thus, in many cases, subprime lending may have encouraged first-time and repeat buyers to "overbuy"—or to buy with less than optimal or highly risky financing terms—rather than simply enabling the purchase of a house, which they may have been able to do with a prime loan. In particular, by allowing for much higher debt-to-income ratios, and by providing more potential variability in these ratios, high-risk loans may essentially make the financial risk in going from renter to owner too large, sometimes by encouraging the borrower to buy "too much" house or to borrow too much on an existing house (Doms and Krainer 2007).

Costs to Borrowers of High Financing Costs and Common Subprime Loan Terms

High-risk loans can reduce the financial return to investments in home-ownership and increase the risk of an involuntary, or forced, exit from homeownership back into the rental market. In some cases, default and foreclosure can mean the loss of substantial owner equity that had been built up in the home and a worsening of the borrower's credit history and lowering of the credit score. This latter phenomenon has growing implications in terms of diminished social and economic opportunities because credit histories and scores are increasingly evaluated in applications for employment, rental housing, and auto insurance, as well as other credit markets. The risks involved in high-risk loans can also compel a borrower to sell her house at an inopportune time, after local values have declined, so that she is unable to weather temporary weaknesses in local prices and sell at a time when values are stronger.

High-risk (and high-cost) loans have been shown to greatly reduce the financial rate of return on homeownership. Belsky, Retsinas, and Duda (2005) have demonstrated that the existence of a high-cost mortgage has a severe negative impact on the probability of homeownership being profitable compared to renting. Some recent studies have found that lower-income and minority homeowners are more likely to exit home-ownership and return to renting, suggesting lower levels of sustainability in lower-income homeownership than for higher income groups. However, Spader and Quercia (2008) found that this pattern does not hold for homeowners with lower-cost, fixed-rate loans and that lower-income borrowers with such loans are no more likely to exit homeownership. Thus, the costs and nature of mortgage debt is a key factor in the stability and sustainability of homeownership as well in whether such homeownership makes households better off financially compared to renting.

Beyond the negative impacts of higher interest rates and fees on the net financial benefits of homeownership, subprime and other high-risk loans often included terms that increased the likelihood of default and foreclosure. Examples include prepayment penalties and balloon payments, both of which have been shown to increase the probability of foreclosure. After controlling for a wide variety of loan characteristics, Quercia, Stegman, and Davis (2007) found that subprime refinance loans with prepayment penalties were 20 percent more likely to experience a foreclosure than otherwise similar loans. Those with balloon payments were 50 percent more likely to experience a foreclosure than otherwise similar loans.

A prepayment penalty requires the borrower to make a substantial payment to the lender if she wants to refinance or pay off a loan, which can make it difficult to refinance into a more affordable loan if one becomes available. Although the balloon payment can result in reduced payments in the short term, it requires the borrower to be able to refinance the loan when the balloon comes due at a specific point in time. If the borrower cannot, she may be forced into foreclosure or forced to sell the house.

Effects of Deteriorated Credit Histories

Beyond the immediate financial loss to the borrower of high-risk lending, there can be longer term costs as well, including those related to weakened credit histories and lower credit scores. The higher level of debt that often accompanies a high-risk loan can also reduce a borrower's credit score. More important, a foreclosure will have a sizeable and long-lasting impact on one's credit history and credit score. Efforts to delay foreclosure, such as filing bankruptcy, can have negative effects as well.

The use of credit histories and, in particular, credit scores has become more widespread and important in many different sorts of key markets that impact the economic and social opportunities of individuals and households. Credit scores are frequently used by employers in evaluating job applicants, by landlords in assessing potential tenants, and by insurance companies in underwriting and pricing automobile insurance. The U.S. Fair Credit Reporting Act (FCRA) allows access to credit data for a wide variety of purposes. Any firm that delivers a good or service prior to receiving payment is effectively acting as a creditor under FCRA and is allowed to access credit reports and scores. Thus, firms providing basic and enhanced utility services, including electricity, water, gas, phone, or cable service, can and sometimes do use credit bureau data. In 2002, TransUnion, one of the three large credit bureau firms, reported that banks and credit unions had been overtaken as the largest users of credit data in the Philadelphia region by nonbank entities such as hospitals, telecommunication firms, and utilities (Furletti 2002).

A substantial deterioration in an individual's credit history, such as that caused by a foreclosure, has the potential to create a substantial web of barriers to employment, quality housing, and basic and affordable goods and services. For example, an estimated 90 percent of auto insurers use credit data in underwriting new policies, although some states prohibit the use of credit data in underwriting and pricing auto insurance (Hartwig and Wilkinson 2003). In many lower-income neighborhoods, auto insurance rates are already higher than average, so a lower credit score may make use of an automobile prohibitively expensive, which in turn can hurt employment prospects.

As landlords have increasingly relied on credit histories, and sometimes on credit scores, former homeowners who have experienced a recent foreclosure and now need rental housing may be excluded from the full array of housing choices to which they might otherwise have access. Given the scarcity of affordable, decent rental housing available in many metropolitan areas, this could make decent rental housing even more difficult to obtain. Employers have also turned to credit data in screening job applicants. In 2003, the Society for Human Resource Management found that 35 percent of the employers it surveyed were using credit data in screening applicants, up from 19 percent in 1996 (Evren 2004).

Consumer credit histories have declined in recent years, a decline that has most likely been aggravated by the growth of subprime mortgage lending—as well as other high-cost credit such as payday loans. Fellowes (2006) found that counties in the United States with relatively low average credit scores saw their scores decline significantly from 1999 to 2004. Counties with average scores falling in the bottom 10 percent of all counties in the country by average credit score saw their cumulative average score drop from 611 in 1999 to 594 in 2004. Meanwhile, counties in the top 10 percent by average credit score only saw a very modest increase in average score from 708 to 710. The typical county saw very little change in credit quality, but in lower-score counties—those most likely to receive higher levels of subprime loans, especially during the first subprime boom—credit scores tended to decline substantially.

Social, Emotional, and Psychological Effects of Foreclosure
and Forced Homeownership Exit

Homeowners going through foreclosure may suffer socially, emotionally, and psychologically. Some commentators on the 2007–08 mortgage crisis suggested that, if an owner-occupier had little equity invested in her home, foreclosure was essentially costless to her (Simon and Patterson 2008). Given such an assumption, homeowners would not be averse to foreclosure and would "ruthlessly" default on their loans if they had little equity in the home. This naïve model of homeowner behavior treats the home as merely a financial investment and ignores the social and economic value that households and families place on residence and ownership as well as the costs imposed by forced relocation. The literature in fact suggests that relatively few owner-occupants default on their mortgage even when "option theory" might suggest that they would, that is, when their outstanding mortgage debt significantly exceeds the market value of their house. Foster and Van Order (1984) found that fewer than 4 percent of borrowers whose mortgage debt exceeded their home value by more than 10 percent defaulted. More recently, researchers at the Boston Federal Reserve Bank found that less than 10 percent of borrowers with negative equity default on their mortgage (Foote, Gerardi, and Willen 2008). (Of course, if a home's value plummets to a very small fraction of the outstanding mortgage amount, e.g., less than 50 percent, then we may expect somewhat higher levels of default.)

Thus, this evidence suggests that there are other reasons—both economic and noneconomic—that borrowers have for staying in their homes and that forced exit from homeownership imposes real costs on borrowers, beyond any obvious loss of financial equity built up in the home. For owner-occupiers, the costs of forced exit and relocation are generally not trivial. One obvious cost is the effect of foreclosure on one's credit score and history. But there are other significant costs as well. Families with children often need to find their children new schools—and may find it difficult to find available rental housing in areas with good schools, making their housing search even more challenging. School mobility—especially in the middle of a school year—can harm student achievement. Increased mobility reduces the chances of high school graduation even when controlling for a large number of family character-istics (Haveman and Wolfe 1994). Moreover, mobility during elementary school has lasting negative impacts on high school performance (Rumberger 2002).

One important cost that has received little attention, and that is difficult to quantify, is the damage that forced relocation can do to social networks and social support systems. This may be particularly true for low- and moderate-income homeowners who may rely on family and friends in their existing neighborhood or nearby for basic needs and support, as well as for emotional support. In their analysis of borrowers receiving commu-nity reinvestment loans (thirty-year fixed-rate loans with near-prime pricing), Spader and Quercia (2008) found that lower-income borrowers actually move less frequently than higher-income borrowers. This may reflect greater premiums put on neighborhood social networks compared to such premiums among higher-income households.

Social ties may be more important to the economic and social oppor-tunity and stability of lower-income households because they may rely more on neighbors and nearby relatives for essential support such as child care and sick care given their constrained access to paid child care and health care. A variety of research has explored the importance of social networks, social capital, and "strong ties" in the lives of lower-income households. Briggs (1998) has suggested that social networks provide critical assistance that help lower-income families cope with a variety of stresses. Consistent with the notion that lower-income households rely more on neighborhood social ties, Dawkins (2006) found that, for lower-income families, social ties are relatively more important in determining residential mobility than is the case for higher-income families, and he suggests that access to daycare, transportation, and recreation are key reasons for this. The existence of nearby relatives is also more important, again with the suggestion that families rely on relatives for essential support and services.

Foreclosure can also be a humiliating or dispiriting event, especially for borrowers who worked hard to achieve homeownership. Journalists have reported on events as severe as suicides that were triggered by mortgage default and foreclosure (Armour 2008). In less grave cases, financial stressors such as mortgage delinquency and default are thought to trigger anxiety, depression, and addictive behaviors.

There has been limited research on the emotional and psychological effects of foreclosure. However, in a study of eighty-eight families going through foreclosure in five cities around the country, Fields et al. (2007) found that those going through foreclosure incur a wide range of attendant hardships and emotional difficulties beyond the harm to their finances and credit histories. Many respondents felt shame, which sometimes discouraged them from seeking support services or even assistance from friends and family. Foreclosure harmed family stability and made it difficult to make long-term plans. In some cases the foreclosure represented a "cascading series of economic and emotional losses that interfere with people's day-to-day lives." Many respondents took on additional employment to try to resolve delinquencies. More broadly, foreclosure sometimes led to increases in "fear, tension, and stress" among family members.

Costs to Lenders and Investors

High-risk lending can be potentially costly to lenders and especially to those investing in mortgage-backed securities. In the case of structured finance, which funded most high-risk lending in the last two decades, investors are more likely to assume the bulk of losses to parties in the mortgage credit supply chain. Lenders are often relatively thinly capitalized, or have limited their exposure to losses. However, in some cases lenders experience losses due to the residual interests they hold in the mortgage-backed securities into which their loans were packaged. In other cases, lenders may be cut off by warehouse lenders or investors due to high default rates, causing them to have to shut down.

It is very difficult to predict the ultimate losses that investors will suffer as a result of the 2007–08 credit crisis. Projections of total losses are built on a complex, interlocking set of predictions about house price trends, future credit availability, policy interventions (or the lack thereof), and other phenomena. Some have made an attempt to estimate likely order-of-magnitude losses to investors. Greenlaw et al. (2008) used three different approaches to arrive at a rough estimate of $400 billion in direct investment losses in mortgage-backed securities and related instruments. Estimates prepared in early 2008 by the Organization for Economic Cooperation and Development were roughly similar, with a range of $350 to $420 billion (Blundell-Wignall 2008).

Such estimates, of course, are very sensitive to how these securities are valued, which is a difficult task when there may be little to no active market for many of the securities at the time of the estimate, despite the securities generating some cash flow, and so analysts must make some key assumptions about what the eventual value of the securities will be. Again, their eventual accuracy will depend on future declines or increases in housing prices and many other issues. Greenlaw et al. (2008) also estimated that U.S. institutions that exhibit significant financial leverage (i.e., that operate with liquid reserves that are only a small portion of their overall assets) accounted for 49 percent of all identified subprime mortgage exposures as of early 2008. Thus, these institutions, which include banks, investment banks, and the GSEs, will be subject to approximately $200 billion in direct losses. However, because these institutions are highly leveraged, the impact of $200 billion is essentially much greater in terms of the financial capacity that has been removed from credit markets in the United States.

Despite the heavy losses to U.S. financial institutions, losses affected many other types of investors as well. Because many securities received triple-A ratings, many traditionally conservative institutional investors, including local and state government bodies and pension funds, suffered significant losses. In the United States a number of public pension funds, state government finance agencies, and others invested in mortgage-related securities, some of which were backed by subprime loans and lost significant value in the credit crisis. Press reports have discussed significant exposure in state-run investment pools, which are used for the investment activities of local governments and school boards, in Montana, Connecticut, and Florida (Evans 2007). In Florida, a state-managed investment pool experienced a run. After it was learned that the fund had significant mortgage-related losses, local governments pulled out almost half the fund's $27 billion in assets before the fund had to be frozen.

Because a substantial portion of investment funds in the U.S. subprime market flowed from overseas, losses were felt in many parts of the world. Blundell-Wignal (2008) estimates that one-third of mortgage-related securities losses will accrue to overseas investors. In Norway, the small towns of Rana, Hemnes, Hattfjelldal, and Narvik lost over $60 million in investments in CDOs that lost almost half their value (Werdiger 2007). In Germany, losses have been particularly acute among the state-owned wholesale Landesbanks, which as of mid-2008 had estimated losses of almost $20 billion in losses in subprime securities (Schultes 2008). In the state of Saxony, in the less affluent eastern part of the country, the Landesbank had to put up approximately $4 billion in public funds to guarantee approximately $60 billion in subprime investments in order to sell the bank (Spiegel 2007). The investments led to the resignation of Saxony's governor (Spiegel 2008).

Costs to Neighborhoods, Cities, and Renters

Effects on Neighborhood Conditions and Property Values

The economic and social costs of foreclosures affect more than the parties directly involved in the financing process. Foreclosures have implications for surrounding neighborhoods and for larger communities. They can also cause the displacement and eviction of tenants from rental properties. Cities, counties, and school districts lose tax revenue from abandoned homes. The costs that rising and concentrated foreclosures impose on neighborhoods and communities have been increasingly recognized and quantified. These costs grow rapidly for properties that are not quickly returned to the market in sound and productive ways.

Since at least the late 1960s, foreclosures of single-family homes have been viewed as a serious threat to neighborhood stability and community well-being, particularly in low- and moderate-income communities (Bradford 1979). Foreclosures can lead to vacant, boarded-up, or abandoned properties. These properties, in turn, contribute to the stock of "physical disorder" in a community that can create a haven for criminal activity, discourage social capital formation, and lead to further disinvestment. Immergluck and Smith (2006a) found that, after controlling for other neighborhood conditions, higher levels of foreclosure are associated with higher violent crime rates. If foreclosures lead to problems such as vacancy and crime, then they are likely to depress property values in their immediate vicinity.

Even without leading to vacancy, blight, and other problems of physical disorder, a jump in concentrated foreclosures over a short period of time creates an excess supply of homes, which, by itself, is likely to lead to lower property values in the area. In a neighborhood with a strong housing market, natural levels of home sales and occasional foreclosures can be easily absorbed by regular in-migration into the neighborhood. But in areas where housing demand may already be weak or modest, a rapid surge in foreclosures among existing residents has the potential to destabilize a neighborhood. Finally, depending on market conditions, foreclosures themselves may sell at significant discounts, either at the completion of the foreclosure process or at a sale of the foreclosed property by the lender. Thus, the comparable values in an area, which are used by buyers and appraisers to establish fair values for local home buying activity, are then depressed.

Immergluck and Smith (2006b) were the first to attempt to directly measure the impact of foreclosures on nearby property values. They sought to discern the independent effect (that is, controlling for other explanatory variables) of a change in the characteristics of the property or its location on the price of property. They used sales and property characteristic data from the Cook County Assessor's office (Chicago) for 1999 and looked at foreclosure activity in 1997 and 1998, during the first high-risk lending boom. The findings suggested that foreclosures did negatively affect the property values of nearby homes, even after controlling for a wide variety of other neighborhood and property characteristics. Each additional foreclosure within an eighth of a mile reduced nearby values by approximately 1 to 1.5 percent. This level of effect was found even during a time of fairly strong housing prices when the ability of the local market to absorb additional housing supply was fairly robust.

Given that low- and moderate-income neighborhoods experience substantially higher levels of foreclosures, and given that such foreclosures may be more likely to result in vacant, abandoned, or blighted property than those in more affluent areas, Immergluck and Smith (2006b) also looked at the effects of foreclosures on neighboring property values in lower-income neighborhoods more specifically, and found that the impact was substantially higher than in other neighborhoods. Under a set of conservative assumptions, the aggregate impact on 1–4 unit single-family homes due to foreclosures in the city of Chicago alone was estimated to be more than $598 million, corresponding to average property value losses to nearby single-family houses of at least $159,000 per foreclosure. And this was during a time when foreclosures were substantially below the very high levels of 2006 through 2008.

More recent studies have confirmed the negative impact that foreclosures have on nearby property values. Lin, Rosenblatt, and Yao (2008) also studied Chicago transactions and found that foreclosures had a negative impact on nearby property values. They noted somewhat larger impacts than Immergluck and Smith (2006b), but the data used were somewhat different, so comparing the precise magnitudes of the two studies is difficult. They also studied different periods—sales in 2003 and 2006 versus 1999—also making comparability difficult.

Lin, Rosenblatt, and Yao (2008) found that the magnitude of the effects, as would be expected, decline as distance from the foreclosure increases and as more time exists between the foreclosure and the sale of the nearby property. They also find somewhat stronger negative effects when the housing market is weaker (2006 versus 2003), which is consistent with the notion that foreclosures may have greater negative impacts in cities or neighborhoods with weaker market conditions or during down cycles in the overall housing market.

Researchers have also looked at the impacts of foreclosures in other cities. Been (2008) examined property sales and proximity to foreclosures in New York City. Similar to the Chicago studies, she found that foreclosures have a negative impact on the sales price of nearby homes, but the effects in New York City during the 2000–2005 period were smaller than the effects in Chicago in the 1997–99 period. Because the housing market in New York City during the 2000–2005 period was very strong, this is consistent with Lin, Rosenblatt, and Yao's finding that effects are larger in weaker housing markets.

In all, the research strongly suggests that foreclosures have sizeable impacts on nearby property values and that these impacts are more severe in areas and cities with weaker housing markets. Other research has looked more specifically at the related problem of the impact of vacant buildings on property values. Shlay and Whitman (2004), for example, examined the impacts of vacant housing units on nearby home values in Philadelphia. They found that properties located within 150 feet of an abandoned housing unit sold for more than $7,000 less than those not located near abandoned units.

Mikelbank (2008) adds to the literature by breaking out the effects of vacant and abandoned homes from foreclosures. He examines data on both in Columbus, Ohio, for 2006—when foreclosures were at very high levels—and finds that, even when controlling for the distribution of vacant homes, the impact of a single foreclosure on housing price is on the order of 2 percent when the foreclosure is within 250 feet of the house and tapers to approximately 1 percent out to 1,000 feet. The impact of a vacant or abandoned house is larger when the vacancy is very close—within 250 feet—with an average loss of 3.5 percent, but quickly tapers off to being insignificant by 750 feet.

The Costs to Local Governments

Foreclosure and any resulting vacancy can impose costs on the public sector in fairly direct fashion. The sorts of costs that foreclosures create include:

- Increased policing due to vandalism and other crime
- Increased burden on fire departments due to arson
- Demolition costs
- Costs of removing trash, mowing lawns, and so forth, for abandoned properties or for properties that mortgage holders do not take care of
- Legal expenses
- Managing the foreclosures process, including record keeping
- Lost tax revenue when borrower or owner stops paying taxes
- Direct lost revenue due to demolished buildings
- Property tax losses due to declining values to building and nearby properties
- Lost economic development benefits due to decreased desirability of community for commercial/industrial development

In a detailed study of foreclosure processes in Chicago, Apgar and Duda (2005) found that these sorts of direct costs to city government in Chicago sometimes exceeded $30,000 per foreclosure. More specifically, they classified foreclosures into ten different scenarios in terms of the complexity and nature of the processes that a property might go through, ranging from a foreclosure that was sold at auction but never became vacant to one that resulted in vacancy, criminal activity, or fire. Costs increase as public demolition is pursued or fire or police services are needed. In some cases nine or ten city agencies can become involved with a single foreclosed property.

The *Cincinnati Enquirer*, Cincinnati's major daily newspaper, conducted its own investigation of the costs of foreclosed properties to the City of Cincinnati (Korte 2007a). The city saw a large increase in real estate owned (REO) properties—those owned by lenders after a completed foreclosure. Deutsche Bank, the largest holder of REOs in Hamilton County (where Cincinnati is located) in 2008, went from having no REOs in the county in 2000 to 188 as of November 2007. The *Enquirer* found that financial institutions owed the City of Cincinnati money for barricading or demolishing more than 155 problem properties since 2004. The *Enquirer* also found that, in numerous cases, foreclosing lenders did not even record the foreclosure transaction so that localities had incorrect information about the ownership of the property. The paper found 140 properties that were sold at foreclosure but for which the new owners—usually the lenders—had not recorded the transfer (Korte 2007b).

The failure of a lender to record title to the property after foreclosure creates all sorts of problems. City and county agencies depend on such recording to identify who is liable for expenses on the property, including taxes and city utilities. Those complaining about nuisance properties cannot identify the correct party responsible for the property. These all add to the hassle and costs of attempting to deal with problems of vacant properties or of redeveloping these buildings.

Some cities have been forced to take extraordinary steps to deal with increasing foreclosures and the resulting vacancies. Chula Vista, California, adopted a local ordinance that requires the mortgage holder to exercise the "abandonment clause" in their mortgage documents (Leeper 2008). The law requires that the mortgage holder, upon recording a notice of default (a legal pre-foreclosure step in California), inspect the property for occupancy. If the property is vacant, the lender must register the property with the city and then maintain it to a certain standard of care. The lender must clearly identify the appropriate contacts responsible for the property, retain the service of a local property management or maintenance company, and post the name of this firm clearly on the premises of the property.

Impacts on Renters

Rarely mentioned in media or policy discussions of the foreclosure problems of recent years has been another party that is not involved in any home finance decisions—renters. High-risk lending, while having large impacts on owner-occupants, also affects tenants. Recent foreclosure surges have almost certainly affected tenants even more than earlier high-foreclosure periods. This is because there was a substantial rise in investor-owned borrowing after 2002, in part driven by the strong demand for rental housing among low- and moderate-income households and declines in the stock of large, affordable multifamily rental buildings. Renters may be even more susceptible to the problems caused by forced relocation than homeowners. They are likely to have little warning of the upcoming eviction and so may have little time to find a new apartment or rental house.

What is often forgotten is that 1–4 unit buildings constitute the majority (59%) of rental units in the country (Joint Center for Housing Studies 2008). Many rental units are owned and operated by individuals with limited resources and so are quite susceptible to foreclosure and the loss of the property. Approximately 30 percent of first-lien purchase loans to non-owner-occupants in 2006 were for subprime loans, with the ratio reaching nearly 50 percent in lower-income minority communities (Joint Center for Housing Studies 2008). Moreover, approximately 20 percent of foreclosures, according to Mortgage Bankers Association data, are small investor properties.

In the city of Chicago in 2007, there were over forty-eight hundred foreclosures filed on 2–6 unit buildings, compared to approximately seventy-three hundred filings on one-unit properties plus another sixteen hundred or so on condominiums (Woodstock Institute, 2008). The 2–6 unit buildings represent many more than forty-eight hundred households potentially displaced. Because most of these units are renter-occupied, it is likely that renters displaced by foreclosures exceeded owners in 2007 in Chicago.

In Massachusetts, 2–4 unit properties accounted for 30 percent of foreclosures on 1–4 unit buildings in recent years (Foote et al. 2008.) Again, given the larger number of units in these buildings, this suggests that the number of renters affected by foreclosures may exceed the number of owners, albeit with different impacts on wealth and credit history. In New York City, the impact on renters has been even greater. In 2007, 60 percent of the properties entering foreclosure were 2–4 unit properties, representing at least fifteen thousand households (Been 2008).

Boom-Bust Lending Markets as an Impediment to Sustainable Metropolitan Development

Even absent the problems caused by foreclosures, subprime and other forms of aggressive, high-risk lending can have impacts on neighborhoods, cities, and metropolitan areas that may be unsustainable. High-risk lending can increase the flow of credit to highly speculative ventures, fraudulent property-flipping scams, and other activities that cause a variety of problems down the road. By allowing borrowers to borrow larger amounts and artificially or temporarily lowering initial monthly payments—only to see payments increase later—adjustable rate loans with teaser rates, negative amortization, or interest-only loans, and other exotic or hybrid structures can increase the run up in housing prices in "hot" housing markets, making such markets even hotter.

When lenders redesign loan products so that they dramatically—but only temporarily—reduce the monthly mortgage payment with the primary purpose of supposedly providing more "purchasing power," some of this increased purchasing power will be extracted in the form of higher prices for homes, especially in markets where demand for housing is strong. Indeed, Doms and Krainer (2007) found that "innovative" home finance products during the 1990s and 2000s increased the proportion of income that households spent on housing. As long as this lending—and borrowing—is sustained, values may continue growing. However, aggressive lending is partly based on continuing appreciation, but this appreciation is in turn dependent upon the continuation of aggressive lending. If either the lending or the valuations stall in some way, the negative impact on credit availability and property values are mutually reinforcing, which can result in a spiraling down of values and neighborhood confidence.

Pavlov and Wachter (2006) find that, in neighborhoods in which more aggressive products are highly prevalent, prices are substantially more volatile. The prevalence of these loans "puts the market at risk as their originations tend to decline on a relative basis faster than the traditional more conservative instruments in the face of a negative demand shock in the underlying market" (Pavlov and Wachter 2006). More specifically, in looking at the impacts of high levels of adjustable rate mortgage lending on neighborhood price trends, they find that, for each 1 percent increase in the share of loans that were ARMs when the market peaked, the amount of price decline increases by 1.3 percent. Aggressive lending can push values up at first, but then pushes them down further when the inevitable market downturn occurs. Property appreciation that is built upon financing gimmicks and short-term teaser rates is not sustainable and, in the long run, discourages the smooth functioning of housing markets and neighborhood economies.

Although further research is needed, it is likely that, in some metropolitan areas, subprime lending also exacerbated problems of rapid single-family residential growth on the fringe of many metropolitan areas, increasing the problems of unplanned growth, traffic congestion, and overall sprawl. By inflating the home purchasing power of households—again often not sustainably—buyers could afford larger lot sizes and homes.

There is some evidence that declines in housing values during the 2006–08 housing downturn were larger in magnitude in many farther out and more recently developed suburban areas than in closer-in suburban and central-city neighborhoods within the same metropolitan areas, suggesting that the boom in high-risk finance facilitated overbuilding and sprawl in at least some metropolitan areas. In examining housing price trends in five large metropolitan areas from the fourth quarter of 2006 to the fourth quarter of 2007, Cortright (2008) found that prices on average declined in distant suburban neighborhoods but only declined in closer-in neighborhoods in two of the five cities. Moreover, in the two cities where close-in prices also declined, the rate of decline was significantly greater in more distant neighborhoods.

Stiff (2008) found that while home prices dropped from September 2005 to the second half of 2007 by 7.3 percent in the Boston metropolitan area, the declines were more severe in areas farther from Boston's financial district. He found similar results in Los Angeles, where between September 2006 and the second half of 2007 the prices of single-family homes in the Los Angeles metropolitan area dropped by almost 9 percent. Home prices fell less in neighborhoods near the city's two large employment centers, West Los Angeles and downtown.

Although the impacts of concentrated subprime lending have been most acute in lower-income central city neighborhoods, newer suburban areas are also susceptible to problems caused by boom-bust lending markets. In sprawling metropolitan areas, where a great deal of moderate-income owner-occupied housing development during the 1990s and 2000s occurred in particular parts of the outer suburban ring, high-risk credit was used to finance, and essentially enable, a great deal of demand for low-density, detached single-family housing.

Perhaps no place is more emblematic of the spatial growth of metropolitan areas in the 1990s and 2000s than the Atlanta region. Figure 5.5 shows building vacancy rate information from the U.S. Postal Service for the ten-county Atlanta region for the first quarters of 2006 and 2008. Comparing the two maps in figure 5.5 shows that many neighborhoods in outer suburban communities, where housing growth was generally strong from 2000 to 2006, saw increased levels of vacancy over a relatively brief

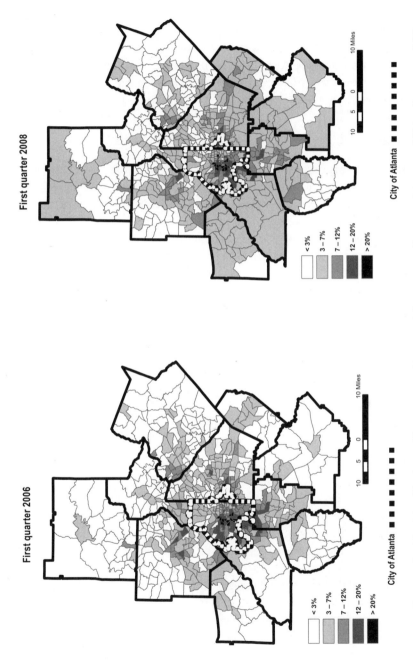

Figure 5.5. Percent of residential and business addresses vacant, 10-county Atlanta metropolitan area, first quarter 2006 to first quarter 2008. *Source:* U.S. Postal Service vacancy data, aggregated to census tract by the U.S. Department of Housing and Urban Development.

two-year period. Although the highest vacancy rates continued to be located in the city of Atlanta and just south of the city, many suburban census tracts—including many located quite far from the core of the metropolitan area—saw significant increases in vacancy rates. Many of these tracts were areas of fairly recent urban growth and development and their development was fueled significantly by increases in credit flows and high-risk loans, especially after 2002.

Mortgage Market Busts, Ripple Effects, and Financial Stability

One important argument for limiting risk levels in mortgage markets is that significant downturns in these markets—especially those on the scale of the 2007–08 crisis—can have substantial destabilizing impacts on broader credit and capital markets and, therefore, on the broader national and international economy. Mortgage markets, especially as they have been structured over the last twenty years, have ties to many parts of the broader economy and their failures can essentially create "contagion" problems in other markets for credit and capital. As late as July 2007, estimates of investor losses in subprime securities were $50 to $100 billion—a figure that some at the time thought exaggerated (Kaiser 2007). By early 2008, the estimated losses were conservatively estimated at $400 billion to $500 billion and growing, and that just included direct losses to holders of mortgage-backed securities and CDOs. Moreover, the complexity and ubiquity of securitization meant that the spreading of risk globally—risk that was largely systematic and not reduced via diversifica-tion—created a much larger amount of uncertainty imbedded in a broad and large set of mortgage investment vehicles. Even beyond RMBS and CDOs, there were an entirely new breed of hedging vehicles, generally called credit default swaps, which investors use to hedge against risk in their mortgage-related (as well as other) investments. Credit default swaps are essentially private insurance arrangements between various parties in the mortgage securitization chain and other investors, where one party agrees to compensate another party based on the performance of a set of mortgages or mortgage-backed securities. These credit default swaps were largely unregulated and their aggregate diffusion and complexity greatly magnified the overall systemic risk of the financial system.

A key reason that the mortgage crisis had such powerful and broad impacts is that many of the mortgage-backed instruments ended up on the books of financial institutions—both banks and nonbanks (e.g., investment firms), where they had the effect of depleting financial equity, thus weakening the balance sheets of the institutions. This, in turn, challenged their solvency or at least made it so that these institutions could not lend or invest at the same levels that they had been. When banks had to write down the value of the RMBS or CDOs that they owned, this meant that they had less equity capital to leverage. A bank (either a depository or a nondepository investment bank) relies upon its equity capital as the fulcrum on which it leverages far greater assets, often at ratios that are substantially greater than ten to one. When a bank's capital gets very low, it becomes subject to significant insolvency risk and regulator scrutiny.

Thus, as Greenlaw et al. (2008) have pointed out, for every one dollar of equity capital that a bank loses, its lending capacity is essentially reduced by $10 to $25, lending that might have gone to homeowners, small businesses, students, government, or others. Of the $400 billion in subprime write-downs, Greenlaw et al. (2008) estimate that banks and other highly leveraged financial institutions will have absorbed $200 billion in losses. These dollars represent equity capital. At a 10–1 leverage ratio, this amounts to a loss of bank assets (including loans) of $2 trillion. At a 25–1 ratio, which is more common for investment banks, the asset loss is closer to $5 trillion.

Even banks that did not suffer large write-downs tightened their credit requirements and loans became more difficult to get in 2007 and 2008. Although some adjustment was no doubt needed, there was substantial evidence that the pendulum had swung into excessive risk aversion.

In the mortgage arena, it was clear by late 2007 and early 2008 that the mortgage crisis had spread well beyond the subprime sector. The Federal Reserve Board (2008) surveys banks quarterly on their lending practices and policies and in April 2008 found that approximately 60 percent of U.S. banks said that they had tightened their requirements on prime mortgages and 75 percent of those offering nontraditional mortgages had tightened their requirements for those products. Approximately 70 percent of banks responded that they had tightened their lending standards for home equity lines of credit, a common prime-loan product where banks tend to dominate the market.

Falling home values that were both a contributor to, and partly the result of, foreclosures put direct pressure on home equity loans, a substantial lending sector that grew even more during the housing boom. This market, unlike the market for subprime loans, was dominated by more depository institutions, including large and medium-sized regional banks (Scholtes and Guerrera 2008). Home-equity and second-lien mortgage loans held by banks increased 43 per cent from year-end 2004 to year-end 2007. For some lenders, home equity loans represent well more than 15 percent of their outstanding loans. These banks were susceptible to problems in other vulnerable lines of business as well, including credit card lending and commercial real estate finance.

Home equity loans—together with prime and subprime refinance loans—were used by many consumers to supplement their regular income, to pay for health care needs, and generally to replace lost earnings due to declining wages. Greenspan and Kennedy (2007) found that one-third of the net proceeds of home equity loans in recent years was used to repay nonmortgage debt, especially credit card debt, and another quarter was used to support direct personal consumption. The remainder was used primarily for home improvements. Cash generated from refinancings was used for similar purposes, with over one-quarter going to pay off credit card and installment debt, and another sixth going to direct personal consumption. In subprime refinancings, however, much higher shares were likely used for paying off credit card and installment debt.

Greenspan and Kennedy (2007) also found that the proportion of personal consumption spending by households funded by the extraction of home equity almost tripled, during the second high-risk boom, rising from 1.1 percent during the 1991–2000 period to almost 3 percent during the 2001–05 period. Of course, these are totals, so that many households used no home equity for financing personal consumption needs (many of course had none to use), but many others extracted substantially more than 3 percent of their personal expenditures in home equity during the latter period.

As home equity loans and refinance loans become harder to obtain, many households are likely to find it more difficult to maintain their standard of living, which will in turn have economic and noneconomic effects on society more broadly. In the case of low- and moderate-income households, this is likely to mean cutting back on basic goods and services, including health care.

By the summer of 2008, it was clear that the downward spiral of the housing market was affecting the bulwarks of the prime mortgage market—the government-sponsored enterprises, Fannie Mae and Freddie Mac, thus threatening the primary sources of liquidity for most mortgage credit in the United States. Although Fannie and Freddie had lost substantial market share in securitized lending during the 2002–07 boom to private-label securitizers, by early 2008 their share of the mortgage-backed securities market had risen to well over 95 percent, because private-label securitization had essentially ground to a halt. Although still not reaching the peaks of 2003, GSE issuance of securities was back up to $130 billion per month by the spring of 2008, while private-label securitization had fallen to a trickle. However, falling home values, spurred by the mortgage crisis, worsened loan performance in prime markets and began hurting the GSEs. Moreover, the GSEs had been allowed by a weak regulator to purchase subprime RMBS as investments and to purchase Alt-A loans, which also weakened their balance sheets. Due to the high levels of leverage that the GSEs were able to operate under, they were unable to withstand large losses on loans, guarantees on securities that they had issued, or in investments that they themselves held, all of which weakened during the crisis. By July, the Treasury Department was forced to propose expanding the lines of credit that would be available to the GSEs and to be allowed to invest federal monies is GSE stock, the latter an unprecedented proposal. This proposal was incorporated and passed as apart of the housing bill that was approved shortly thereafter.

The GSEs suffered from the interaction of weak safety and soundness regulation and plummeting housing values. In the mid-2000s, in order to counteract falling profits from declining market share, the GSEs responded by chasing high-risk RMBS investments and expanded their purchases of Alt-A and other high-risk loans. The bulk of mortgages purchased by the GSEs remained relatively conservatively underwritten prime loans. However, as home values dipped in many populous regions by 30 percent or more, foreclosures increased. Moreover, the housing bill appeared to have a negative impact on the companies' ability to raise equity capital, because investors feared that any government rescue of the companies would—due to political constraints—require shareholders to lose their investment. By August, Treasury Department officials and the new regulator of the GSEs were planning for a likely takeover of one or both of the firms. In September, the Treasury Department and the new GSE regulator placed the GSEs into federal conservatorship.

Thus, the decline of the financial strength of the GSEs was driven directly by weak safety and soundness regulations, which would have required higher capital ratios that, in turn, would have helped the firms withstand falling housing prices. Of course, stronger regulation of the mortgage market overall would have moderated housing prices and also mitigated problems at the GSEs.

The mortgage crisis affected a wide variety of other credit markets, including student loans, small-business loans, and municipal finance. As banks' balance sheets became significantly weaker, they began to look much more closely at the risk of all of their lines of business. As of May 2008, approximately seventy student lenders, including about one third of the top one hundred, had quit offering government-insured loans through programs such as the Stafford student loan program (Quinn 2008). This was because lenders had difficulty raising the necessary capital. Some student lenders also cut out many community colleges and other schools that disproportionately serve less advantaged students.

In the commercial and small-business-loan arena, the Federal Reserve quarterly loan officer survey for April 2008 found that approximately 55 percent of U.S. banks reported tightening lending requirements on commercial and industrial loans. Moreover, approximately 70 percent said that they had increased the spread between loan rates and the cost of bank funds, suggesting a significant tightening in loan markets. For very small firms, owners have often relied on home equity loans, a source that was increasingly difficult to tap beginning in late 2007. The Federal Reserve survey also found that 80 percent of U.S. banks tightened requirements on commercial real-estate loans, the highest rate since the question was first asked in 1990.

Backlash Effects

One major concern that some observers have voiced regarding the failures of high-risk mortgage markets is that efforts to extend credit to lower-income and minority homebuyers and homeowners will fall out of favor. For example, at a speech in March 2008, Janet Yellen, the president of the Federal Reserve Bank of San Francisco, stated:

> There has been a tendency to conflate the current problems in the subprime market with CRA-motivated lending, or with lending to low-income families in general. I believe it is very important to make a distinction between the two. Most of the loans made by depository institutions examined under the CRA have not been higher-priced loans, and studies have shown that the CRA has increased the volume of responsible lending to low- and moderate-income households. We should not view the current foreclosure trends as justification to abandon the goal of expanding access to

credit among low-income households, since access to credit, and the subsequent ability to buy a home, remains one of the most important mechanisms we have to help low-income families build wealth over the long term. (Yellen 2008)

The risk that many may "conflate" community reinvestment lending and high-risk and high-cost subprime lending is real and should, in itself, be considered a cost of the 2007–08 mortgage crisis. Unless policymakers are disabused of such notions, a great deal of progress in responsible community reinvestment and fair lending may be undermined.

Notwithstanding the problems in subprime and other high-risk mortgage sectors, there has been a good deal of progress in the sound and affordable extension of home loans to historically underserved populations and communities. These programs have generally involved loans that have been at prime or near-prime interest rates and fees and have not used exotic terms or structures. Community reinvestment loans have relied on relatively traditional underwriting practices, including full documentation of income and assets, as well as standard, low-risk loan structures, including long-term fixed interest rates, fully amortizing payment schedules, and reasonable debt-to-income ratios that typically do not exceed 40 or 45 percent. These programs have often employed down payments that are well under the 10 to 20 percent often used for middle- and upper-income borrowers, but most have generally still involved some significant down payment of at least 3 to 5 percent.

Spurred in part by some increased attention to the Community Reinvestment Act, fair lending laws, as well as a more general effort to maintain and improve public relations in the late 1980s and early 1990s, many banks and thrifts increased their lending to, or invested in third-party collaborative loan programs that made loans to, lower-income and minority borrowers and communities. Federal Reserve Bank of Chicago researchers found that banks increased lending to low- and moderate-income communities substantially from 1993 to 1994, by thirty-five thousand loans and $2.7 billion, even though interest rates rose substantially between the two years (Evanoff and Segal 1996). Of course, this increase was nothing like the sort of increases during the second subprime boom, but that suggests the initiatives were much more cautious and responsible than those of subprime lenders. The 1993–94 span occurred during a period of substantial policy attention to lending to underserved communities. It was shortly after the release of the Boston Federal Reserve study on mortgage market discrimination, which received a great deal of public attention. The Clinton administration announced its proposal in 1993 to strengthen CRA regulation. In 1992, the Federal Housing Enterprise Financial Safety and Soundness Act (FHEFSSA) authorized HUD to establish affordable housing goals for Fannie Mae and Freddie Mac.[2]

Despite the success of community reinvestment and prime lending programs aimed at underserved markets, the intense media coverage that accompanied the mortgage crisis may have left an impression among some policymakers and some of the public that efforts to improve or maintain access to credit for moderate-income and traditionally underserved groups are ill advised. Some commentators even went so far as to suggest that laws such as the Community Reinvestment Act were a principal cause of the mortgage crisis.[3] Yet these critics of CRA have offered no serious evidence to support such a notion. If anything, there is a strong argument that the limitations of these laws—especially the failure to extend CRA to mortgage companies and their incomplete or anemic implementation and enforcement—were significant long-term contributors (in combination with other forces) to the crisis as well as to problems in the subprime market during the first boom.

---

2. Later on, especially after 2002, the GSEs became significant purchasers of subprime RMBS and were rewarded for such purchases under HUD's regulations implementing the FHEFSSA. This helped fuel the market for subprime lending generally and is widely considered a policy mistake (Leonnig 2008). Consumer advocates argued that any subprime loans or securities that the GSEs purchased should be held to high standards, but such comments were largely rebuffed.

3. For example, in testimony before the House Financial Services Committee in April 2008, Brian Wesbury, chief economist of First Trust Portfolios LP, argued that the Community Reinvestment Act was partly to blame for the mortgage crisis: "In a 2007 speech, the former Federal Reserve Board Governor [Edward Gramlich] outlined factors that led to rapid growth in subprime loans. One of those forces was the Community Reinvestment Act, which forced banks that operated in areas with low-income populations to make mortgages available to that community" (Wesbury 2008). Yet the speech to which Wesbury referred did not blame the Community Reinvestment Act for subprime problems. Rather, it credited the law with increasing lending to low- and moderate-income borrowers by prime-lending banks, which did not suffer the large losses that subprime mortgage companies did: "And there were changes on what might be called the supportive side of the market too—one of the biggest was the Community Reinvestment Act, which gave banks an incentive to make low- and moderate-income mortgages. To their surprise, most banks found that CRA lending was pretty good business" (Gramlich 2007b).

Successful Community Reinvestment
and Affordable Mortgage Programs

There has been significant research on the impacts and performance of community-reinvestment-oriented and related home lending initiatives (Immergluck 2004; Barr 2005). None of this literature suggests that community reinvestment lending programs, which are not structured as subprime product lines and which are generally not originated through subprime channels, have had anywhere near the sorts of performance problems that the subprime market has had. Moreover, the volume of such initiatives pales in comparison to the rapid growth in subprime lending, especially the growth of subprime lending from 2002 to 2006.

In a study by Federal Reserve Board staff, researchers found that special, customized community reinvestment single-family loan programs had mean ninety-day delinquency rates that were only slightly higher (1 percent versus 0.78 percent) than conventional mortgage programs, and that the median delinquency rate for the special programs was actually substantially lower (0.07 percent versus 0.53 percent) (Avery, Bostic, and Canner 2000). The study also looked at the profitability of community reinvestment lending overall, including regular loans to low- and moderate-income borrowers and neighborhoods, as well as special programs. Bank respondents reported that 94 percent of community reinvestment home purchase and refinance lending programs were at least marginally profitable.

Tholin (1993) took an approach similar to the Federal Reserve researchers and examined loans made by a set of banks with specialized community reinvestment programs. She found that the lenders' single-family loans had lower delinquency rates than for the overall single-family loan market. Although multifamily delinquency rates were somewhat higher than market comparables, foreclosure rates were not.

Canner and Passmore (1997) examined the lending patterns of banks that made significant numbers of mortgage loans. This study covered lending preceding the first boom in subprime lending and looked at banks, which made essentially no subprime loans during the study period. The authors found that banks making more loans to lower-income borrowers were no less profitable than those that made fewer lower-income loans. They obtained similar results for banks that made more loans to lower-income areas.

Ding et al. (2008) compared the default rates of community reinvestment loans that go through a large secondary market program to otherwise similar subprime loans using a propensity-scoring approach. They find that community reinvestment loans were roughly 70 percent less likely to default than comparable subprime loans. They attribute the large differences in performance in large part to the role of mortgage brokers and risk-inducing loan terms.

Researchers at the Federal Reserve Board analyzed HMDA data, disaggregated by lender type, and found that, in 2006, 94 percent of higher-priced loans were not eligible for CRA consideration for three reasons (Canner 2008). First, most such loans were not made to lower-income borrowers or to lower-income areas. Second, only a modest portion of the higher-priced loans made to lower-income borrowers or lower-income areas were made by banks, thrifts, or their affiliates, and, third, most of these were not in the institutions' CRA assessment areas, so that they would receive little to no CRA credit for them.

Public policy has been effectively used to promote sound lending to underserved communities in a variety of ways that extend beyond, and are complementary to, the Community Reinvestment Act and fair lending laws. A good example of such programs are those of locally based nonprofit housing organizations around the country that are affiliated with the NeighborWorks program and that assist modest-income homeowners in purchasing and maintaining owner-occupied housing. The most recent annual report of NeighborWorks shows that in the fourth quarter of 2007, during a time of rising foreclosures across the country, its foreclosure rate remained one-tenth that of the subprime market (NeighborWorks 2008).

Not only is sound, affordable, community-reinvestment-oriented lending to underserved communities feasible, it can be a strong preventative to high levels of high-risk subprime lending and thus help expand and preserve homeownership when it makes sense to do so. An and Bostic (2006) found that increased purchasing of prime-priced loans by Fannie Mae and Freddie Mac in a neighborhood effectively displaced subprime lending. Thus, community reinvestment lending can create a healthier and less risky local mortgage market. An and Bostic also found that increases in GSE purchase activity are associated with larger declines in subprime lending in neighborhoods with significant minority populations. They estimate that a 10 percent increase in GSE market share could lead to twenty thousand borrowers receiving prime instead of subprime loans, at a cost savings of approximately $100 million.

High-Risk Lending and Public Policy, 1995–2008

Much of the media coverage of the 2007–08 mortgage crisis gave the impression that the problems of high-risk lending had come as a total surprise to policymakers. There was little mention of well-documented problems in the high-risk mortgage market and the decadelong policy battle over regulating subprime loans. Federal regulators were said to be "asleep at the wheel" and somehow missed this major development in credit markets (Levitt 2008.) In fact, major problems in the subprime mortgage market had been recognized as early as the 1990s, and significant policy debates had occurred continually since then.[1] The increase in subprime lending from 2002 to 2007 was not the first boom in subprime lending. Although there were some minor changes in federal regulation in 2001, the financial services industry successfully fought off most calls for increased regulation and even had the assistance of some federal regulators in overriding state attempts to regulate lending more strongly.

In this chapter I will focus on just some of the many debates over the regulation of high-risk lending since the late 1990s. In fact, many efforts to increase regulation of subprime and other high-risk mortgage lending preceded the national media furor over the mortgage crisis that began in 2007. Consumer groups had pointed to problems from the first high-risk lending boom and already evident problems of high foreclosure rates and unfair and abusive lending practices well before the 2002–07 second boom

---

1. An example of regulators' early knowledge of serious problems in the subprime market can be found in a guidance from the U.S. Comptroller of the Currency (1999): "A number of institutions have incurred significant losses and other problems because of poorly structured subprime lending programs. Generally, these institutions underestimated the higher default rates and loss-on-default rates involved with subprime lending, as well as the higher overhead costs."

had even developed. Of course, from a national perspective, the extent of the problems became much more severe and evident in 2007, ascending to the top of the federal policy agenda.

Among the policy debates that received substantial media attention in 2007 and 2008 were those concerning proposals to assist distressed borrowers in foreclosure or at risk of foreclosure. Although I will address some of these proposals in this chapter, I will focus more on earlier policy debates around increased regulation of the mortgage lending industry. To establish policy proposals for reforming and restructuring mortgage markets going forward, which will be covered in the final chapter, it is critical to understand the policy debates that have occurred in recent decades.

Policy Debates over Regulating High-Risk Mortgage Lending, 1995–2008

As problems of predatory lending and higher foreclosure rates among subprime loans came to light in the late 1990s, consumer and community groups around the country became increasingly focused on the issue. There were concerns and policy debates over predatory and high-cost lending before the late 1990s, however. In the late 1980s and early 1990s, Washington, D.C.-based consumer advocates such as the National Consumer Law Center and others worked to get the Home Ownership and Equity Protection Act (HOEPA) passed in 1994. HOEPA had been focused on increasing regulation of very high-cost home equity and refinancing loans. It established a threshold of loan pricing, with loans priced over this threshold becoming subject to special disclosures, and it prohibited certain loan practices and terms. Consumer advocates argued for stronger restrictions on high-cost loans, but were successful only in obtaining regulations that relied primarily on increasing disclosures to borrowers.

Although HOEPA may have had some effect on small, "hard-money" lenders that charged interest rates in the high teens and low twenties, it did not restrain subprime lending in any meaningful way and may have, in fact, provided the regulatory context for the growth of the market. Besides relying mostly on additional disclosures as the fundamental way to protect borrowers, HOEPA employed pricing thresholds or "triggers" over which proscriptive regulations would kick in. However, these thresholds were generally much too high to address the vast majority of subprime loans and easily could be avoided by pricing just under the threshold or by shifting pricing from interest rates to up-front or contingent fees that were not included in the pricing calculations. The subprime market actually grew faster after 1995, especially for refinance lending, the primary target of HOEPA. With the explosion of the subprime market came the growth of predatory lending and, soon, an increase in defaults and foreclosures as well.

In 1997, the Federal Reserve Board, which is responsible for adopting regulations under HOEPA, examined early implementation of the law. The following year, the Board, together with the Department of Housing and Urban Development, issued a joint report to Congress that addressed issues such as loan flipping, credit insurance, and related issues of abusive and predatory lending. However, few of the recommendations were implemented.

Some states moved to increase regulation of subprime lending in the mid- to late 1990s (Bostic et al. 2008). Some restricted the use of prepayment penalties or balloon payments in mortgages. Other states tightened mortgage broker and banker licensing and regulation. However, these laws were generally not very comprehensive and attacked only small pieces of the abusive and predatory lending problem.

As subprime lending reached a critical mass in the late 1990s, the disproportionate concentration of high-risk loans in urban neighborhoods began to be felt more acutely, especially in the form of foreclosures and abandoned housing. Moreover, subprime and predatory lending became not just a consumer issue but also posed problems for community development. Concentrated foreclosures hurt neighborhoods and cities, adding to the unfairness of the loss of homes to individual families.

North Carolina Makes the First Move toward Comprehensive Regulation

Advocates for stronger mortgage regulation found success first at the state and local levels. In North Carolina, a state with a strong history of community reinvestment activism, a number of organizations became involved in the issue. These included the country's largest community development credit union, the Center for Self-Help, as well as the Community Reinvestment Association of North Carolina and the North Carolina Fair Housing Center. This group formed the hub of the Coalition for Responsible Lending, which was able to gain the support of a major statewide elected official, the attorney general, who played a significant role in the legislative campaign. The legislature's black caucus was also supportive.

Advocates for increased regulation of subprime home loans in North Carolina developed a bill that would go far beyond HOEPA in limiting the practices that could be used in making high-cost loans. In the summer of 1999 the North Carolina legislature passed the first comprehensive antipredatory-lending state legislation in the country. The bill followed the threshold approach of HOEPA but set the triggers significantly lower so that the law would capture a substantial segment of subprime loans while avoiding prime loans. It then prohibited certain lending features that, in the case of high-cost lending, were often viewed as predatory. Surprisingly, especially in the light of the later fierce battles in other states, the bill was supported by both the Mortgage Bankers Association of North Carolina and the North Carolina Association of Mortgage Brokers.

Following passage of the North Carolina law, two states, New York and Massachusetts, issued regulations aimed at the predatory lending problem, although these measures were substantially weaker than the North Carolina legislation. Other states began debating similar measures. On the local level, the City of Chicago and Cook County, Illinois, each proposed local ordinances aimed at the problem in early 2000. Unlike the North Carolina legislation, the Chicago and Cook County ordinances did not call for regulating lenders. Rather, the proposals relied on a significant history of local laws aimed at encouraging banks to be socially responsible by linking government financial business to responsible banking. Chicago, for example, had an ordinance dating back to 1974 that required banks accepting municipal deposits to disclose data on their lending in the city.

The Chicago ordinance and others like it in Oakland, Atlanta, Dayton, Cleveland, and Detroit sought to withdraw municipal business from firms engaged in predatory lending. These laws followed earlier municipal deposit ordinances aimed at encouraging banks to reinvest in urban neighborhoods. They also bore close resemblance to antiapartheid ordinances that many cities passed in the 1980s, in which cities refused to do business with firms that invested in South Africa. The industry responded quickly by appealing to state legislatures, where they had more lobbying experience and relationships, to override the local ordinances. Some of the local predatory lending ordinances—including those in Detroit, Dayton, and Cleveland—were soon overridden by state legislation or court decisions. By preempting these incentive ordinances, state legislatures or courts told local governments that they did not have a right to choose the financial institutions with which they did business.

Stiff Opposition: Lenders, the GSEs, and the Credit Rating Agencies Fight State Regulation of High-Risk Lending

Following the initial actions of a few early states, other states continued to consider more comprehensive antipredatory lending regulations. By 2003, the National Conference of State Legislatures listed more than thirty states as having passed predatory lending statutes, and by the beginning of 2007 only seven states had no sort of "mini-HOEPA" statutes or sets of laws restricting prepayment penalties, balloon payments, or predatory practices or terms (Bostic et al. 2008; National Conference of State Legislatures 2003). However, there was great variation in both what sorts of loans these statutes covered and the extent to which the laws proscribed certain practices or products. Many state statutes were not very comprehensive or very strong. Some essentially just re-created HOEPA protections in state law. Many so-called antipredatory lending laws at the state level had been heavily influenced by state banking lobbyists. The result was that the pricing thresholds over which the regulations would kick in were often the same as the very high federal HOEPA thresholds and the restrictions themselves were often very minimal.

When consumer advocates and community organizations made efforts to strengthen lending regulations, they were often thwarted by industry advocates and lobbyists. Banking and financial services lobby groups have traditionally had a great deal of influence on state legislatures in the mortgage regulation arena. Moreover, federal banking laws put pressure on state legislatures to accommodate banking interests. Banks are allowed to "export" interest rate and fee regulations from their "home" state. As a result, banks aggressively lobby state legislatures for favorable regulations that they can then use to override regulations in other states.

Economic development has frequently been used as a major argument in such lobbying. Lenders sometimes agree to maintain facilities—or simply the "main office" location—in the home state in exchange for favorable regulations. Some states have gone so far as passing laws aimed at encouraging bank locations and facilities by reducing regulations in exchange for economic development commitments by the institutions. Delaware passed a law in 1981 that eliminated fee and rate restrictions on consumer loans and reduced income taxes in exchange for employing at least one hundred people in the state. Other banks have worked to win regulatory concessions on mortgage regulations, which they can then export around the country. A very large bank lobbied the Illinois legislature unsuccessfully in 2000 and 2001 to gain exemption from essentially any regulations on fees for second mortgages, a freedom that it would then be able to export to other states. The bank holding company argued that economic development would occur as a result of the policy and threatened to locate its new main charter in Ohio or another state if the deregulatory bill did not pass (Hinz 2001).

A key set of actors in the state-level policy debate were the GSEs Fannie Mae and Freddie Mac and the three primary credit rating agencies, Standard & Poor's, Moody's, and Fitch. These firms had significant leverage over state policymakers. The GSEs could refuse to purchase certain types of loans in the state. The rating agencies could refuse to rate mortgage-backed securities containing loans covered by certain state laws, essentially eliminating the regular liquidity and marketability for such loans—or for even greater numbers of loans due to the mixing of loans in securitized pools. Beginning in Georgia in early 2003, the GSEs and the credit rating agencies became actively involved in influencing state legislation by proclaiming that it would not rate securities containing any loans covered by the state's new antipredatory lending law.

In 2001, on the heels of the hearings held around the country on predatory lending by federal agencies, Senator Vincent Fort introduced an antipredatory lending bill in the Georgia legislature. In the next session in 2002, Governor Roy Barnes, an ally of Fort's on the predatory lending issue, introduced what was to become the Georgia Fair Lending Act (GFLA). After undergoing a number of changes, the bill was passed and went into effect in late 2002. The law was immediately considered one of the strongest state antipredatory lending laws in the country. Based on North Carolina's statute, the Georgia law was stronger, especially because it held purchasers of loans accountable for violations of the law, in what is known as assignee liability, something the North Carolina law lacked. Assignee liability was a key issue, because it meant that a regulatory violation followed the loan through the securitization process and affected subsequent parties in the chain of capital. This essentially overrode the problem created by the holder-in-due-course doctrine, which enabled funders of loans to shield themselves from liabilities created by predatory and abusive practices in the origination process.

Immediately after the law went into effect, the lending and mortgage brokerage industry began a concerted campaign to overturn it, especially after Governor Barnes lost his reelection bid in late 2002 (Milligan 2004). They were aided by a prominent local conservative radio host and others in this effort. But they gained their most important ally in early 2003, when Standard & Poor's issued a press release saying that it would not rate

securities backed by Georgia mortgages for fear that some of the underlying loans might violate GFLA:

> Loans governed by the GFLA are categorized as "Home Loans,"
> "Covered Home Loans," or "High Cost Home Loans," with each
> category having its own requirements and, in the case of Covered
> Home Loans and High Cost Home Loans, fees, points, and annual
> percentage rate tests. According to Standard & Poor's, violations of
> the statute will subject non-complying parties to potentially severe
> liability. Most importantly, however, the GFLA subjects assignees
> of Home Loans that violate the Act to potential liability. Thus,
> transaction parties in securitizations, including depositors, issuers
> and servicers, might all be subject to penalties for violations under
> the GFLA. (Mortgage Bankers Association 2003)

This press release, which was later followed by similar actions by
Moody's and Fitch, was the critical factor in enabling opponents of GFLA
to severely weaken the law by essentially removing the assignee liability
provision. In a letter to S&P's chief executive officer, Senator Fort pointed
out that S&P misconstrued the original GFLA assignee liability provision, which actually only applied to high-cost loans (Fort 2003). The
letter also asked S&P to identify and explain the firm's financial relationships with lenders, issuers, and brokers, suggesting that the firm may have
been suffering from conflicts of interest and benefiting from continued
securitization of high-risk products. It was not long before lending
industry advocates had managed to replace GFLA with a much weaker
law that effectively gutted the assignee liability provisions.

Contrary to some of the media discussion that followed the Georgia
debate, rating agencies could rate securities with assignee liability provisions, as long as the potential damages from the provisions could be
quantified (Engel and McCoy 2007; Reiss 2006). Nonetheless, efforts to
create assignee liability provisions in state or federal regulations, even
when damages were made quantifiable, were a key flashpoint for industry
advocates in mobilizing against regulation.

*Federal Agencies Study Abusive Lending and Regulators Warn
of Subprime Risks to Banks*

In 1999 and 2000, a variety of developments were putting pressure on
federal regulators to act on the predatory lending problem. In 1998 lower

mortgage rates and higher prepayment rates lowered subprime lender profitability. Moreover, many subprime lenders experienced higher default rates than they had anticipated (U.S. Office of the Comptroller of the Currency 1999). On top of this the Asian and Russian financial crises of 1997 and 1998 made raising capital much more difficult. The result was that a significant number of subprime lenders failed.

On the policy front, states were looking closely at the North Carolina law and a variety of localities were considering local ordinances aimed at slowing abusive lending. In 1999, the U.S. Department of Housing and Urban Development and the U.S. Treasury Department created a task force to develop federal policy recommendations to address "predatory lending," which includes excessive or unnecessary charges, prepayment penalties, repeated refinancings, and other abuses. The HUD-Treasury Task Force held hearings in five large cities in the spring of 2000 and issued a report in June containing a number of federal policy recommendations, including calling on the Federal Reserve Board to use more of its authority under HOEPA to outlaw predatory practices.

In Congress, separate and opposing bills were introduced backed by consumer and industry interest groups. In May 2000, the House Banking Committee held a hearing on predatory lending in which the Federal Reserve Board was chastised by Chairman Jim Leach (R-IA) for not using its authority to act on the issue. The Federal Reserve had not acted on the recommendations made in the 1998 joint Federal Reserve-HUD HOEPA report. Chairman Leach asked "if there is a problem out there, if Congress has given very strong authority to regulators and the Federal Reserve, our regulators, is the Federal Reserve AWOL? That is a question that I think demands a response" (Leach 2000).

Even before the surge of federal policy activity in 1999 and 2000, federal bank regulators had recognized the growth of subprime lending and at least its risks to lenders. In March 1999, the four bank and thrift regulators issued an "Interagency Guidance on Subprime Lending" (U.S. Office of the Comptroller of the Currency 1999). However, this guidance was clearly focused on the need for depository institutions to minimize any institutional risk that they may have in holding high-risk subprime loans on their balance sheets. The eight-page guidance devoted less than half of a page to concerns over consumer protection, and much of this was concerned with how well banks "identify, monitor and control the consumer protection hazards associated with subprime lending." The guidance did address some of the risks that originators faced in making and securitizing subprime loans, but it did not address the risks that banks and thrifts took on in purchasing subprime mortgage-backed securities to hold on their balance sheets.

State and local policy developments, the HUD-Treasury report, and public and congressional concern led the Federal Reserve Board to hold public hearings in four large cities in the summer and fall of 2000 on potential revisions to HOEPA regulations. At the end of 2000, the Board proposed some significant, albeit modest, changes to the HOEPA rules. The largest changes in the rules involved classifying single-premium credit insurance (SPCI) within the definition of fees under HOEPA and lowering the interest rate threshold at which a loan would be classified as "high-cost." The former meant that almost any loan with single-premium credit insurance would be classified as a high-cost loan under HOEPA (since SPCI typically exceeds the 8 percentage point fee trigger in the law), thereby increasing the disclosures and protections associated with the loan. The latter meant that more high-rate loans would be covered by HOEPA.

The most successful effort by consumer and community advocates was the push to effectively ban single-premium credit insurance. Considered by many to be an egregious predatory practice, SPCI involved selling people insurance that covers loan payments should some calamity (e.g., death or disability) occur. However, SPCI was relatively unique among insurance products in that it was financed completely up-front into the loan. With SPCI, rather than pay the premiums monthly or some other periodic way, the borrower paid the entire 5–10 years of insurance up front via the premium being added onto the mortgage amount. The lump-sum premiums for such policies could easily amount to 15 percent of the principal amount of the loan. This increased the loan amount and reduced borrower equity. Moreover, unlike in the case of insurance that is paid monthly, if the borrower got into trouble, she could not stop paying the insurance portion of her monthly payment without defaulting on the mortgage.

Consumer and community groups began focusing on problems with the product as a key focus of their antipredatory lending campaigns. By the summer of 2000, consumer activism on SPCI, and the inherent problems with the product, compelled Fannie Mae and Freddie Mac to pledge not to purchase loans containing the product. Following this, the product was condemned in the HUD/Treasury report, and later in 2000 the Federal Reserve recommended including SPCI in the HOEPA definition of points and fees. Then, by the summer of 2001, three large sellers of single-premium credit insurance voluntarily announced that they would no longer offer it. By the end of 2001, the Federal Reserve finalized its proposal to include SPCI in the definition of points and fees, which essentially made any loan with SPCI a high-cost loan under HOEPA and therefore subject to heightened regulation.

The OCC and OTS Preempt State Regulation of High-Risk Lending

As more states began to adopt predatory lending regulations in 2001 and 2002, lenders began to turn to Washington to push for lender-friendly federal policies that would override state laws. Lenders argued that state laws would create a "patchwork" of regulation across the country that would reduce the efficiency of the banking system by making it difficult for lenders and secondary-market firms to operate national lending operations. Advocates of state laws, including governors and legislators, countered that states have a right to protect their citizens, especially when it came to something as important as protection of homeowners and borrowers. Moreover, a good deal of real estate law—including foreclosure law—already varied by state, and lending markets had accommodated such differences without causing significant harm to loan availability. In fact, by the early 2000s vendors had begun marketing software that enabled lenders to monitor compliance with various state antipredatory lending laws. One firm, for example, marketed a product called the "Predatory Lending Monitor," which interfaced with major loan origination systems. From September 2002 to March 2003, the company completed nineteen installations of the product (Experity 2003).

To block state antipredatory lending laws in the early 2000s, the lending industry pursued a mixed strategy of seeking a federal statute aimed at preempting state laws and, at the same time, trying to get federal bank regulators to preempt state laws. The first approach would remain difficult as long as Democrats held significant power in the Senate and, perhaps more important, as long as Senator Paul Sarbanes, a supporter of increased mortgage regulation, retained the ranking Democratic seat on the Senate Banking Committee. Therefore, lenders—particularly banks, thrifts, and bank-owned mortgage companies—also adopted the second strategy. Both thrifts and national banks appealed to their federal regulators (the Office of Thrift Supervision and the Office of the Comptroller of the Currency, respectively) to preempt state predatory lending regulations. The OTS regulates federal thrifts and the OCC oversees national banks. Federal law gave both regulators significant ability to preempt state consumer protection regulations. In the late 1990s and early 2000s, they wielded such power aggressively, rebuffing states' attempts to adapt consumer protection laws to a changing financial marketplace—something Congress and federal regulators were not doing.

Unfortunately for those who favor state authority in this arena, some federal regulators have a vested interest in preempting state consumer protection laws. The ability to preempt state law is perhaps the greatest source of value in the federal thrift and national bank charters. Regulators can gain political power based on the number and size of the banks that fall under their regulatory supervision. In some cases, a regulator's operations are funded by levying fees on the institutions they regulate. This can encourage an agency to pursue policies that are friendly to banks—especially larger ones. If a regulator does not use its ability to allow banks under its supervision to preempt state consumer protection regulations, the bank may change its charter so that it is regulated by a more lender-friendly agency. The impacts of charter changes can be significant. Even one very large bank shifting its charter to another regulator can significantly affect an agency's revenues. When Chase Manhattan Bank (now J.P. Morgan Chase) merged with Chemical Bank in 1995 and changed from a national to a state charter, it was estimated that the OCC lost 2 percent of its budget in fees (Rosen 2002). Even if an agency's funding is not directly tied to the banking assets under its supervision, if fewer and fewer institutions fall under its supervisory umbrella, its power and relevance will be called into question. In the long run, this could jeopardize the agency's very existence.

The more power that a regulator has to effectively override state regulations—and the more it exercises such power—the more likely it is that institutions will want to be chartered under that regulator's authority. In the past, competition between regulators was mostly restricted between the national bank (OCC) charter and the state charter (FDIC, Federal Reserve, and state regulators). However, as thrifts were allowed to behave more like commercial banks, and banks became more involved in mortgage markets, the thrift-bank distinction became less meaningful, increasing the competition between regulators.

In 1974, Arthur Burns, chairman of the Federal Reserve Board, expressed concerns over a "competition in laxity" among the regulators (Scott 1977). Since then, there have been repeated concerns that banks "forum shop" to find the most comfortable regulator (Dennis 1978; Matasar and Pavelka 1998). Since at least the late 1990s, this "race for the bottom" includes regulators vying to offer banks as much preemption power as they can.

Demonstrating the importance of preemption to the value of a charter type, a banking attorney was quoted in the *American Banker* regarding the OCC's preemption actions as asking, "Why would you want a national charter but for the preemption authority?" (Davenport 2003).

The OTS moved first to override state mortgage regulations by preempting key provisions of Georgia's antipredatory lending law in January 2003, making federal thrifts were exempted from the law. A week later, it preempted New York's predatory lending law. State regulators immediately objected to the OTS moves. Community groups saw the OTS's action—under Bush appointee James Gilleran—as particularly antagonistic, given that the preceding director of the OTS, Clinton appointee Ellen Seidman, had voiced some of the strongest concerns over predatory lending among federal regulators (Blackwell 2003).

The OCC was not about to let the thrift charter gain a clear regulatory advantage over the national bank charter. It had issued a letter to national banks in November 2002 asserting its jurisdiction over all state regulators and asked banks to inform it if a state regulator had asserted its authority over a national bank. In comments to the press after the OTS decision, the OCC pointed out that it needed a request from a bank before it could follow the OTS's preemption move (Blackwell 2003).

It was not long before a national bank, National City Bank of Cleveland, requested that the OCC preempt the Georgia law. Community groups, governors, attorneys general, and state legislatures argued that the OCC should not move to preempt state consumer protection laws. In the summer of 2003, the OCC did preempt the Georgia antipredatory lending law, even after industry interests had succeeded in weakening the law at the state level. The agency went on to suggest that it would preempt all similar state laws, and issued proposed regulations to do so. The OCC's move in some ways was a more assertive move in defense of banks to ignore state laws, because its authority under banking statutes to preempt state consumer protection laws was less well established.

Federal regulators went even further and argued that even mortgage lenders that were subsidiaries of national banks or federal thrifts would benefit from federal preemption. The federal courts upheld this position when challenged by state regulators. The financial services regulator for the state of Michigan challenged the ability of a mortgage company subsidiary of a national bank to escape state regulation (U.S. Supreme Court 2007). The state regulator argued that, because the mortgage company, Wachovia Mortgage, was not itself a national bank but only the subsidiary of a national bank, Michigan's laws should not be preempted.

In 2007, the U.S. Supreme Court found in favor of the bank, stating that the preemption powers given by the National Banking Act covered subsidiaries of national banks as well as the banks themselves.

The policy debate between state and federal regulators over preemption became quite heated, with some advocates for state regulation being particularly outspoken. Foremost among these was Elliott Spitzer, attorney general for New York. In 2003, Spitzer threatened to sue the OCC over its preemption activities (New York Times 2003). However, after he initiated an investigation into racially discriminatory behavior by national banks in New York, the OCC joined an industry trade group in suing him and effectively prevented his investigation (Bloomberg News 2005). Although Spitzer had a higher profile than other advocates for the rights of states to regulate lending, he was not alone. Many other state regulators and attorneys general also argued against the federal agency's aggressive preemption practices.

Notwithstanding the aggressive use of preemption powers by some federal regulators, it is not true that most states took aggressive actions to stem the tide of high-risk lending. Mortgage banker and broker lobbies at the state level were generally successful in repelling substantive efforts to improve mortgage regulation in the late 1990s and early 2000s. The laws that did pass were often quite weak. Of course, the actions in the early 2000s most likely blunted any ongoing efforts by states to improve or strengthen regulations after about 2002, knowing that their laws would cover only a portion of the industry and that national banks and federal thrifts could, if necessary, acquire state-regulated lenders to move them out of the state regulatory umbrella.

During the second high-risk boom in the mid-2000s, exotic mortgage products became more widespread in both the prime and subprime markets. As banks and thrifts increasingly became drawn into higher-risk markets, and as the performance of such products began to show some weaknesses, banking regulators issued some warnings about their use. In 2003, the OCC issued another warning about the risks posed by subprime loans to the banks it regulated. The agency was particularly concerned that national banks might suffer "legal, reputation and other" risks in acquiring loans through mortgage brokers or by purchasing loans from originators (U.S. Office of the Comptroller of the Currency 2003a).

Despite their warnings about the risk to lenders involved in subprime lending, with the exception of the modest changes to HOEPA in 2001, federal policymakers made essentially no substantive changes in regulations aimed at curbing lending abuses and the growth of excessively risky lending practices in the subprime market. In fact, federal regulators facilitated the expansion of high-risk lending and paved the way for the second high-risk boom by actively preempting states' attempts to increase lending regulations when federal policymakers would not.

The second high-risk boom saw an increase in the use of "alternative" or exotic loan structures, including interest-only, negative amortization, and payment-option loans. These structures were applied to both the subprime and prime markets. Subprime loans increasingly were structured as hybrid adjustable rate loans in which the interest rate would be fixed for two or three years and then allowed to adjust. Many prime loans were also structured with adjustable rates. As different exotic features were layered on top of each other, many observers became increasingly worried about the underlying risk in the mortgage marketplace.

In the early to mid-2000s, consumer advocates and the U.S. General Accounting Office called on federal regulators to do more to regulate the affiliates and subsidiaries of banks that were increasingly dominating the subprime and high-risk loan markets. In general, the supervision of these lenders was left to state financial service regulators and to the Federal Trade Commission, both of which did not have nearly the level of supervisory resources as the federal banking regulators. In early 2004, the General Accounting Office issued a report calling for stronger regulatory supervision in the subprime market and specifically calling for giving the Federal Reserve more explicit power to conduct regular examinations of lenders affiliated with banks through bank holding company structures (U.S. General Accounting Office 2004). Earlier in 2000, Edward Gramlich, a Federal Reserve Board governor, had urged Federal Reserve chairman Alan Greenspan to direct examiners to examine the lending of bank-affiliated mortgage companies on a pilot basis (Andrews 2007). The suggestion was rebuffed by Greenspan.

More generally, even though federal regulators had issued cautions to banks holding subprime loans directly on their balance sheets, they generally supported the growth of the subprime mortgage market. The most important support came in the form of the preemption of state consumer protection laws. But key federal regulators also issued statements and studies that argued that subprime lending was enabling increased homeownership among minority and lower-income groups, which in turn gave support to similar arguments made by industry lobbyists working against efforts to increase regulation in Congress. The evidence presented for these claims, however, was quite limited, and there was little analysis of the benefits and costs associated with subprime lending or even whether subprime-financed homeownership was economically beneficial to borrowers.

In July 2003, the OCC released a controversial working paper, "Economic Issues in Predatory Lending," during the agency's decision making over its first preemptions of state consumer protection laws (U.S. Office of the Comptroller of the Currency 2003b). The OCC study argued that state antipredatory lending laws reduced levels of subprime lending and suggested that this was a negative outcome because it reduced "credit availability." It now looks quite likely that subprime markets were, in fact, providing socially inefficient amounts and types of credit. The OCC report relied primarily on a study by the industry-funded Credit Research Center at Georgetown University, which found that the number of subprime originations in North Carolina had declined by approximately 14 percent as a result of the state passing the first antipredatory lending law. The OCC paper suggested that this was an undesirable effect of the law. However, many would now likely question whether a decline in subprime lending of 14 percent was an undesirable result. By restricting abusive practices and reducing the number of loans with excessive up-front fees, such laws are likely to discourage the riskiest loans.

The OCC was not alone in its support for the booming subprime industry. Federal Reserve governor Edward Gramlich gave a speech in 2004 that, while acknowledging the problems of higher foreclosure rates in the subprime market, clearly came down on the side of viewing higher levels of subprime lending as a positive trend: "Despite the caveats, the net social evaluation of these trends is probably a strong positive" (Gramlich 2004). Only three years later, Gramlich seemed much less certain on this count (Gramlich 2007a). Gramlich had also argued in 2004 that "subprime lending represents a natural evolution of credit markets." Gramlich was clearly not alone in this opinion, especially among economists at the federal regulatory agencies. Subprime lending was often viewed as generally an organic, natural outgrowth of technological and financial innovation that was somehow purely the product of unfettered free markets. Yet the history of deregulation and supportive policies supporting structured mortgage finance tells us otherwise. Housing finance markets are politically and socially constructed. They are the products of decades of lobbying and policy debates at the state and federal level.

In late 2005, as the market for exotic loans boomed and increasingly involved both prime and subprime loans, the four banking regulators issued a proposed guidance on "nontraditional" mortgage products—what many called exotic loans—and issued a final guidance in October 2006

(U.S. Office of the Comptroller of the Currency et al. 2006). In responding to the late 2005 proposal, consumer groups warned that regulators were not going nearly far enough. In particular, they argued that regulators should direct lenders to underwrite adjustable rate loans using the maximum interest rate to which a loan might adjust. In fact, many subprime and other adjustable rate loans were approved based on initial, low fixed introductory or "teaser" interest rates that later could adjust upward a great deal. Advocates also generally called for the essential prohibition of no-documentation or stated-income loans, while regulators merely discouraged the use of such products. Of course, the guidance was inherently limited in its impact on the mortgage market, because it applied only to depository institutions directly regulated by the four regulators and not to the many affiliate and independent mortgage companies that were, on average, more active in the subprime and high-risk markets.

In 2006 and early 2007, as problems in subprime and higher- risk market segments became much clearer and caused significant disruptions to broader financial markets, regulators responded with additional proposals and hearings. The Federal Reserve Board held hearings related to subprime and predatory lending in both 2006 and 2007. In early 2007, it issued a draft proposal for increased regulation of the subprime market. After the 2007 hearings, the Board issued a more complete set of regulatory proposals with particular attention to using HOEPA to regulate a substantially broader segment of the subprime market, rather than just the very high-cost segment that HOEPA had been used to address previously.

After the fall 2006 election, when Democrats gained control of the House of Representatives and Barney Frank took over as chair of the House Financial Services Committee, there was also some movement in the legislative arena. Frank sponsored a bill that contained many substantive regulations that consumer advocates had been proposing for over a decade. However, the bill that eventually passed the House in 2007 also contained some key language that would preempt some state efforts to impose assignee liability in a stronger way than the federal law would. Despite the fact that the 2007–08 subprime crisis had been caused in large part by breakdowns in the mortgage supply chain—which is precisely what assignee liability is designed to guard against—industry lobbyists had once again successfully weakened the law in this regard.

Of course, by late 2007 a good deal of the damage done by the second boom in high-risk lending had already been put in motion and the subprime market had been substantially shut down. Therefore, proposals to increase regulation would be relevant in the longer term, to prevent a repeat of mortgage market excesses and abuses. Many of the proposals both in the Frank bill and in the proposed HOEPA regulations would constitute significant regulatory improvements and help set the stage for sounder lending markets. These sorts of proposals will be discussed in the last chapter in the broader context of establishing policies for promoting sound and fair lending markets.

Foreclosure Mitigation Responses to the 2007–2008 Mortgage Crisis

A good deal of attention by policymakers during the mortgage and foreclosure crisis of 2007 and 2008 concerned what could—or should—be done to assist homeowners who were in danger of, or in the process of, losing homes through foreclosure. As foreclosure rates increased dramatically during 2007 and into 2008, policymakers, lenders, investment firms, and consumer advocates offered numerous policy proposals to stem the tide of foreclosures, assist homebuyers, and, in some cases, slow the fall of the overall housing market. The debates over these proposals were very high profile, especially compared to most issues in the arena of housing policy, which have often been relegated to the pages of specialized media and policy publications. By late 2007 and early 2008, daily newspapers covered national policy debates on a regular basis about voluntary interest-rate freezes, plans to use the FHA to refinance unaffordable loans, foreclosure moratoria, and a variety of more complicated proposals. The mortgage crisis spawned a number of specialized websites and blogs that tracked the extent of the crisis but also were focused heavily on the debate over various proposals to reduce foreclosures or their impact.[2]

Although I make no attempt here to exhaustively list all of the various plans to address mounting foreclosures, I will address some key proposals. These received different levels of support, but all of them ran into a variety of obstacles. It took until the summer of 2008 to finally pass a housing bill that contained some relief for households facing foreclosure and for neighborhoods pockmarked with vacant, foreclosed homes.

Although the precise date of the beginning of the 2007–08 mortgage crisis is difficult to pinpoint, many would point to April 2007, when New Century Financial, one of the largest subprime lenders in the country,

---

2. Prominent examples include Housing Wire at http://www.housingwire.com and Calculated Risk at http://calculatedrisk.blogspot.com.

filed for bankruptcy. Smaller players in the subprime industry, such as Ownit Mortgage Solutions and People's Choice, had filed for bankruptcy in preceding months, but the failure of a lender the size of New Century revealed the scale of the crisis. In the same month, Senator Charles Schumer, the chair of the Joint Economic Committee, called attention to the impact that foreclosures were having on local neighborhoods and communities by issuing a report, "Sheltering Neighborhoods from the Subprime Foreclosure Storm," and calling for federal intervention to help distressed borrowers (U.S. Senate Joint Economic Committee 2007b).

Initially, in the late spring and early summer of 2007, policymakers such as Fed Chairman Ben Bernanke and HUD Secretary Alonzo Jackson called for federal funding for foreclosure prevention counseling. In June, the investment banking firm Bear Stearns revealed that it was pledging over $3 billion to bail out one of its hedge funds that had lost money on subprime mortgage investments, and in July the rating agencies begin to downgrade some subprime RMBS. Two Bear Stearns hedge funds declared bankruptcy and investors filed suit against the parent company. Things deteriorated even more in August, as more investors, in the United States and Europe, announced large losses in RMBS and CDO investments. By mid-August, credit markets had essentially seized up, as more investment losses were revealed and financial stock prices fell. The Federal Reserve quickly moved to lower interest rates. However, by late 2007 the securitization market for subprime mortgages had essentially shut down.

As delinquencies grew and foreclosure rates increased dramatically in late 2007, with some increases in the prime as well as subprime markets, policymakers introduced a variety of proposals to help delinquent homeowners keep their homes. One of the first legislative proposals introduced separately in the House and Senate in the fall of 2007 was a measure to allow bankruptcy judges to modify the outstanding balance on home loans for borrowers in bankruptcy.

When distressed homeowners do not file for bankruptcy, lenders may voluntarily modify the terms of distressed loans. But lenders often are reluctant to do so, and the complex structured securitization of mortgages created many barriers to loan modifications. Under Chapter 13 bankruptcy, borrowers file debt reorganization plans with the bankruptcy court. Federal bankruptcy law gives the court the ability to modify certain outstanding loans. In the case of most secured loans, bankruptcy judges have the authority to "cram down" the principal balance of the loan without the lender's permission, with the lower limit on such cram-downs typically being the fair market value of the collateral. However, this ability does not extend to loans secured by owner-occupied residences. Bankruptcy judges can modify the loan balance on a vacation home or on an investment property, for example, but not for a borrower's principal residence.

Bills introduced by Senator Richard Durbin (D-IL) in the Senate and Representatives Brad Miller (D-NC) and Linda Sanchez (D-CA) in the House aimed to temporarily remove the exclusion from the cram-down of owner-occupied mortgages, which would have allowed bankruptcy judges to modify loans on owner-occupied homes as a way of reducing foreclosures and keeping people in their homes. Given the challenges of voluntary loan modifications for securitized loans, there was a strong argument for using bankruptcy courts—which, after all, are in the business of restructuring consumer debt—to facilitate the modification of loans to affordable levels.

The key argument in favor of Chapter 13's special protection for lenders making loans on owner-occupied properties is that it enables them to offer lower interest rates and thus encourages home ownership. This presumption, however, was not empirically established prior to the development of the owner-occupancy exception. Only recently have any researchers examined the evidence on the impact of cram-downs on interest rates.

In strongly opposing the bankruptcy cram-down proposals, lending industry representatives argued that the proposal would raise interest rates on owner-occupied loans by 1.5 percentage points (Mortgage Bankers Association 2008). As evidence for this claim, they cited higher interest rates for investment property mortgages (whose interest rates are not generally 1.5 percentage points higher) but also factored in higher down-payment requirements and higher origination fees. Yet, the greater financing costs for such loans are due more to the greater risks involved in investor property mortgages.

Levitin and Goodman (2008) measured the impact of cram-down on interest rates using historical data. From 1979 to 1993, federal judicial districts varied in the degree to which they allowed for mortgage cram-downs on principal residences. These differences allowed Levitin and Goodman to identify the impact that cram-downs have on mortgage rates. They found that mortgage cram-downs resulted in, at most, only a 0.05 to 0.15 percentage point increase in interest rates, a far cry from the 1.5 percentage points asserted by the Mortgage Bankers Association.

Despite the evidence suggesting that permitting bankruptcy cram-downs for owner-occupied loans would not have a significant impact on overall mortgage rates, industry advocates continued to maintain otherwise. Industry lobbyists lobbied aggressively against these proposals, even though they were designed to be temporary. Consumer advocates continued to argue that this proposal would be an important and efficient tool in slowing foreclosures, but by April 2008 congressional proponents of the proposal had largely conceded defeat. The proposal to allow bankruptcy cram-downs continued to be discussed throughout 2008 as foreclosures continued to mount.

Hope Now—the Bully Pulpit Runs into Structural Obstacles

In late November and early December 2007, after the administration had opposed the bankruptcy cram-down proposals, Secretary of the Treasury Henry Paulson introduced the Hope Now initiative, a voluntary initiative developed in cooperation with the securities and loan servicing industry to develop ways to speed up and "streamline" loan modifications of subprime adjustable rate mortgages. Hope Now was coordinated by the Homeownership Preservation Initiative of Minneapolis, a lender-funded coalition that had been managing a national foreclosure hotline.

The Hope Now proposal was heavily criticized by consumer advocates as being a meager response in part because it was entirely voluntary on the part of servicers and investors. The plan merely laid out a proposed set of methods to identify borrowers for speedier consideration for loan modifications. Although the plan was generally described as one focused on freezing interest rates on adjustable rate loans for five years, the voluntary nature of the plan and the constraints imposed by securitization schemes made such arrangements unlikely in most cases. The proposal was also structured to target a narrow band of homeowners who met specific criteria; even for these borrowers, though, there was no strong incentive for investors to agree to modify loans. The very narrow segment of borrowers eligible to be *considered* for streamlined modifications had to meet the following conditions:

1. borrowers had to be living in the residences covered by the mortgage;
2. loans had to be hybrid ARMs with initial fixed interest rate periods of thirty-six months or less;
3. borrowers had to be no more than thirty days past due at the time that the loan modification is being considered and no more than sixty days past due more than once over the past twelve months;

4. loans had to be included in securitized pools;
5. loans had to be originated between January 1, 2005, and July 31, 2007;
6. loans had to have an adjustable interest rate that would reset between January 1, 2008, and July 31, 2010;
7. payments had to be scheduled to increase by more than 10 percent after the reset;
8. the amount of the first-lien loan had to be greater than 97 percent of the home's value;
9. borrowers had to have credit scores below 660 and less than 10 percent higher than their scores at the time of origination.

Estimates of the proportion of subprime ARM borrowers that would fit these requirements fell in the range of 3 to 12 percent.

The focus of Hope Now on borrowers that were current with mortgages prior to an interest rate reset was not well aligned with the scope of the foreclosure problem. A very large number of delinquent subprime borrowers—on the order of 30 percent or more depending on different estimates—had not even encountered their initial interest rate reset. Rather, the loans were so badly underwritten that they were unsustainable even at the introductory rates. Hope Now was also criticized, including by the Office of the Comptroller of the Currency, for not being able to provide standardized, reliable progress reports on how many borrowers were receiving loan modifications of different sorts or on the success of those modifications (U.S. Office of the Comptroller of the Currency 2008).

As discussed in Chapter 4, one of the difficulties in modifying distressed loans that have been securitized is that the cash flows to investors in different tranches are derived differently, so that reducing the interest rate on a loan may hurt one type of investor more than the other. Conversely, lengthening a loan term to reduce payment amounts or reducing the outstanding principal will impose different costs on different investors, again potentially causing a sort of "tranche warfare" (Eggert 2007).

Another obstacle to loan modifications was the heavy use of junior mortgages in the subprime market. As Rosengren (2008) has pointed out, the junior mortgages were often securitized separately from the senior mortgages, even if the same lender originated both loans. This means that modifying a borrower's mortgage debt may involve working with two different servicers and two different securitization structures, greatly compounding the complexity of satisfying securitization agreements and investors. Second-lien mortgages were very prevalent in some markets. The proportion of senior mortgages that had associated junior mortgages increased in Massachusetts from 26 percent in the second quarter of 2003 to 65 percent in the third quarter of 2005 (Rosengren 2008).

The legal agreements and arrangements that undergird structured finance are also obstacles to negotiating large numbers of loan modifications. The pooling and servicing agreements that allow servicers to modify loans often have limits of how many loans can be modified in different ways. Frequently, the agreements stipulate that modifications cannot be made unless the loan is in default or default is reasonably expected, a decision that generally was designed to be made on a case-by-case basis. If mass modifications are made, some servicers may fear litigation by investors. As Rosengren (2008) has argued, the legal structure for securitization "clearly did not foresee the widespread emergence of distressed borrowers, delinquencies, and foreclosures."

In the "old days" of originate-to-hold lending, a distressed borrower would be able to contact the lender that originated the loan. Given the physical costs of the foreclosure process, the interests of the borrower and lender would often align over avoiding a foreclosure and modifying the loan in such a way that the borrower could afford it. Even when GSE securitization began to dominate, the relatively unstructured nature of pass-through securities meant that investor and borrower interests could be rather easily aligned and servicers' decision making and constraints in modifying loans were much less complicated. Although the engineers of structured finance products may have correctly predicted that these products would increase the flow of capital into higher-risk mortgage markets, they clearly did not consider their impacts on the difficulty of modifying mortgages, especially in the event of a need to modify hundreds of thousands of mortgages in a fairly short period of time.

Congressional Foreclosure Rescue Proposals Move Slowly

While the Bush Administration pushed the voluntary Hope Now investment-industry-led partnership as an alternative to the bankruptcy bill or other legislative proposals, and especially after the bankruptcy bill failed, some members of Congress continued to push for a more active role for the federal government in mitigating foreclosure, arguing that such intervention was necessary in part to slow the flood of vacant housing spilling into an already weak housing market. A variety of proposals were put forward, including various programs to use the FHA to offer refinance loans to finance 80 to 90 percent of the outstanding balance of distressed loans. The FHA had earlier in late 2007 announced its "FHA Secure" program that would make refinance loans to borrowers with subprime adjustable rate loans. However, the program was relatively restrictive, requiring borrowers to be current on their loans prior to any reset in their interest rate—even though many subprime foreclosures were due to defaults occurring well before the reset period. The FHA Secure Program did not constitute a substantial change to existing FHA refinance products. Nonetheless, the agency did increase the overall number of refinance loans significantly after it announced the program. Thus, although the program may not have served borrowers in proximate danger of losing their home, it likely led to refinancing a substantial number of borrowers into safer, fixed-rate loans.

Notwithstanding FHA's increased refinancing activity, foreclosures continued to rise in late 2007 and 2008. Despite the continuing problem, those arguing for a more muscular federal role in refinancing distressed borrowers met with substantial opposition. Critics of such proposals argued that many borrowers were actually "speculators" and therefore should be held responsible for their fate. Although, depending on the local market, significant portions of foreclosures were non-owner-occupied properties, held either for investment or vacation home purposes (or both), this "speculator" argument was a distraction, because the proposals for refinancing distressed borrowers were all designed only for borrowers who could document owner-occupancy.

There were also suggestions that some large portion of distressed owner-occupants were well-informed, knowledgeable borrowers who had knowingly taken on loans that they knew they could not afford but were betting that their property would appreciate so quickly that they would be able to refinance or sell before their interest rate reset. Again, however, little to no evidence was provided to show that such borrowers were a very sizable portion of distressed homeowners. Although some borrowers might have fit this scenario, many certainly did not, especially in many parts of the country that did not see wild rises in property values but still had experienced large increases in foreclosures.

Some critics argued that assisting distressed borrowers would create a "moral hazard," in that risky behavior would be rewarded rather than punished, suggesting that borrowers receiving such help would go right out again and take out another risky loan because they would now assume that they would be "bailed out" once again. Such arguments were quite effective with the media and the general public, even though there was little evidence of a moral hazard in the case of most owner-occupiers. There may be cases when moral hazards may present themselves in taking out risky loans, but these are much more likely to involve investment properties. Homeowners are less likely to view their home as purely a financial investment and to willingly reengage in activity that put them into high-cost loans and subjected them to the heavy personal costs and humiliation of mortgage default.

Many media reports suggested that owner-occupants whose property values had declined below their outstanding mortgages were walking away from their homes, in what pundits called "jingle mail," implying that homeowners would just send their house keys to the lender and walk away from the house and the mortgage even if they could afford their existing mortgage payments. Again, it is important to distinguish investors from owner-occupants here. Investors are much more likely to walk away from a property whose value has declined significantly. This explains the inherently greater risk of lending to non-owner-occupied properties.

In the case of owner-occupant loans, however, there is substantial evidence that the great majority of borrowers in "negative equity" situations do not abandon their homes. Based on data for Massachusetts, Rosengren (2008) pointed out that the percentage of borrowers who default on loans when the loan amount exceeds home value is only on the order of 6 to 10 percent. This supports the notion that homeowners do not view their home as only a highly liquid investment that they will dump as its value falls. Rather, there are a wide variety of social and economic factors, many of which were discussed in chapter 5, that a homeowner will take into consideration. If values drop very far, many owner-occupants may decide to default, especially if their mortgage payments are large relative to their income.

None of this to say that home values are unimportant factors in determining foreclosure rates. But weak housing markets are typically not sufficient causes for very high foreclosure rates among owner-occupants. An increase in borrower risk—which can be caused by loan features and terms as well as economic conditions and shocks—will increase the number of borrowers in distress. Subprime and high-risk loans are more vulnerable to borrower economic shock such as unemployment, health crises, and divorce. There is less cushion in large part due to the higher debt-to-income ratios in such loans. But when house prices are rising, distressed borrowers can usually find ways to either refinance their loans or sell their homes. Flat or declining housing prices will leave such borrowers with little alternative but foreclosure, unless lenders or policy-makers step in to somehow help reduce monthly debt burdens.

Finally, by July 2008, with the spillover of the mortgage crisis affecting the economy more broadly and a national election coming up in the fall, there was more pressure to do something about the foreclosure problem. On top of this, there were now concerns that the GSEs might need federal intervention in the form of borrowing or even an equity invest-ment from the federal government. The administration, which had initially opposed any funding in the legislation for local governments struggling with vacant and abandoned properties due to foreclosures, finally dropped its opposition in order to get the bill approved. The result was a complex, multifaceted legislative package—labeled the Housing and Economic Recovery Act (HERA) of 2008—that contained tax breaks for residential builders, a complicated first-time-homebuyers tax credit, provision for a $300 billion FHA loan program to restructure the loans of distressed homeowners. The bill also contained a provision allowing the Treasury to extend credit to and possibly invest in the GSEs. Finally, it contained almost $4 billion for the Neighborhood Stabilization Program (NSP). The NSP is an eighteen-month program of block grants to state and local governments for reclaiming and redeveloping vacant, foreclosed homes.

The $300 billion "Hope for Homeowners" program, which went into effect in October 2008 and was run by the FHA, required lenders to write down mortgages and refinance borrowers into loans up to 90 percent of the current value of the home. The program also required borrowers to share a portion of their equity gain with the FHA when they sell the property.

The $4 billion in NSP funds was allocated according to a formula based on foreclosure-related activity, although each state was given a minimal level of funding, even if it had experienced few foreclosures. Local governments can use the NSP funds to purchase, reclaim, or demolish vacant homes.

Despite the July 2008 HERA bill and the Hope for Homeowners program, which began operations in October, mounting foreclosures and continued weakening in the housing market continued to press on the larger economy. In early September, Fannie Mae and Freddie Mac were placed into a government "conservatorship," giving their regulator control over the firms. A week later, Merrill Lynch, the investment bank, was sold to Bank of America and Lehmann Brothers filed for bankruptcy after seeking and being rejected for federal aid.

In the third week of September, the Federal Reserve Board rescued the large financial services firm AIG. AIG had been a heavy participant in the credit default swap market, a market that was hit hard by, and amplified the aggregate damage from, the mortgage crisis. The Board made the firm an $85 billion loan and essentially took control of the firm.

As commercial paper markets froze after the collapse of Lehman Brothers, officials in the Treasury Department quickly introduced a $700 billion proposal to allow it to purchase troubled financial assets, including mortgage-backed securities, from financial institutions. After only two weeks of high-profile debate and an initial defeat in the House of Representatives, the Emergency Economic Stabilization Act (EESA) was passed and signed into law on October 3. Together with many earmarked tax breaks and initiatives not clearly related to the financial crisis, EESA contained, as its principal component, the Troubled Assets Recovery Program (TARP). EESA gave the Treasury Department unprecedented authority to purchase distressed financial assets through TARP. It also gave the department the ability to make equity investments in financial institutions. Soon after the bill was approved, various European governments, led by the United Kingdom, began making equity investments in large banks. The U.S. approach of relying more on purchasing mortgage- and asset-backed securities was widely criticized as being an inefficient approach to unfreeze credit markets. By mid-October, the Treasury Department announced that it would use $250 billion in TARP funds to purchase equity in financial institutions and that half of these funds would go to nine very large financial institutions.

State Responses to the Foreclosure Crisis

As the mortgage crisis emerged in late 2006 and early 2007, state governments, many of which had been active in earlier efforts to regulate subprime lending, adopted a number of policies and programs to respond to rising foreclosures and related problems. States had learned that they could not afford to count on a rapid and vigorous response from the federal government, especially having witnessed the efforts of federal banking regulators to preempt many of their earlier attempts to increase lending regulations. A number of states, including some that were particularly hard hit by increased foreclosures, passed new laws, set up new programs, or established high-profile task forces to address the issue.

Before the Treasury Department announced its Hope Now initiative, for example, California governor Arnold Schwarzenegger had already announced a similar, though perhaps somewhat more forceful, plan for major loan servicers to work with borrowers to provide them with adjustable rate loans with interest-rate freezes (Pew Charitable Trusts 2008). Governor Ted Strickland of Ohio formed the Ohio Foreclosure Prevention Task Force in early 2007 to develop ways to reduce foreclosures in the state.

In the summer of 2007, a group of eleven state attorneys general, the bank regulators of New York and North Carolina, and the Conference of State Bank Supervisors formed the State Foreclosure Prevention Working Group (State Foreclosure Prevention Working Group 2008).[3] Its goal was to "identify ways to work together to prevent unnecessary foreclosures." The Foreclosure Prevention Working Group collaborated with federal regulators and industry participants to develop a system for collecting and reporting data to measure the size of the foreclosure problem and servicers' responses to it.

The Pew Charitable Trusts (2008) identified a number of actions that states took to address the foreclosure crisis through the spring of 2008. These included, but were not limited to, the following:

1. Twenty states had partnered with the Homeownership Preservation Foundation, the group that coordinated Hope Now counseling efforts to provide around-the-clock foreclosure counseling hotlines.
2. Fourteen states had created foreclosure task forces.
3. Nine states had adopted or implemented mortgage refinance loan programs aimed at helping borrowers retain their homes.
4. A few states, including California, Ohio, and Massachusetts, had worked with lenders to encourage them to modify the loans of distressed homeowners.
5. A few states had required lenders to give delinquent borrowers early notice of foreclosure initiation and information on any assistance that was available.
6. Nine states had implemented regulations to prevent "foreclosure rescue scams," in which consultants typically charge distressed homeowners substantial fees promising to save the home but having very little ability to do so.

---

3. The State Working Group consisted of representatives of the attorneys general of Arizona, California, Colorado, Iowa, Illinois, Massachusetts, Michigan, New York, North Carolina, Ohio, and Texas; two state bank regulators (New York and North Carolina); and the Conference of State Bank Supervisors.

States also adopted new regulations covering mortgage brokers and lenders in an effort to prevent future occurrences of excessively risky or abusive lending. Although these efforts are important, they will have to contend with the continuing ability of federal regulators to preempt such rules for many lenders, unless federal preemption laws are altered.

Mallach (2008) describes the sorts of things that states could do to respond to the foreclosure crisis. He argues that, while state attempts to directly refinance distressed borrowers through state loan funds were well intentioned, the scale of such programs, which cumulatively amounted to no more than a few hundred million dollars, were far too small to have a meaningful impact on a problem as large as the 2007–08 foreclosure crisis. Mallach recommends that states focus more on providing high-quality counseling and short-term emergency loans where appropriate, ensuring a fair foreclosure process to enable borrowers to negotiate with lenders, and encouraging lenders to work with borrowers toward sustainable loan modifications. An important ingredient to effective counseling is access to legal expertise that can ensure that borrowers are receiving the full protections of the law.

State Foreclosure Laws and Their Impacts on Foreclosure Mitigation and Recovery

One of the key parts of the mortgage process over which states do retain substantial policy influence and control is foreclosure law. The foreclosure process, other than issues related to bankruptcy protection, is largely governed by state law and state foreclosure laws generally cannot be preempted (or has not yet been preempted) by federal banking laws. Mallach (2008) recommends that state foreclosure law provide for sufficient time for borrowers to seek alternatives to foreclosure. Adequate periods of time between foreclosure notice and final sale provide homeowners with more opportunities to obtain the financial resources needed to cure the default, or to negotiate a loan modification (perhaps with legal assistance), or to sell the house at a price sufficient to pay off the mortgage.

Given the complexity of modifying securitized loans, brief foreclosure periods can severely impede loan modification and the ability of borrowers to obtain substantial assistance. Some states provide for as little as one month between the time a foreclosure notice is delivered and the foreclosure sale, making foreclosure mitigation more difficult.

Rapid and lender-friendly foreclosure regimes work to lower the effective costs that foreclosing lenders face. Given that foreclosures impose substantial social and public costs, lender/investor foreclosure costs should not be set too low. Lender-friendly foreclosure law may work to facilitate higher levels of high-risk lending than is socially optimal.

After controlling for other demand and supply side factors, Clauretie (1987) found that states with judicial foreclosure and longer foreclosure periods have lower foreclosure rates and suggested that more expensive foreclosure processes deter lenders from foreclosing and encourage them to use alternatives to foreclosure, such as loan modifications, repayment plans, or short sales. Others have argued that lender-friendly foreclosure laws create a highly conducive environment for high-risk lenders. For example, the president of Consumer Credit Counseling Services of Atlanta was quoted in the *Atlanta Journal-Constitution* as saying, "Our state is very attractive to lenders, and part of that is our non-judicial foreclosure process. . . . There have been a number of incredibly aggressive products [loans] marketed to consumers over the past five to eight years. Now we're starting to see the fallout of that aggressive marketing" (Hairston 2006). Moreover, while not addressing credit risk directly, Pence (2006) found that, controlling for other factors, loan sizes were larger in states with lender-friendly foreclosure laws. Although she interprets this as a negative impact of stronger foreclosure laws because borrowers are more constrained in the amount they can borrow, others may interpret her findings differently. Higher-risk lenders are likely to lend at higher debt-to-income ratios. Thus, Pence's findings are consistent with a scenario in which riskier lenders market more aggressively in states with lender-friendly foreclosure laws. Whether this outcome is perceived as in the public's interest is, of course, likely to be a point of debate.

Although rapid foreclosure processes and lender-friendly foreclosure laws may encourage high-risk lending and make alternatives to foreclosure more difficult, there are also reasons to avoid excessively slow or bureaucratic foreclosure processes. If foreclosure processes cause properties to sit vacant for very long periods of time, they may exacerbate the negative effects of foreclosures on surrounding communities (Mallach 2008). Thus, it is likely that, depending on market conditions and the regulatory climate, a period of well more than a few months but less than a year is the appropriate period of time between the foreclosure notice and the final consummation of the foreclosure sale.

The next and final chapter will first discuss broad principles for restructuring and regulating mortgage markets to create markets that are stable, fair, and affordable. It will also go into some particular issues and details that are particularly important or illustrative of the need to regulate mortgage markets more carefully and comprehensively. Such measures are key to preventing the sorts of economic and social damage done by the boom-bust lending markets that were precipitated by the steady march toward deregulation and regulatory preemption over the last three to four decades.

Policies for Fair, Affordable, and Sustainable Mortgage Markets

Mortgage market regulation, and financial services regulation more generally, has always been highly contested in the United States (Hoffman 2001; Immergluck 2004). Even in the earliest years of the nation, various founding fathers—including Alexander Hamilton and Thomas Jefferson—debated the form of the country's financial infrastructure and governance. They recognized the importance of credit and capital to the economic and social well-being of a nation's citizens. Time and again, from the Panic of 1907 to the 2007–08 mortgage crisis, the country has been forced to revisit its financial systems, their fundamental structures, and the extent of public control that should be exerted over different segments of the financial markets. Financial calamity has often triggered the reinvention, or at least the restructuring, of financial markets. The Panic of 1907 paved the way for the Federal Reserve System, and President Roosevelt's response to the Great Depression ushered in the large-scale development of the thirty-year fixed-rate mortgage and a more vigorous federal role in mortgage markets. Financial and economic calamities can, but do not always, help spur the political will to break through the very powerful special interests that work to resist fundamental changes in market structures or regulation. Hopefully, the 2007–08 mortgage crisis will bring a similar sort of fundamental restructuring and paradigm shift in the structure and regulation of mortgage markets in the United States.

Markets in consumer finance are quite different from most other consumer markets. They are not derived out of thin air and are not described well by some Robinson Crusoe model of people trading coconuts. They are politically and socially constructed. We only have to look at how drastically mortgage markets vary across countries. In Germany, for example, home loans are, at least at this writing, not sold in any sort of secondary markets. Securitization, at least as it developed in the United

States in the late twentieth century, has taken hold on a large scale in only a few places, and nowhere—as of this writing at least—did it engender the kinds of transactional failures and market collapse that it did in the United States in recent years. Although they vary greatly over time and across nations, the rules of exchange in financial markets—including mortgage markets—are complex and multifaceted. The products and the consumers are often highly heterogeneous. And, perhaps most fundamentally, many of the decisions people make in consumer finance markets are often not well predicted by simple rational choice models of utility maximization.

In this final chapter I aim to do four things. First, I lay out a set of broad principles for mortgage market regulation. Second, I propose a set of fundamental policy changes that would provide for sound, fair, and affordable home finance. Some of these are likely to be viewed as politically naïve, and that may be a legitimate criticism. My goal in this second section, however, is to lay out policy proposals without too much regard for political viability, at least in the near term. Of course, libraries and think tanks are littered with failed proposals in this arena, and I recognize the substantial political resources that are likely to work against some of these suggestions. However, there are two reasons for not being too focused on near-term political viability here. First, the dynamic nature of legislative and regulatory policy debates means that a book like this is not the best place to put forth highly detailed policy proposals. Second, the problems with mortgage markets have been so large and have had such devastating consequences that calling for only marginal steps is insufficient. Incremental policies alone, while perhaps helpful, are unlikely to prevent another boom-bust cycle and the resulting damage to families, neighborhoods, cities, and national and international economies.

At the same time, some of these broader principles and policies will be extremely difficult to adopt, especially without more fundamental political reform. Therefore, rather than merely dismiss more incremental approaches out of hand, I address some recent measures that have been taken by the Federal Reserve Board to tighten mortgage regulations, partly in response to the 2007–08 mortgage crisis. Although I do not discuss all such proposals in detail, I provide some examples of where these efforts fall short and how they might be improved.

Even after the dramatic breakdown in mortgage markets that occurred in 2007 and 2008, the current regulatory regime is one marked by a strong preference against proscriptive regulation and in favor of continuing to rely on the fundamental approach—consumer disclosure—that brought us the mortgage crisis. And regulatory agencies are not solely to blame here. Congress has been unable to move away from this approach as well, and, as of this writing, has not delivered any substantive legislation strengthening mortgage regulation for the president's signature, or veto.

Finally, I turn to two nonregulatory topics. First are some of the policy issues arising from the surge and concentration of vacant and abandoned properties spurred by foreclosures. Second, in order to reduce the dependence of low- and moderate-income households on homeownership in their attempt to secure decent affordable housing, I recommend redesigning housing subsidy and tax policy in the United States to provide for a wider array of housing tenure options.

Principles for Mortgage Market Regulation and Structure

The Costs of Failing to Regulate Are Very Large

Much of the debate over mortgage market regulation during the last thirty to forty years has operated largely within a frame of balancing the immediate protections to individual consumers against the regulatory burden or costs of imposing or maintaining regulations on the mortgage industry. Industry advocates have been quick to come up with alleged dollar figures for these costs and argue that net social welfare will be diminished if the choices of borrowers are restricted in any way. The scale of the 2007–08 mortgage crisis and the impacts that it has had on the broader economy provide an opportunity to reorient this debate.

The 2007–08 mortgage crisis has made it clearer than ever that failing to regulate mortgage markets sufficiently can have very large and systemic costs to mortgage and housing markets, credit markets more broadly, the stability of federally insured commercial banks and thrifts, the quality of life of neighborhoods and localities, and the overall national economy. Policymakers, including state and federal regulators and legislators, have often been swayed by arguments that proscriptive regulation of mortgage lending will discourage mortgage market innovations and reduce access to credit. Yet, at least before 2007, little weight has been given to the actual and potential harms that deregulation or a lack of regulation can bring.

Communities as Well as Individuals Are Hurt by Irresponsible, High-Risk Lending

Much of the policy debates around mortgage lending regulation are framed solely as consumer protection debates. Although this frame is a valid one, especially in an arena as critical to lifetime economic welfare as mortgage finance, it is not sufficient. The negative externalities—or spillovers—of high-risk lending are now generally well established. Even beyond government's responsibility to protect homeowners against lending abuses and overly risky lending practices, there is a need to consider the negative impacts on neighbors and local communities. Thus, while many lending regulations are aimed primarily at owner-occupants, non-owner-occupied properties are even more likely to be susceptible to foreclosure and vacancy, so that high-risk lending on such properties can cause problems for entire communities. As a result, lending regulations should not be focused exclusively on owner-occupied properties.

Consumer Disclosure Is Severely Limited as a Policy Tool

The federal policy tool of choice for consumer protection regulation in the United States over the last forty years has been individual consumer disclosure. The Truth in Lending Act, for example, relies on the disclosure documents that the borrower must read and understand. The primary alternative approach to consumer disclosures as a policy tool is proscriptive regulation, under which various sorts of loan terms or practices are prohibited, either for all home loans or for some subset of loans. The Home Ownership and Equity Protection Act (HOEPA) has some proscriptive content, but the pricing thresholds at which these protections kick in are so high that the law has had little impact. Moreover, the law gave the Federal Reserve Board authority to add proscriptive regulations, which it chose not to do until 2008. Some states have been more aggressive in adopting a proscriptive approach, but these laws can suffer from inconsistent coverage, weak enforcement regimes, and, for many lenders, federal preemption or the threat of preemption.

The theoretical basis for relying on consumer disclosure as the primary method of consumer protection lies in the notion that, given adequate disclosures, borrowers will make choices that suit their needs and that increasing the amount of information about the loan that is disclosed will help the borrower "shop around" and receive the best available loan. However, this reasoning fundamentally confuses information with knowledge and, as Barr, Mullainathan, and Shafir (2008) have pointed out, the success of this approach requires "fully rational agents who make intelligent choices about their options."

The available evidence from behavioral economics and finance shows that individuals who face complex financial decisions such as those involving mortgage terms often simplify them into one or two basic decisions, when, in fact, mortgage-related decisions involve a set of myriad, interdependent decisions (Barr, Mullainathan and Shafir 2008). Partly as a result of this complexity, borrowers tend to trust—or at least rely on—mortgage brokers or lenders to direct them to the most suitable loan product, even when these actors have incentives to do otherwise.

One of the underlying premises of the disclosure-based regulatory paradigm is that, because disclosure increases information and does not eliminate options for borrowers (because it is not proscriptive), it maximizes product availability and choice, which, given good information, should maximize consumer satisfaction. However, especially in complex arenas such as mortgage finance, more options may not increase consumer satisfaction or welfare. A large number of choices can intimidate borrowers and discourage them from making well-thought-out choices, instead relying on highly simplistic decision or default rules or relying too heavily on the advice of a broker or lender. Moreover, the context in which a decision is made becomes very important. By introducing more options, the borrower may get confused and be more easily steered by the broker or lender to an inferior product.

Regulation Should Promote Lender and Investor Accountability for Sound Lending

Regardless of the source and structure of capital and credit flowing into mortgage markets—including whether the credit supply chain is vertically integrated (as in the case of originate-to-hold portfolio lenders) or vertically disintegrated—lenders and their funders must be accountable for origination policies and behavior. Thinly capitalized originators should not be able to be used as shields against financial or legal liabilities.

Financial accountability, so that originators, securities issuers, investors, and other parties in the credit supply chain have "skin in the game," is an important component of ensuring accountability. Structured finance arrangements were thought to provide at least some level of financial accountability. For example, originators would typically be obligated by representation and warranties on loans they sold or securitized to buy back at least some of the loans that suffered from early defaults or other defects. However, if originators were thinly capitalized and these "kickouts" reached high levels, the originator could file for bankruptcy, thereby limiting accountability. In addition, originators might be required to retain the most junior, or residual, tranche in the RMBS in which its loans were securitized. However, the lender could avoid this accountability mechanism by selling off its residual interest to a CDO investor, shedding its longer term financial stake in the securitized loans.

Beyond financial accountability, nonoriginators (issuers and investors, for example) in the credit supply chain should have legal, and not just financial, accountability and be responsible for illegal or unfair and deceptive loans that underlie mortgage-related securities. In practice, this is typically implemented through some sort of assignee liability provision in regulation. A vigorous regime of legal liability through civil action is a critical and necessary complement to administrative regulation and supervision by government agencies. Government regulatory supervision, as has been clearly shown by the mortgage crisis, can be weak, uneven, and subject to regulatory capture. This is not to argue that administrative supervision and regulation are unnecessary or cannot be effective. Given the resources and leadership, such an approach can be a powerful tool in controlling irresponsible lending. However, the tool of civil litigation—at the federal and state levels—remains an important one.

Ability-to-Pay Underwriting Must Be Paramount

The key breakdown in mortgage markets over the last ten years has been a substantial movement away from sound underwriting and the use of reasonable and stable debt-to-income ratios. Mortgage markets will only function well when originators, and not borrowers, are held responsible for determining whether a borrower has the ability to repay a loan. It is important to move beyond the frivolous arguments over "personal responsibility" that have dominated so many of the popular debates over the foreclosure crisis. A sustainable system of mortgage finance depends upon lenders, and not borrowers, making the underwriting decisions, including those concerning affordability and loan size. Subprime default and foreclosure rates did not increase many times in the 2000s because levels of personal financial responsibility or financial literacy somehow spontaneously suffered a precipitous decline. Certainly, the United States has severe problems of declining wages, income inequality, and financial illiteracy, and reducing these problems would reduce mortgage market inequities. But these problems, while real, were not the proximate or primary cause of the recent crisis. Excessive financial innovation and declining underwriting standards were the dominant, direct culprits and must be addressed directly.

*Any Policy Goals concerning Homeownership Should Focus
on Sustainable and Beneficial Homeownership*

As pointed out in chapter 5, there is no substantive evidence that government policy—such as the Fair Housing Act or the Community Reinvestment Act—aimed explicitly at promoting access to affordable lending for minority or lower-income households had a significant role in the mortgage crisis of 2007 and 2008, as some critics of such policies have implied. The relatively minor policy permitting the GSEs to count investments in subprime RMBS toward their affordable housing goals may have given some additional support to the subprime market. Nonetheless, this policy was clearly not a principal factor in the 2007–08 mortgage crisis.

Much of the political support for promoting subprime lending, however, and for opposing increased regulation of subprime lending, has employed an argument that subprime lending was a key force in increasing homeownership rates, especially for minority and lower-income households. Thus, the regulation of subprime lending was portrayed as having negative impacts on minority and lower-income homeownership rates. Yet, the very high default foreclosure rates of subprime loans, even before 2007 and 2008, strongly suggest that subprime homeownership is excessively risky for the borrower. And the downsides of such risk are substantial.

The other, less well understood issue with the argument that subprime lending increased homeownership is whether homeownership financed by a high-cost, high-risk loan is likely to be financially beneficial for the homebuyer, even when there is no default or foreclosure. High-cost loans are likely to reduce the net present value of the home buying (versus renting) decision so much that the odds of ownership being a wise financial decision become quite small.

None of this is to say that homeownership cannot be beneficial for lower-income households. However, it is clear that the financing costs and sustainability of the ownership experience are key determinants of whether homeownership makes sense for a household.

*Fair Lending and Community Reinvestment Policy
Should be Expanded and Reinvigorated*

In the first high-risk lending boom, a good deal of the focus of the policy debates concerned racial disparities in the distribution of subprime or abusive loans. In part because the impacts of the 2007–08 mortgage crisis were felt by a broader and more affluent segment of the population—

including investors and the securities industry—the focus on the disproportionate concentration of these problems in minority households and communities received relatively less attention. Also, the scale of the crisis and its spillovers beyond mortgage markets meant that regulators and policymakers were concerned with large systemic financial failures. Notwithstanding the importance of some of these concerns, very large disparities in the impacts of high-risk lending and its associated costs persisted before and through this crisis. In dealing with the aftermath of the crisis—in terms of both individual impacts on credit histories and housing conditions as well as community-wide problems of vacant and abandoned housing—these disparities should be a focus of policy attention.

There are at least three aspects of policymaking that come into play here. First, resources for addressing the aftermath of irresponsible high-risk lending—especially in regard to vacant properties—should be directed especially to communities that were particularly hard hit by the crisis. Blanket, aspatial policies such as generic homebuyer tax credits are likely to be highly inefficient at solving problems caused by concentrated foreclosures. Federal and state programs should avoid being overly prescriptive so as not to tie the hands of local agencies, but resources are likely to be scarce relative to the scale of the problem nationally. Thus, wise subnational targeting of resources and the ability of local governments and nonprofits to craft their own solutions and targeting at the local level will be important.

Second, as discussed in chapter 5, one of the effects of the 2007–08 crisis, and of other periods of mortgage market failure, has been policy backlash. Again, by this I mean the possibility that government or private sector financial institutions will institute policies that have disparate negative impacts on lower-income or minority neighborhoods. Although some of the overall pullback in credit markets will harm these communities, it is important to avoid policies that exhibit redlining tendencies. The crisis has the potential to give political cover to policies that, in other times, would likely not pass muster from a fair lending or Community Reinvestment Act perspective. Such policies are likely to worsen the disparities that the crisis has produced. If lenders, mortgage insurers, or others need to tighten their underwriting criteria or loan-to-value limits, then they should, but these changes should be across the board. Any attempt to address weak housing prices that may play out spatially should be done through an individual appraisal process and not through policies that institute different standards for some neighborhoods over others.

Finally, whatever the regulatory infrastructure looks like in the future, there should be an emphasis on expanding and enforcing fair lending and community reinvestment law. These laws should not vary in their coverage or enforcement depending on the source of mortgage credit (bank, thrift, affiliated mortgage company, or independent mortgage company). All lenders should be regularly examined for compliance with these laws and the results of these examinations should be publicly available. The dual regulatory structure, in which some lenders are subject to much more scrutiny than others, facilitates dual lending markets and should be abandoned.

Fundamental Proposals for Rationalizing Mortgage Market Structures and Regulation

Revamping the Regulatory Infrastructure

Regardless of how capital and credit markets recover over the next several years, the lessons from the 1990s and 2000s in terms of mortgage regulation are quite powerful. A fragmented system of regulation that enables lenders to shop for the kindest and gentlest regulators does not promote a sustainable, robust, or fair mortgage market. The system that exists is one built on internecine struggles between regulatory fiefdoms and not on a highly rational plan of pluralistic regulation that some suggest. There certainly is a case to be made for multiple regulators, especially for overlapping federal and state jurisdiction. There is much less rationale for the hodgepodge of federal regulators that serve as a menu from which lenders select their preferred set of supervisors and rules. This system has not produced strong results.

Although some have proposed fundamental regulatory consolidation or reform before, these proposals have often been proposed in order to reduce regulatory "burdens" on financial institutions. Most notable here is a 2007 proposal from the Treasury Department, the formulation of which predated the mortgage crisis, and was admittedly designed for furthering the "economic competitiveness" of U.S.-based financial institutions and not for improving consumer protection or sound lending. My proposals are not aimed at such a goal, but at producing a rational and universal set of federal consumer protection regulations that are applied uniformly to all mortgage lenders, which also gives state government the ability to overlay a stronger set of regulations or supervision on lenders operating in their states should they choose to do so.

1. Create a system of more uniform federal regulation and supervision, including severe restrictions on the ability to preempt state consumer protection and fair lending regulations.

Uniform federal regulation means that all consumer protection laws and fair lending laws should govern the activities of all mortgage lenders equally. This is generally the case—TILA, HOEPA, ECOA, and the Fair Housing Act apply to all lenders, although the vigor of their enforcement and the interpretation of these laws can vary depending on the supervising regulator. However, there are exceptions, most notably the Community Reinvestment Act, which currently applies only to banks and thrifts and, as it is implemented, includes a separate, less rigorous set of regulations for smaller institutions.

Uniform federal regulation, however, also means that the ability to preempt state consumer protection and fair lending laws should not vary. Although there may be a rationale for retaining the national bank or the federal thrift charters, these should not include the ability to preempt state consumer protection laws. The ability to choose among different federal charters has created a "competition in laxity" between the Office of the Comptroller of the Currency and the Office of Thrift Supervision. This is a strong argument for consolidating these two federal charters. However, policymakers should go further in severely limiting the ability of nationally chartered depositories to ignore state consumer protection or fair lending policies.

As important as uniform federal regulations are, expanding the sort of routine and proactive supervision for compliance with consumer protection and fair lending laws that depository lenders undergo to nondepository lenders is critical. There are alternative ways that this could be done. One way is for an existing federal agency to expand its purview over certain additional lenders. In July 2007 the Federal Reserve and the Office of Thrift Supervision announced plans to begin a "pilot" program of conducting consumer-protection compliance reviews of mortgage companies that are subsidiaries of bank or thrift holding companies. Unfortunately, these reviews were announced about the time that the subprime market was grinding to a halt. Moreover, going forward, independent mortgage companies would not be subject to such reviews and, as the mortgage industry recovers, such partial coverage would give lenders and incentive to move out from under holding company structures and federal regulatory authority by reorganizing as an independent lender.

I propose a somewhat more fundamental approach: a new regulatory agency focused on consumer protection in financial services that would be given broad examination and enforcement authority regarding consumer protection and fair lending laws. Although the Federal Trade Commission appears to be the agency most suitable to take on this role, it would need to be given a clearer mandate, substantially broader coverage, and much greater resources to fill this role. Elizabeth Warren has suggested a Financial Products Safety Commission, which would review and endorse products from the perspective of the consumer (Warren 2007). Although this would be a useful entity, I am suggesting a more muscular agency with broad powers to regularly monitor and evaluate the lending practices of all mortgage lenders, but with a primary focus on consumer and community protection. This agency would analyze lending data, conduct matched-pair tests for discriminatory treatment, examine delinquency and foreclosure rates at both national and local levels, and enforce laws such as the Community Reinvestment Act, fair lending laws, and all consumer protection laws. A key component would be annual or biennial on-site examinations with broad authority. Moreover, any funding and operating schemes for such an agency should avoid perverse incentives that might bias the agency toward lenient enforcement.

There are two primary reasons for creating a new agency—or for creating a new, much stronger unit within the FTC—that would proactively and routinely examine all lenders. One is the need for an agency focused on consumer protection and responsible lending as its primary mission. This does not negate or override the safety and soundness responsibilities of the Federal Reserve or other regulators. Second, even if federal laws apply uniformly to all lenders, if their enforcement varies depending on the type of charter (e.g., state bank, mortgage company, national bank), then lenders are still likely to engage in shopping around for the most lenient regulator, resulting in another form of competition in laxity, this time based on the rigor of detailed enforcement. Sufficient care must be given to providing the sufficient, sustainable funding and independence of this regulator. Ideally, it would not be subject to the annual appropriations process, but be funded through some sort of widespread tax or fee on financial assets. However, such funding schemes must be applied broadly to all institutions and not provide for any perverse incentives to seek a more lax regulator.

2. Move toward proscriptive regulation of all mortgage loans, not just "high-cost" loans.

As discussed above, the focus on consumer disclosure laws as the only form of consumer protection for all but very high-cost loans is misplaced. Policymakers should fundamentally revise the HOEPA approach, in which pricing thresholds are used to attempt to parse out only certain loan segments for proscriptive regulation, and move toward more comprehensive regulation. One of the clear problems with this approach is that, as markets change and evolve, these thresholds are easily avoided or made obsolete. Even as the Federal Reserve lowered the interest rate threshold modestly for coverage under HOEPA in 2001, the flood of capital flowing into mortgage markets in 2002 and 2003 lowered market rates for high-risk loans, so that very few loans exceeded the HOEPA threshold that triggered proscriptive regulations, even with the lower interest rate threshold. Moreover, many of HOEPA's protections do not apply to home purchase loans and, in 2001, there was little focus on problems with subprime purchase loans. Yet, a good portion of the problems in the second boom occurred in the home purchase market.

One can almost always identify some reasonable uses for a particular loan feature, including prepayment penalties, payment-option terms, and others. However, the benefits of offering such products in the mortgage market must be weighed again the sizeable risk and damage that these products impose on large numbers of borrowers, and on the stability of mortgage markets more generally. The benefits are usually quite marginal and diffuse while the harms can be quite large and highly concentrated. If such loan terms are allowed, the risk lenders take on in offering such products should be substantially higher than for loans that do not feature them as suggested by the default product approach that follows.

3. Create a set of favored, default mortgage products.

This proposal follows basically from one developed by Barr, Mullainathan, and Shafir (2008). They propose that lenders be required to offer qualified borrowers a standard mortgage product—or menu of standard products—such as a thirty-year fixed-rate loan. Other products on such a menu might include a simple adjustable rate loan without any exotic features that would have to be underwritten at the maximum rate to which it might adjust. Any alternative mortgage product not contained in the list of standard products would require exercising a nontrivial "opt-out" provision.

Barr, Mullainathan, and Shafir (2008) are not naïve about the potential for brokers and lenders to manipulate borrowers into frequently choosing

opt-out alternatives. The opt-out loans would trigger heightened disclosures and, more importantly, additional "legal exposures." In this way, the
default products would be "sticky" in that lenders would have substantial
incentives to prefer originating the default loans. The expected losses or
risks of opt-out products would be greater due to greater liability, so
lenders would likely charge more for such products, but this would help
internalize some of social costs associated with products that have higher
foreclosure rates.

4. End federal preemption of state consumer protection and fair lending laws.

Chapter 6 described the role of federal preemption of state consumer
protection laws in promoting the high-risk loan market. States should
have the ability to supplement consumer protection and fair lending laws
to protect their citizens. If such regulations create impediments to certain
types of credit in states that impose stronger regulations, the regulated
states will bear the bulk of the associated costs and benefits of such
impediments. Setting aside the merits of the policy itself, in Georgia the
state legislature moved to overturn the state's strong state anti-predatory-
lending law after the credit rating agencies compelled a drastic curtailment
of the subprime market by refusing to rate securities containing Georgia
subprime loans. However, the Office of the Comptroller of the Currency
stepped in as well to preempt the law to show that it had the power to do
so and to therefore enhance the value of the OCC charter. State policymakers should have the ability to move beyond federal regulations in
order to protect consumers; they are more accountable for the impacts of
such decisions than are federal policymakers. At the same time, there is a
strong argument for a uniform base level of regulation that would protect
all borrows in the United States regardless of state action.

*5. Extend the Community Reinvestment Act (CRA) to all financial services
firms involved in providing capital or credit in residential, small business, or
consumer finance markets, and improve the Home Mortgage Disclosure Act to
provide more comprehensive data on mortgage lending products and practices.*

The CRA, which now covers only banks and thrifts, misses many of
the most important providers of credit and financial services, including
mortgage and finance companies, insurance companies, securities firms,
and credit unions. The application of the CRA only to federally insured
depositories exacerbated the problem of a dual regulatory system in which
prime lenders were scrutinized more heavily than subprime lenders. Given
the blending and intermixing of all sorts of financial institutions, and the

unclear lines between depositories and nondepositories, the choice must be made between maintaining a policy system that explicitly articulates a social contract concerning lower-income communities, on the one hand, and abandoning the social, contract on the other. The Community Reinvestment Act—however limited in its implementation—has been that contract for federally insured depositories.

Limiting CRA to institutions utilizing deposit insurance has been justified as suggesting that CRA is a quid pro quo for the benefits of deposit insurance. Some argue that uninsured institutions—or parts of them—receive no similar benefits. Yet these so-called non-banks have received many government-related benefits, not least of which is the regulatory and financial institution infrastructures that had been built up since the early twentieth century, including via the FHA, the GSEs, the Federal Reserve, and the other federal actors and agencies. Large mutual fund and securities firms invested regularly in federal and GSE securities and state and local bonds. And, in the case of larger institutions, there is a strong argument that some firms benefit from the perception that they are "too big to fail" or at least that their creditors would be protected, as was the case in the purchase of Bear Stearns by J. P. Morgan Chase, which was engineered by the Federal Reserve.

These policies and programs provide the resources and confidence that financial firms cannot provide themselves. It is arguable that the larger the explicit and implicit benefits that an industry receives from government action, the larger its obligation under its social contract should be. But it is difficult to argue that any consumer financial services activity does not receive substantial benefits of this sort. Some forms of government benefits, like deposit insurance, may be easier to measure, but this does not mean that the others are any less real or important.

Of course, since the heavy federal assistance given to a variety of financial services firms in 2008, there is a much clearer argument for expanding CRA coverage. Most clearly, the provision of resources through TARP should be matched with an explicitly community reinvestment obligation on the part of participating firms.

The most obvious way to extend CRA would be through a form of "functional" regulation. Any financial institution that makes housing, consumer, or small-business loans should be subject to the act, regardless of its status as a depository. The next logical extension of CRA would be in the coverage of institutions competing with banks in offering retail investment and money market account services. Functional CRA regulation would mean that mortgage companies would be evaluated primarily for their lending performance in housing markets, while issuers of mort-gage-backed securities or other "wholesale" entities involved in the mortgage supply chain would be evaluated using something like the current CRA investment test, in which banks receive CRA credit for nondebt investments in community development projects. Securities firms would need to have national-level assessment areas, or areas that reflect the distribution of their investments.

Rationalizing Securitization

Private-label structured finance was a driving force in the growth of irresponsible, high-risk mortgage lending in the United States. On the other hand, GSE securitization, especially before the GSEs began to lose substantial market share to the private-label market, was largely a successful financial innovation. If private-label securitization is going to return to being a substantial source of mortgage credit, it needs to be subjected to a significant number of changes.

1. Reduce the complexity and increase the transparency of mortgage-related securitizations.

The resecuritization of mortgage-backed securities through collateral-ized debt obligations should generally be avoided, especially for high-risk loan products. As Mason (2007) argues, using complex securitization structures for complex mortgage instruments makes little sense. Securi-tization of mortgages—especially high-risk ones—should be relegated to simple securitization structures and ideally to pass-through securities. In addition, all mainline parties in the vertical credit supply chain, including originators and issuers, should be required to retain a more substantial collateralized interest in the security and not be allowed to sell off such interests. This will increase the incentives for different parties to demand and scrutinize underlying loan information more carefully. Assignee liability, discussed below, is an important complement here.

2. Create an affirmative obligation for issuers of mortgage-related securities to provide for simplified protocols for loan modification, especially in the event of overall high default rates.

Any securitization structures used in the mortgage market should provide for a straightforward set of incentives to modify distressed loans and avoid the inter-investor tranche warfare that is embedded in most structured finance vehicles. Securitization agreements should provide for interparty compensation, especially when large numbers of loan modifications are required, and should not limit the ability of servicers to modify large numbers of loans. The inability of servicers to modify loans quickly and in ways that maximize net social benefit severely aggravated the 2007–08 crisis. The designers of complex structured finance products thought little about this problem, especially in the context of very high default rates. The SEC should reject mortgage-backed securities offerings that do not provide for simple and high-volume loan modifications.

3. Provide for quantifiable assignee liability in all mortgage secondary markets.

Assignee liability is an important tool to increase the functioning and information flow in the securitization process. The holder-in-due-course doctrine has enabled issuers and investors to shield themselves from being held accountable for enabling irresponsible and abusive lending. The rating agencies have made it very difficult for states to include assignee liability in their state laws. However, Engel and McCoy (2007) have persuasively argued that carefully crafted assignee liability that allows the potential damages to be quantified by rating agencies should not be a barrier to the rating of a mortgage-backed security.

4. Create a system of much more robust and routine supervision and regulation for credit rating agencies.

Securities and bank regulators give special status to nationally recognized credit rating agencies, and the functioning of even a reformed mortgage securitization market is likely to continue to depend on the integrity, consistency, and accuracy of their ratings. Some have suggested that introducing more competition in the ratings industry would solve the problems described in chapter 4. Although increased competition may have some benefits, it will not solve the major problems here, and could, without increased regulation, actually exacerbate these sorts of problems. What is called for is a much more extensive system of regulation and associated supervision of the credit rating agencies. Although the Securities and Exchange Commission has primary regulatory responsibilities over the agencies, up until 2008 at least their regulatory authority was quite limited and did not address most of the problems that have come to light. Even after the 2007–08 mortgage crisis, the SEC introduced only modest reforms to stem conflicts of interest and did not address the fundamental systemic problem in the issuer-pays model of agency compensation. Rating agencies should be required to conduct and publish detailed analyses of loan-level data in all mortgage-related securitizations of any sort. Regulators should require and ensure that rating agencies update ratings using current performance data and conduct more rigorous stress tests on securities using broader assumptions of house price declines and economic weakness.

Providing for Sustainable and Affordable Sources of Mortgage Credit

The history of mortgage capital sources in the United States is one of ebbs and flows, with different sources of mortgage credit being encouraged or discouraged by regulatory decisions and policies supporting one source over another. Although relying solely on an originate-to-hold model is not feasible and would likely restrict mortgage credit excessively, given the recent mortgage crisis it would have been advantageous to have more originate-to-hold capacity in U.S. financial institutions to mitigate the effects of the crisis in the securitization market. Thus, there is a need for more alternative but sound ways for portfolio lenders to remain liquid and to access capital, including, for example, the use of more on-balance-sheet mortgage-backed bond financing, which is sometimes referred to as debenture or "covered-bond" financing.[1]

Such financing had been used in the United States quite commonly in the early twentieth century and, as of 2008, is still a dominant way for banks to access capital in some parts of Europe, where the debenture market is on the order of $2.75 trillion in 2008 (Solomon 2008).

Also called for is a stronger role for the Federal Housing Administration in the mortgage market as suggested by White (2008). Historically, the FHA essentially laid the groundwork for GSE securitization by helping to standardize loan products. Before this, the FHA enabled the proliferation of whole-loan secondary market transactions by mainline institutional investors such as insurance companies. However, to remain robust and to serve as a standard-setting institution, the FHA should avoid products and practices that have been shown to encourage excessively risky lending. Most recently this included seller-funded down-payment programs, in which developers' contributions to nonprofit agencies are then used to provide down-payment-assistance grants to households purchasing homes from these developers. Such programs threaten not only the solvency of the agency but also its ability to

---

1. Federal regulators began calling for banks to utilize "covered-bond" financing methods during the spring and summer of 2008 (Solomon 2008).

encourage high-road lending standards in the broader marketplace. In the summer of 2008, Congress took action to curtail seller-funded down payments in FHA loans, although various actors tried to reinstate the program after this action.

There will remain a need for the GSEs—or their successor—to provide liquidity in the mortgage market. In September, the GSEs went into federal conservatorship. This fundamentally leaves four choices. First, the GSEs can be held in conservatorship until the housing market strengthens and then returned to the traditional GSE model, essentially private firms with very minimal government oversight and supervision. This seems unlikely given the federal intervention thus far. The second approach would be to permanently nationalize the GSEs, turning them into a public entity that provides a primary vehicle for securitization and secondary market activity for a large portion of the mortgage market. The third option, one that is being advocated by deregulationists, is to break apart their operations and sell them off to private firms, essentially ending federal involvement in the secondary market process.

The final option would be to reconstitute the GSEs as some form of public-private partnership or public utility. The utility model would involve a new private firm but one that is tightly regulated, with, most likely, some form of public regulatory commission overseeing detailed regulations. The utility's profit and/or pricing would be regulated and policy advocacy would be severely limited. A similar option would be to reconstitute the GSEs along the lines of the Federal Home Loan Banks, essentially a firm owned cooperatively by the mortgage originators who utilize the firm's secondary market functions. Such a firm would still be subject to federal regulation.

Regardless of whether or not the GSEs remain as one or more private, government-supervised firms—either in their previous form or as some sort of public utility or lender cooperative—regulatory scrutiny of the institutions needs to be increased, including examining loan-level and securities-level data and performance and setting standards and guidelines for loan purchases, securities guarantees, and other activities. Given that the implicit guarantee that the GSEs had has become an explicit guarantee, there would now need to be a stronger quid pro quo both for the agencies themselves and for the lenders that utilize the GSEs for their lending activities. The regulator should be required to regularly issue public versions of comprehensive examinations of the new entities both for safety and soundness, as well as for progress toward their missions of providing for affordable and responsible mortgage credit.

In the long run, given the explicit guarantee that has now been provided to the GSEs, there is a strong argument that the firms should be consolidated and nationalized. As public entities, the firms would function primarily to purchase and aggregate loans and securitize similar to the way they have done in the past, although with much greater care for downside risk. While the U.S. taxpayer essentially absorbed much of the downside risk of the traditional GSEs, the new public ownership structure would allow taxpayers to receive upside, and not just downside, risk—the profits generated by issuing successful securities. It would also provide for limiting downside risk more directly.

Pure privatization is clearly the least desirable option, as it would leave mortgage secondary markets to the private securitization and secondary market system that produced the high-risk mortgage market that precipitated the larger mortgage crisis. Some will argue that Wall Street and the private secondary market will be reformed by the larger credit crisis and that market forces will create a more stable system in the future. There is no evidence for such claims. It remains entirely likely that, given the opportunity, many of the systems that created the high-risk mortgage debacle can be easily reestablished over time, albeit with somewhat different tools and mechanisms. Global savings gluts will provide continual pressure for international financial markets to satisfy their need to find lucrative, short-term profits. Federally governed secondary market firms have the ability to control and mediate the flow of mortgage market capital into the neighborhoods and households that are ill equipped to be connected directly to the spigot of global capital markets.

Some Key Details in Recent Federal Regulatory Initiatives

During 2007 and 2008, the Federal Reserve Board issued proposed modifications to regulations under the Home Ownership and Equity Protection Act. These moves followed public hearings in 2006 and 2007 by the Board around issues of abusive and irresponsible mortgage lending. Consumer advocates had been calling on the Board to strengthen regulations under HOEPA since the law's adoption thirteen years earlier. Although the Board did adopt some changes, including a slight lowering of the high-cost loan threshold, in 2001, the regulations increasingly affected a smaller and smaller share of the home loan market, even as the subprime market grew. In July of 2008, the Board issued its final revised rules.

Although the 2008 final regulations did expand the coverage of HOEPA so that more loans are subject to the law's protections, the new rules are likely to have only a moderate impact on controlling abusive or irresponsible lending in the long term. Of course, the mortgage crisis temporarily resulted in a curtailment of most high-risk mortgage lending. But without fundamental regulatory change, another boom-bust cycle is likely to occur, bringing with it much of the same types of damage stemming from the recent crisis.

Although my purpose here is not to provide an exhaustive discussion of the revised HOEPA regulations, some notable strengths and weaknesses of the revised rules include:

1. The revised rules require lenders to conduct an ability-to-repay analysis for all mortgage loans. This is a key step. While the original proposal put the burden on borrowers to show that lenders engaged in a "pattern and practice" of not conducting such analyses, many consumer advocates, as well as the chairman of the Federal Deposit Insurance Corporation, successfully argued against such a requirement. Requiring borrowers to show a pattern and practice on the part of lenders in order for them to defend their individual homes against foreclosure would have made this key part of the regulation essentially unworkable.

2. The rules do not ban yield spread premiums (YSPs). YSPs are payments made to brokers based on the difference between the rate the borrower pays and the current wholesale lending rate that the lender is charging. YSPs provide an incentive for brokers to steer borrowers into higher-cost—and higher-risk—loans. The new rules did not even go so far as to require a complete, up-front disclosure of YSPs to borrowers, which had been proposed in draft regulations.

3. The rules do not cover all mortgages. Consumer advocates called on the Federal Reserve to ensure that abuses in the prime and home equity loan markets are covered by the rules, but the final rules did not do so (National Consumer Law Center et al. 2008). The fundamental problem here goes back to the basic model of threshold-based regulatory systems that are unable to anticipate the future structure and pricing of mortgages. Even if the thresholds address problem loans in the current or recent mortgage market, lenders are likely to find ways to craft loans to evade coverage under the rules as markets evolve.

There are other strengths and weaknesses in the Federal Reserve's recent regulatory rule-making. However, an exhaustive discussion of all such flaws is beyond the scope of this book. Moreover, whatever the incremental changes to the current regulatory schemes, policymakers have not addressed the more systemic failures in the federal approach to mortgage regulation that were raised earlier in this chapter. Without addressing these issues, only marginal improvements in outcomes are likely, and there will be little to stop further boom-bust cycles in mortgage and housing markets.

Helping Neighborhoods Recover from Foreclosures

As detailed in chapter 5, spatially concentrated foreclosures can, especially when foreclosures surge in a neighborhood, result in a jump in vacant and abandoned homes. This is one of the ways that high-risk lending affects entire communities, including many that were not involved in the lending transactions at all. This problem is a classic example of market failure— where the costs of a transaction are spread out beyond the parties directly involved in a transaction. Although the prevention of such problems in the future requires the sort of improved, proscriptive regulation described above, once vacant properties occur, they can become significant catalysts of community decline.

The problem of spatially concentrated vacant properties is not a new one, although the levels resulting from the second high-risk lending boom are, in the aggregate, somewhat unprecedented. There can be many challenges to reclaiming vacant and abandoned properties for productive use or, in some cases, for demolishing such properties (Keating 2007; Mallach 2006). Many properties have become tax delinquent. For others, clear ownership may be difficult to establish.

In addition to the large numbers of vacant properties resulting from the 2007–08 foreclosure crisis, the complexity of structured finance can make reclamation of vacant properties and neighborhood recovery a much more daunting task. In previous periods of high vacancies in the 1970s or 1980s, the volume of foreclosures tended to be lower. More important perhaps, the holder of the foreclosed property was easier to identify and negotiation over price and disposition was much simpler. In the case of portfolio lending, the lender's interest would often align quite closely with the community's. Neither would want the property to sit idle for long, because foreclosed properties can deteriorate rapidly and bring down the values of nearby properties. Since the portfolio lender was likely to have a good number of other loans in the neighborhood, this mattered to the lender. In the case of FHA lenders, neighborhoods and cities could put pressure on the agency to do what was necessary to keep the property secure and to get it back into productive use.

With the dominance of private-label securitization and structured finance vehicles, the problems of reclaiming vacant foreclosed properties are less straightforward. The securitization agreements that govern the disposition of the foreclosed property can make it difficult for the servicing companies managing the real estate owned (REO) properties to reduce prices of the REOs to the point where reclamation is feasible. Moreover, the REO properties in a particular neighborhood may be held in many disparate trusts with different rules regarding any ability to sell the properties at a discount, especially if the properties' true value is below the amount technically owned on the property.

Some localities are taking steps to address increased foreclosures and the problems they can pose. One set of approaches is to strengthen their local housing codes, or their enforcement, or create or improve vacant property registries, in which owners (including servicers) of vacant properties must register houses with the locality—usually at some cost—and agree to keep them maintained and secured up to a certain requirement. By requiring lenders to keep properties secure and free from blight, these laws are essentially internalizing the spillover costs of foreclosures, putting the social costs of vacancy on the lender. This may encourage lenders to avoid excessively risky lending, as foreclosures become more costly, and to seek alternatives to foreclosures when borrowers become delinquent.

A particular problem of vacancies resulting from high-risk lending is their spatial concentration. Redeveloping one property may be difficult unless the other nearby vacant properties are also reclaimed. After all, many homeowners or renters do not want to live in a neighborhood with many vacant properties. This creates barriers to development for both conventional developers and nonprofit community developers. Acquiring and rehabilitating a substantial number of vacant properties in a small area can entail significant risks and require substantial resources.

Much of the detailed planning and policy development focused on the recovery of neighborhoods pockmarked with vacant and abandoned buildings must be developed at the local level. Cities, counties, and community-based organizations understand local real estate markets, local capacity, and the barriers to development. However, local communities often do not have the financial capacity to acquire and rehabilitate substantial numbers of vacant properties. This is especially true because foreclosure problems tend to hit communities during overall weak economic times when public budgets are tight. Moreover, the vacancy effects cause even additional declines in revenues. Therefore, funding property reclamation and neighborhood recovery is an appropriate role for federal assistance. Moreover, to the extent that these problems were precipitated by a lack of regulation by federal policymakers and the preemption of state regulations, there is a strong argument that the federal government should assist in the recovery process. The Housing and Economic Recovery Act passed in July 2008 included $3.9 billion for the Neighborhood Stabilization Program, which provides funds for states and cities to purchase and rehabilitate or demolish foreclosed, vacant homes. However, there is some significant concern that the constraints on the use of the funding—especially a requirement to spend or commit the funds in a relatively short eighteen-month time frame—will make it difficult to leverage these funds to greatest effect.

Another challenge in trying to return substantial numbers of vacant properties to productive use of some kind is that of acquiring, holding, and developing the properties. Although some local governments have developed land bank authorities for this purpose, these are relatively rare and often have limited capacity. The scale of the vacant property problem precipitated by the 2007–08 mortgage crisis suggests the need for a national-scale intermediary that can assist local actors—governments and nonprofits—acquire vacant properties. In 2008, a coalition of national community development groups, including Enterprise Community Partners, the Local Initiatives Support Corporation, and NeighborWorks, proposed a "National Community Stabilization Trust" (Enterprise Community Partners 2008). The Trust would be capitalized with public and private resources and charged with acquiring distressed loans and properties. Its national scale would enable it to attract the involvement of lenders and investors and enable it to exercise significant bargaining power in acquiring and selling properties. Its financial resources and expertise would allow it to handle substantially more project risk in holding properties than most local community development groups or local governments.

At the state and local level, policymakers can support efforts to create state or local land banks and to capitalize these organizations. Another key area of state and local policy that can impede or assist recovery is property taxation. High levels of foreclosures and vacant properties can reduce property values. Local tax assessors should modify their assessment systems to address depressed values. In particular, many property tax systems do not consider lender sales of foreclosed properties to reflect market value and thus do not use such properties as comparables for determining local market values. However, in many heavily affected neighborhoods, lender sales of foreclosed homes have become a substantial share of total neighborhood home sales (Immergluck 2008). Thus, to automatically exclude these sales may distort assessed values, leading to unfair effective property tax rates, which may in turn inhibit redevelopment.

Rethinking Housing Policies That Limit Affordable Tenure Options

The mortgage crisis of 2007–08 has given some pause to rethink the national ethos of expanding homeownership as a goal of U.S. public policy. This is a reasonable and appropriate exercise. There are many reasons to question whether homeownership, by itself, is an appropriate goal for urban or housing policy. This is not to suggest that homeownership cannot bring significant benefits to households and neighborhoods. But, as argued earlier, policies and programs aimed at encouraging homeownership should specifically aim at *sustainable* and *financially beneficial* homeownership.

In the United States, most households essentially face a choice of two tenure options—renting or owning. There are other options in some places, including limited equity cooperatives, community land trusts, or affordability-restricted housing, but for most Americans in most places these alternatives are not available or are very scarce. Moreover, for many Americans, the choice between renting and owning is inextricably tied to other residential needs and preferences, including the size, quality, and location of available housing. In many parts of the country, if one wants to live in a detached, single-family home in a predominantly residential area with strong public schools, much of the housing stock meeting this description is likely to be for sale. Even if a household has no particular desire to own a home, and receives little financial benefit from ownership itself (e.g., for example, it does not itemize income taxes so does not benefit from the mortgage interest or property tax deductions), it may find that in order to access certain public services (e.g., a particular public school system), it is essentially compelled to purchase a home.

Making housing markets more efficient means encouraging a variety of housing types and location options across a variety of tenure options. In this way, families are not forced to choose ownership simply because they want to live in a particular type of community or in a particular type of structure, where there are few rental or other tenure alternatives. Too often, detached single-family rental options, for example, are located almost exclusively in lower-income neighborhoods, in part because of the implicit and explicit subsidies and policies that discourage rental housing in more affluent communities.

As Apgar (2004) suggests, the rental-ownership dichotomy can "divert attention away from larger policy goals, including the overarching goal of ensuring that all families and individuals have access to decent and affordable housing in a suitable living environment." Housing policy should not particularly favor ownership over other tenure options, although to the extent that unreasonable barriers to ownership exist, it is an appropriate role for government to reduce those barriers. Rather, public policy should look to promote long-term, affordable, and sustainable housing that offers low- and moderate-income families access to a wide variety of neighborhoods and housing choices. For those who want to pursue ownership, and where sustainable and beneficial ownership opportunities are feasible, homeownership programs are appropriate. But a locality's housing programs should offer other tenure options. Localities that focus solely on supporting homeownership, for example, could be encouraging tenure decisions that do not make sense for many households.

Some policy choices that discourage alternative tenure options are not as explicit as the design of subsidy programs. One important area for state and local policymakers, for example, is the structure of local property taxes. Many local property tax systems implicitly or explicitly favor owner-occupied housing, either through very generous homestead exemptions or through other assessment schemes that result in higher tax rates for multifamily rental housing. Property tax issues can be a particular deterrent to the less common forms of housing tenure. For example, community land trusts, in which homeowners own the building but not the land on which their houses sit, essentially lower the cost of housing by removing the underlying land from the conventional ownership market. By separating land tenure from building tenure, community land trusts can make housing much more affordable over a very long period of time, but they also limit the extent to which homeowners can realize capital gains on their ownership. Yet, if the land of a community land trust is taxed as if property owners own the land and can realize high levels of appreciation of the land, the land trust will have to pass on these high taxes in the form of higher land rents to the building owners. Thus, the building owners would have to pay property taxes similar to conventional property owners, even though they will never benefit from the appreciation assumed in the tax assessor's appraisal. In the end, property tax systems must be adaptable to alternative tenure structures.

Moving Forward

The history of mortgage markets in the United States is one in which periods of stability and incremental progress toward access to affordable and sound credit and capital have involved a strong, proactive role for the public sector, both in providing and standardizing mortgage credit and in providing a regulatory infrastructure that constrains market booms and busts. The rise of stable and risk-limiting mortgage markets in the broad middle part of the twentieth century—epitomized perhaps by the long-term dominance of the plain-vanilla thirty-year fixed-rate mortgage—was due to a persistent and substantive role for the federal government. These markets and products were not without the serious and pervasive problems of discrimination and redlining. However, their basic structure constituted a sound base upon which to build a fairer system, and in the late 1960s and into the 1970s, a number of federal statutes—the Fair Housing Act, the Home Mortgage Disclosure Act, the Equal Credit Opportunity Act, and the Community Reinvestment Act—were adopted toward this end. Although the implementation and enforcement of these laws was frequently lackluster, there were periods of time when significant progress toward fair, affordable, and sustainable home finance was made—especially in the late 1980s and early 1990s. This progress, however, was soon overwhelmed by a flood of high-risk credit.

This flood of credit, in turn, was fundamentally enabled by a strong deregulationist push by the financial services industry as well as many policymakers to avoid state and federal regulation and constraints that had resulted in a risk- and cost-limiting mortgage finance system. Since the 1980s, deregulationist forces typically dominated consumer and mortgage finance policy at both the state and federal levels, especially in the specific area of consumer protection.

Even when some states stepped in to fill the regulatory vacuum—and many did not—federal policymakers generally rebuffed them, preempting state consumer protection laws. Deregulation—which was both active and passive—favored the growth of structured residential finance. These policies paved the way for the connection of unrestrained global capital markets to create investment structures designed primarily to speed the flow of high-risk and high-cost credit to local communities, and especially to neighborhoods that were most vulnerable to such costs and risks.

The market structures developed in the absence of government oversight or regulation were able to ignore the very powerful negative spillovers of excessively risky and irresponsible lending. The result was that mortgage lending was treated no differently than markets for some mass-marketed consumer product. There was little thought given to the fundamentally different nature of real estate and housing, or to the impacts of foreclosure on households' long-term economic prospects and on neighborhoods and cities. Although structured finance greased the wheels of global capital flowing into lower-income neighborhoods, policymakers and financial engineers gave little thought to the "back-end" problems of what would happen if many loans failed and many houses were left vacant.

The silver lining to the 2007–08 crisis may be that it catalyzes a new way of thinking about mortgages, housing, and local real estate, and, perhaps, a new approach to related policies. This approach is based on recognizing a number of precepts. First, deregulation or the lack of regulation of mortgage markets over the last twenty to thirty years has imposed heavy costs on borrowers, neighborhoods, and broader credit markets and the economy. Given the very substantial costs imposed on local communities by high-risk lending, there is a very strong argument that states should have the authority to regulate such lending, in order to mitigate and limit such risks given the costs that are borne by local and state government and residents.

Second, it has become apparent that the fundamental approach of consumer disclosure is not a sufficient one for developing and sustaining affordable and fair mortgage markets. Borrowers do not necessarily benefit from receiving more choices; in fact, greater choice can confuse borrowers and make sound financial decisions even more difficult.

Third, the nature, extent, and form of consumer protection and fair lending regulation in mortgage markets should not depend on the path that capital takes into the retail mortgage market. A dual system of financial regulation, in which prime lenders are subject to closer supervision and scrutiny than subprime lenders, makes little sense.

Finally, if homeownership is to be encouraged, particularly for low- and moderate-income households, policymakers must be sure that such programs promote homeownership that is sustainable and financially beneficial for the households who choose it. But it is also important to increase the tenure options—including rental, ownership, and various limited equity schemes—that are available in a wider variety of communities.

These are the critical principles that will provide the basis for a sound, risk-limiting, and affordable mortgage marketplace and for promoting sustainable homeownership as well as affordable housing options more generally. Although incremental improvements in policy are always valuable, until these fundamental principles are accepted and acted upon, we are unlikely to have seen the end of boom-bust cycles and crises in mortgage and housing markets, with all of their attendant damages and costs.

References

Abrams, C. 1955. *Forbidden Neighbors: A Study of Prejudice in Housing.* New York: Harper and Brothers.

Adelson, M., and D. Jacob. 2008. "The Subprime Problem: Causes and Lessons." Long Island: Adelson and Jacob Consulting, LLC. January 8. www.adelson andjacob.com.

Alexander, W., S. Grimshaw, G. McQueen, and B. Slade. 2002. "Some Loans Are More Equal Than Others: Third Party Originators and Defaults in the Subprime Mortgage Industry." *Real Estate Economics* 30: 667–97.

American Dialectic Society. 2008. "'Subprime' Voted 2007 Word of the Year." January 4. http://www.americandialect.org/Word-of-the-Year_2007.pdf.

American Housing Survey. 1999, 2005. "American Housing Survey Data, U.S. Census Bureau." http://www.census.gov/hhes/www/housing/ahs/national data.html (accessed December 20, 2006).

An, X., and R. Bostic. 2006. "Have the Affordable Housing Goals Been a Shield against Subprime? Regulatory Incentives and the Extension of Mortgage Credit." Lusk Center for Real Estate Working Paper 2006–1006. Los Angeles: University of Southern California. http://www.usc.edu/schools/sppd/lusk/ research/pdf/wp_2006-1006.pdf (accessed June 1, 2008).

Andrews, E. 2007. "Fed and Regulators Shrugged as the Subprime Crisis Spread." *New York Times,* December 18.

Apgar, W. 2004. "Rethinking Rental Housing: Expanding the Ability of Rental Housing to Serve as a Pathway to Economic and Social Opportunity." December. Working Paper W04–11. Cambridge: Harvard Joint Center for Housing Studies. http://www.jchs.harvard.edu/publications/markets/w04-11.pdf (accessed May 20, 2008).

Apgar, W., A. Calder, and G. Fauth. 2004. "Credit, Capital, and Communities: The Implications of the Changing Mortgage Banking Industry for Community-Based Organizations." Cambridge: Joint Center for Housing Studies of Harvard University. March 9.

Apgar, W., and M. Duda. 2005. "Collateral Damage: The Municipal Impact of Today's Mortgage Foreclosure Boom." Washington, D.C.: Homeownership

Preservation Foundation. http://www.hpfonline.org/images/Apgar-Duda %20Study%20Final.pdf (accessed August 20, 2005).

Apgar, W., and A. Fishbein. 2004. "The Changing Industrial Organization of Housing Finance and the Changing Role of Community-Based Organizations." Cambridge: Joint Center for Housing Studies of Harvard University. May.

Appraisers' Petition. 2002. http://appraiserspetition.com/ (accessed April 10, 2008).

Armour, S. 2008. "Foreclosures Take an Emotional Toll on Many Homeowners." *USA Today*, May 16.

Ashcraft, A., and T. Schuermann. 2008. "Understanding the Securitization of Subprime Mortgage Credit." Federal Reserve Bank of New York. Staff Report no. 318. March. http://www.newyorkfed.org/research/staff_reports/sr318.pdf.

Austin, K. 2007. "Zero Down-payment Mortgage Default." Office of Federal Housing Enterprise Oversight. http://mpra.ub.uni-muenchen.de/5370/MPRA Paper No. 5370 (accessed December 2, 2007).

Avery, R., R. Bostic, and G. Canner. G. 2000. "CRA Special Lending Programs." *Federal Reserve Bulletin*. November. http://www.federalreserve.gov/pubs/ bulletin/2000/1100lead.pdf (accessed April 2, 2008).

Avery, R., K. Brevoort, and G. Canner. 2007. "The 2006 HMDA Data." *Federal Reserve Bulletin*, December: 73–109. http://www.federalreserve.gov/pubs/ bulletin/2007/pdf/hmda06final.pdf (accessed November 8, 2008).

Barr, M. 2005. "Credit Where It Counts: The Community Reinvestment Act and Its Critics." *New York University Law Review* 80 (May): 101–233. http://ssrn. com/abstract=721661 (accessed June 2, 2008).

Barr, M., S. Mullainathan, and E. Shafir. 2008. "Behaviorally Informed Home Mortgage Credit Regulation." Harvard Joint Center for Housing Studies UCC08-12. April. http://www.jchs.harvard.edu/publications/finance/under standing_consumer_credit/papers/ucc08-12_barr_mullainathan_shafir.pdf.

BasePoint Analytics. 2006a. "Broker-Facilitated Fraud—the Impact on Mortgage Lenders. Unpublished white paper. Carlsbad, Calif.: BasePoint Analytics.

——. 2006b. "A Study of Mortgage Fraud and the Impacts of a Changing Financial Climate." Unpublished white paper. Carlsbad, Calif.: BasePoint Analytics.

Bean, B. 2008. "Enhancing Transparency in the Structured Finance Market." *Supervisory Insights* 5, no. 1 (Summer): 4–11. http://www.fdic.gov/regulations/ examinations/supervisory/insights/sisum08/sisum08.pdf.

Been, V. 2008. "External Effects of Concentrated Mortgage Foreclosures: Evidence from New York City." Testimony before Committee on Oversight and Government Reform Subcommittee on Domestic Policy. May 21. http:// domesticpolicy.oversight.house.gov/documents/20080522105505.pdf.

Belsky, E., N. Retsinas, and M. Duda. 2005. "The Financial Returns to Low-Income Homeownership." Harvard University Joint Center for Housing Studies. Working Paper W05-9. September. http://www.jchs.harvard. edu/publications/finance/w05-9.pdf (accessed April 22, 2008).

Bernanke, B. 2005. "The Global Savings Glut and the U.S. Current Account Deficit." Remarks at the Homer Jones Lecture, St. Louis, Missouri, April 14. Federal Reserve Board of Governors. http://www.federalreserve.gov/boarddocs/speeches/2005/20050414/default.htm.

Blackwell, R. 2003. "Second OTS Preemption: Predator Law in N.Y." *American Banker*, January 31.

Bloomberg News. 2005. "Court Blocks Spitzer Inquiry into Loan Data." *New York Times*, October 13.

Blundell-Wignall, A. 2008. "The Subprime Crisis: Size, Deleveraging, and Some Policy Options." Financial Market Trends Paper ISSN 0378-651X. http://www.oecd.org/dataoecd/36/27/40451721.pdf.

Bostic, R., K. Engel, P. McCoy, A. Pennington-Cross, and S. Wachter. 2008. "State and Local Antipredatory Lending Laws: The Effect of Legal Enforcement Mechanisms." *Journal of Economics and Business* 60: 47–66.

Bradford, C. 1979. "Financing Home Ownership: The Federal Role in Neighborhood Decline." *Urban Affairs Quarterly* 14: 313–35.

——. 2002. *Risk or Race? Racial Disparities in the Subprime Refinance Market.* Washington, D.C.: Center for Community Change, May.

Bradford, C., and D. Marino. 1977. *Redlining and Disinvestment as a Discriminatory Practice in Residential Mortgage Loans.* Report to the U.S. Department of Housing and Urban Development, Office of Assistant Secretary for Housing and Equal Opportunity. Chicago: University of Illinois Center for Urban Studies.

Briggs, X. 1998. "Brown Kids in White Suburbs: Housing Mobility and the Many Faces of Social Capital." *Housing Policy Debate* 9: 177–221.

Brooks, R. 1999. "Unequal Treatment: Alienating Customers Isn't Always a Bad Idea, Many Firms Discover; Banks, Others Base Service on Whether an Account Is Profitable or a Drain." *Wall Street Journal*, January 7, p. A1.

Brooks, R., and R. Simon. 2007. "Subprime Debacle Traps Even Credit-Worthy." *Wall Street Journal*, December 3, 1.

Calem, P., K. Gillen, and S. Wachter. 2004. "The Neighborhood Distribution of Subprime Mortgage Lending." *Journal of Real Estate Finance and Economics* 29, no. 4: 393–410.

Calem, P., J. Hershaff, and S. Wachter. 2004. "Neighborhood Patterns of Subprime Lending: Evidence from Disparate Cities." *Housing Policy Debate* 15, no. 3: 603–22.

Callahan, D. 2005. "How Widespread Appraisal Fraud Puts Homeowners at Risk: Borrowing to Make Ends Meet." Paper No. 4. March. Washington, D.C.: Demos.

Canner, G. 2008. "CRA and the Subprime Crisis." Presentation to the Federal Reserve Board's Consumer Advisory Council. October 22. Washington, D.C.: Federal Reserve Board.

Canner, G., and W. Passmore. 1997. "The Community Reinvestment Act and the Profitability of Mortgage-Originated Banks." Finance and Economic Discussion Series, Federal Reserve Board. February.

Canner, G., and D. Smith. 1991. "Home Mortgage Disclosure Act: Expanded Data on Residential Lending." *Federal Reserve Bulletin* 77 (November): 863–64.

Carr, J. 2007. "Responding to the Foreclosure Crisis." *Housing Policy Debate* 18: 837–60.

Chinloy, P. 1995. "Public and Conventional Mortgages and Mortgage-Backed Securities." *Journal of Housing Research* 6, no. 2: 173–96.

Clauretie, T. 1987. "The Impact of Interstate Foreclosure Cost Differences and the Value of Mortgages on Default Rates." *AREUEA Journal* 15, no. 3: 152–67.

Cleveland Advocate. 1917. "Chicago Lays Plans for Race Segregation." *Cleveland Advocate*, April 14, 1.

Colton, K. 1983. "The Report of the President's Commission on Housing: The Nation's System of Housing Finance." *Real Estate Economics* 11: 133–65.

———. 2002. "Housing Finance in the United States: The Transformation of the U.S. Housing Finance System." Working Paper W02–5. Cambridge: Joint Center for Housing Studies, Harvard University. July.

Cortright, J. 2008. "Driven to the Brink: How the Gas Price Spike Popped the Housing Bubble and Devalued the Suburbs." Washington, D.C.: CEOs for Cities. http://www.ceosforcities.org/newsroom/pr/files/Driven%20to%20the %20Brink%20FINAL.pdf.

Creswell, J., and V. Bajaj. 2007. "A Mortgage Crisis Begins to Spiral, and Casualties Mount." *New York Times*, March 5, C-1.

Crossney, K., and D. Bartelt. 2005. "The Legacy of the Homeowners Loan Corporation." *Housing Policy Debate* 16: 547–72.

Cuomo, A. 2007. "The People of the State of New York against First American Corporation and First American eAppraiseIT." Supreme Court of the State of New York, County of New York. November 1. http://www.oag.state. ny.us/press/2007/nov/EA%20Complaint.pdf (accessed May 15, 2008).

Curry, T., and L. Shibut. 2000. "The Cost of the Savings and Loan Crisis: Truth and Consequences." *FDIC Banking Review* 13, no. 2: 26–35.

Dane, S. 1993. "Eliminating the Labyrinth: A Proposal to Simplify Federal Mortgage Discrimination Laws." *University of Michigan Journal of Law Reform*, Spring.

Davenport, T. 2003. "Why OCC May Tread Lightly on Georgia Law." *American Banker*, April 9.

Dawkins, C. 2006. "Are Social Networks the Ties That Bind Families to Neighborhoods?" *Housing Studies* 21: 867–81.

Dedman, W. 1988a. "Atlanta Blacks Losing in Home Loans Scramble: Banks Favor White Areas by 5–1 Margin." *Atlanta Journal-Constitution*, May 1, A1.

———. 1988b. "A Test That Few Banks Fail—in Federal Eyes." *Atlanta Journal-Constitution*, May 3, A1.

Dennis, W. 1978. "The Community Reinvestment Act of 1977: The Legislative History and Its Impact on Applications for Changes in Structure Made by Depository Institutions to the Four Federal Financial Supervisory Agencies." Credit Research Center Working Paper No. 24. Washington, D.C.: Pottinger and Company.

Ding, L., R. Quercia, J. Ratcliffe, and W. Li. 2008. "Risky Borrowers or Risky Mortgages: Disaggregating Effects Using Propensity Score Models." Chapel Hill: University of North Carolina Center for Community Capital. http://www.ccc.unc.edu/documents/RiskyBorrowers_RiskyMortgages_1008. pdf (accessed November 9, 2008).

Dinham, H. 2007. "Subprime and Predatory Lending: New Regulatory Guidance, Current Market Conditions, and Effects on Regulated Financial Institutions." Testimony before the Subcommittee on Financial Institutions and Consumer Credit Committee on Financial Services, United States House of Representatives, March 27. http://www.house.gov/apps/list/hearing/ financialsvcs_dem/htdinham032707.pdf (accessed December 2, 2007).

Doan, M. 1997. *American Housing Production, 1880–2000: A Concise History.* Latham, Md.: University Press of America.

Doms, M., and J. Krainer. 2007. "Innovations in Mortgage Markets and Increased Spending on Housing." Federal Reserve Bank of San Francisco Working Paper 2007–05. July.

Downs, A. 2007. "A Niagara of Capital into Real Estate Markets." Speech to the Berkeley Real Estate Advisory Council, Pebble Beach, Calif. April. http:// www.anthonydowns.com/niagaracapital.html (accessed June 10, 2008).

Eggert, K. 2007. "Testimony before the Senate Banking, Housing, and Urban Affairs Committee's Subcommittee on Securities, Insurance, and Investments at a Hearing Regarding Subprime Mortgage Market Turmoil: Examining the Role of Securitization." April 17. http://banking.senate.gov/public/_files/ eggert.pdf (accessed May 12, 2008).

Engel, K., and P. McCoy. 2007. "Turning a Blind Eye: Wall Street Finance of Predatory Lending." *Fordham Law Review* 75: 102–62.

Enterprise Community Partners. 2008. Presentation to National Association of Local Housing Finance Agencies. April 17. http://www.nalhfa.org/meetings/ 2008SpringConf/Presentations/ThursPMForeclosure.pdf.

Ernst, K., D. Bocian, and W. Li. 2008. *Steered Wrong: Brokers, Borrowers, and Subprime Loans.* Durham, N.C.: Center for Responsible Lending. April 8. http://www.responsiblelending.org/pdfs/steered-wrong-brokers-borrowers- and-subprime-loans.pdf.

Evanoff, D., and L. Segal. 1996. "CRA and Fair Lending Regulations: Resulting Trends in Mortgage Lending." *Federal Reserve Bank of Chicago Economic Perspectives.* November–December.

Evans, D. 2007. "Montana, Connecticut Hold Downgraded by Moody's." Bloomberg. December 3.

Evren, E. 2004. *SHRM Workplace Violence Survey.* January. Alexandria, Va.: Society for Human Resource Management.

Experity. 2003. Press release, www.experity.com/press_releases/PR_3_19_2003. html (accessed June 23, 2003).

Fannie Mae. 2001. *2001 National Housing Survey.* Washington, D.C.: Fannie Mae.

Federal Housing Finance Board. 2006. "Monthly Interest Rate Survey." Washington, D.C.: FHFB.

Federal Reserve Board of Governors. 1980. "Information Statement re: Community Reinvestment Act." *Federal Reserve Bulletin*, January. Washington, D.C.: Federal Reserve Board of Governors.

———. 2008. "Senior Loan Officer Opinion Survey on Bank Lending Practices." April.

Fellowes, M. 2006. "Credit Scores, Reports, and Getting Ahead in America." Washington, D.C.: Brookings Institution. http://www.brookings.edu/~/media/Files/rc/reports/2006/05childrenfamilies_fellowes/20060501_creditscores.pdf (accsssed May 20, 2008).

Fields, F., F. Justa, K. Libman, and S. Saegert. 2007. "American Nightmare." *Shelterforce* no. 150 (Summer). http://www.nhi.org/online/issues/150/americannightmare.html.

Fishbein, A. 1993. "The Community Reinvestment Act after Fifteen Years: It Works, but Strengthened Federal Enforcement Is Needed." *Fordham Urban Law Journal* 20 (2): 293–310.

———. 2003. "Filling the Half-Empty Glass: The Role of Community Advocacy in Redefining the Public Responsibilities of Government-Sponsored Housing Enterprises." In *Organizing Access to Capital: Advocacy and the Democratization of Financial Institutions*, edited by Gregory Squires, 102–18. Philadelphia: Temple University Press.

Fishbein, A., and P. Woodall. 2006. "Exotic or Toxic? An Examination of the Non-traditional Mortgage Market for Consumers and Lenders." Washington, D.C.: Consumer Federation of America. May. http://www.consumerfed.org/pdfs/Exotic_Toxic_Mortgage_Report0506.pdf (accessed June 20, 2006).

Fisher, E. 1950. "Changing Institutional Patterns of Mortgage Lending." *Journal of Finance* 5: 307–15.

Fitch Ratings. 2005. "Operational Risks in New RMBS Products." Residential Mortgage Special Report. New York: Fitch. September 7.

———. 2007. "The Impact of Poor Underwriting Practices and Fraud in Subprime RMBS Performance." New York: Fitch. November 28. http://www.fitchratings.com/corporate/reports/report_frame.cfm?rpt_id=356624 (accessed April 22, 2008).

Foote, C., K. Gerardi, L. Goette, and P. Willen. 2008. "What (We Think) We Know about the Subprime Crisis and What We Don't." Federal Reserve Bank of Boston. Public Policy Discussion Paper No. 08–2. http://www.bos.frb.org/economic/ppdp/2008/ppdp0802.pdf.

Foote, C., K. Gerardi, and P. Willen. 2008. "Negative Equity and Foreclosure: Theory and Evidence." Federal Reserve Bank of Boston. Public Policy Discussion Paper No. 08–3. http://www.bos.frb.org/economic/ppdp/2008/ppdp0803.htm.

Fort, V. 2003. "Letter to Leo C. O'Neill, President, Standard & Poor's." January 28. http://www.federalreserve.gov/secrs/2006/august/20060808/op-1253/op-1253_5_1.pdf (accessed May 20, 2008).

Foster, C., and R. Van Order. 1984. "An Option-Based Model of Mortgage Default." *Housing Finance Review* 3: 351–77.

Fredericksen, D. 1894. "Mortgage Banking in America." *Journal of Political Economy* 2: 203–34.

Furletti, M. 2002. "An Overview and History of Credit Reporting." Philadelphia: Federal Reserve Bank of Philadelphia. June.

Gale, D. 2001. "Subprime and Predatory Mortgage Refinancing: Information Technology, Credit Scoring, and Vulnerable Borrowers." Presented at the "Housing and the New Economy" sessions of the American Real Estate and Urban Economics Association Midyear Meeting. Washington, D.C., May 31.

Garwood, G., and D. Smith. 1993. "The Community Reinvestment Act: Evolution and Current Issues." *Federal Reserve Bulletin* (April): 251–67.

Geisst, C. 1990. *Visionary Capitalism: Financial Markets and the American Dream in the Twentieth Century.* New York: Praeger.

Goering, John, and Ron Wienk. 1996. *Mortgage Lending, Racial Discrimination, and Federal Policy.* Washington, D.C.: Urban Institute Press.

Golding, E., R. Green, and D. McManus. 2008. "Imperfect Information and the Housing Finance Crisis." UCC 08-6. Cambridge: Joint Center for Housing Studies. February. http://www.jchs.harvard.edu/publications/finance/under standing_consumer_credit/papers/ucc08-6_golding_green_mcmanus.pdf.

Goolsbee, A. 2007. "'Irresponsible' Mortgages Have Opened Doors to Many of the Excluded." *New York Times*, March 29.

Gordon, A. 2005. "The Creation of Homeownership: How New Deal Changes in Banking Regulation Simultaneously Made Homeownership Accessible to Whites and Out of Reach for Blacks." *Yale Law Journal* 115: 186–226.

Gorton, G. 2008. "The Panic of 2008." Federal Reserve Bank of Kansas City, Jackson Hole, Wyoming, conference. August. http://www.kc.frb.org/publicat/ sympos/2008/Gorton.08.04.08.pdf.

Gramlich, E. 2004. "Subprime Mortgage Lending: Benefits, Costs, and Challenges." Speech before the Financial Services Roundtable Annual Housing Policy Meeting, Chicago. May 21. http://www.federalreserve.gov/boarddocs/ speeches/2004/20040521/default.htm (accessed June 22, 2008).

——. 2007a. *Subprime Lending: America's Latest Boom and Bust.* Washington, D.C.: Urban Institute Press.

——. 2007b. "Booms and Busts: The Case of Subprime Mortgages." Presented in Jackson Hole, Wyoming. August 31. http://www.urban.org/Uploaded PDF/411542_Gramlich_final.pdf (accessed May 2, 2008).

Green, R., and S. Wachter. 2007. "The Housing Finance Revolution." Prepared for the 31st Economic Policy Symposium: Housing, Housing Finance, and Monetary Policy. Kansas City: Federal Reserve Bank of Kansas City. http:// www.kansascityfed.org/publicat/sympos/2007/PDF/2007.08.21.Wachterand Green.pdf (accessed April 2, 2008).

Greenlaw, D., J. Hatzius, A. Kayshap, and H. Shin. 2008. "Leveraged Losses: Lessons from the Mortgage Market Meltdown." Unpublished manuscript. February 29. http://www.chicagogsb.edu/usmpf/docs/usmpf2008confdraft. pdf.

Greenspan, A., and J. Kennedy. 2007. "Sources and Uses of Equity Extracted from Homes." Finance and Economics Discussion Series Number 2007–20. Washington, D.C.: Federal Reserve Board. http://www.federalreserve. gov/pubs/feds/2007/200720/200720pap.pdf (accessed June 1, 2008).

Gries, J., and J. Ford. 1932. *Home Finance and Taxation, Reports of the Committees on Finance and Taxation.* Washington, D.C.: Presidents Conference on Home Building and Home Ownership.

Gruenstein-Bocian, D., K. Ernst, and Wei Lei. 2008. "Race, Ethnicity, and Subprime Home Loan Pricing." *Journal of Economics and Business* 60: 110–24.

Grynbaum, M. 2008. "Study Finds Flawed Practices at Ratings Firms." *New York Times,* July 9.

Hagerty, J., R. Simon, M. Corkery, and G. Zuckerman. 2007. "At a Mortgage Lender, Rapid Rise, Faster Fall." *Wall Street Journal,* March 13.

Hairston, J. 2006. "Home Foreclosures Soar." *Atlanta Journal-Constitution,* May 12. http://www.ajc.com/search/content/auto/epaper/editions/yesterday/business_4446b195956b22a100fe.html (accessed August 5, 2006).

Hallahan, K. 1992. "The Mortgage Lending Controversy: National People's Action Takes on the Lenders and Wins Anti-Discrimination Legislation in Congress." Paper presented at meeting of the Association for Education in Journalism and Mass Communication, Montreal. August.

Harris, R., and C. Hamnett. 1987. "The Myth of the Promised Land: The Social Diffusion of Home Ownership in Britain and North America." *Annals of the Association of American Geographers* 77: 173–90.

Hartwig, R., and C. Wilkinson. 2003. "The Use of Credit Information in Personal Lines Insurance Underwriting." New York: Insurance Information Institute. June. http://server.iii.org/yy_obj_data/binary/729782_1_0/credit.pdf (accessed May 20, 2008).

Haveman, R., and B. Wolfe. 1994. *Succeeding Generations: On the Effects of Investments in Children.* New York: Russell Sage Foundation.

Hays, R. A. 1995. *The Federal Government and Urban Housing: Ideology and Change in Public Policy.* 2nd ed. Albany: State University of New York Press.

Helper, R. 1969. *Racial Policies and Practices of Real Estate Brokers.* Minneapolis: University of Minnesota Press.

Hillier, A. 2001. "Redlining and the Home Owners' Loan Corporation." Paper presented at the Fall Colloquium Series, University of Pennsylvania Population Studies Center.

Hinz, G. 2001. "Lobbying Bid Falls Short for Bank One. *Crain's Chicago Business,* November 19.

Hoffman, S. 2001. *Politics and Banking: Ideas, Public Policy, and the Creation of Financial Institutions.* Baltimore: Johns Hopkins University Press.

Hornstein, J. 2005. *A Nation of Realtors®: A Cultural History of the Twentieth-Century American Middle Class.* Durham, N.C.: Duke University Press.

Hutchinson, J. 2000. "Shaping Housing and Enhancing Consumption: Hoover's Interwar Housing Policy." In *From Tenements to the Taylor Homes: In Search of Urban Housing Policy in Twentieth Century America*, edited by J. Bauman, R. Biles, and K. Szylvian. University Park: Penn State Press.

Immergluck, D. 2004. *Credit to the Community: Community Reinvestment and Fair Lending Policy in the United States.* Armonk: M. E. Sharpe.

———. 2008. "More Subprime-Induced Inequities: Spatially Concentrated Property Market Problems and Property Tax Assessments." Presentation to the Association of Collegiate Schools of Planning. Chicago. July 9.

Immergluck, D., and G. Smith. 2006a. "The Impact of Single- Family Mortgage Foreclosures on Crime." *Housing Studies* 21, no. 6: 851–66.

———. 2006b. "The External Costs of Foreclosure: The Impact of Single-Family Mortgage Foreclosures on Property Values." *Housing Policy Debate* 17, no. 1: 57–80.

Immergluck, D., and M. Wiles. 2000a. "Where Banks Do Business: An Analysis of Small Business Lending Patterns from 1996 to 1998 in the Chicago Area." Chicago: Woodstock Institute.

Interagency Task Force on Fair Lending. 1994. "Policy Statement on Fair Lending." *Federal Register*, April 15, 59 FR 18266-01.

Ip, G. 2007. "Did Greenspan Add to Subprime Woes?" *Wall Street Journal*, June 9, B-1.

Jackson, K. 1985. *Crabgrass Frontier: The Suburbanization of the United States.* New York: Oxford University Press.

Jacobides, M. 2005. "Industry Change through Vertical Disintegration: How and Why Markets Emerged in Mortgage Banking." *Academy of Management Journal* 48: 465–98.

Joint Center for Housing Studies. 2008. *America's Rental Housing: The Key to a Balanced National Housing Policy.* Joint Center for Housing Studies. Cambridge: Harvard University. http://www.jchs.harvard.edu/publications/rental/rh08_americas_rental_housing/rh08_americas_rental_housing_bw.pdf.

Kaiser, E. 2007. "Subprime Losses Could Hit $100 Billion: Bernanke." Reuters. July 19. http://www.reuters.com/articlePrint?articleId=USN1933365020070719 (accessed April 20, 2008).

Keating, W. D. 2007. "Preserving Properties on the Edge: Rapid Recycling of Distressed and Abandoned Properties." March. Paper RR-07-16. Cambridge: Harvard Joint Center for Housing Studies. http://www.jchs.harvard.edu/publications/rental/revisiting_rental_symposium/papers/rr07-16_keating.pdf (accessed June 1, 2008).

Keys, B., T. Mukherjee, A. Serus, and V. Vig. 2008. "Did Securitization Lead to Lax Screening? Evidence from Subprime Loans 2001–2006." January. http://ssrn.com/abstract=1093137.

Khademian, A. 1996. *Checking on Banks: Autonomy and Accountability in Three Federal Agencies.* Washington, D.C.: Brookings Institution Press.

Kim-Sung, K. and S. Hermanson. 2003. "Experiences of Older Refinance Mortgage Loan Borrowers: Broker- and Lender-Originated Loans." Washington, D.C.: AARP Public Policy Institute. January.

Klaman, S. 1961. *The Postwar Residential Mortgage Market*. Princeton: Princeton University Press. http://www.nber.org/books/klam61-1 (accessed May 1, 2008).

Korte, G. 2007a. "City Foots Bill on Foreclosures." *Cincinnati Enquirer*, November 25.

Korte, G. 2007b. "Who Cares for Foreclosures?" *Cincinnati Enquirer*, December 14.

Lea, M. 1996. "Innovation and the Cost of Mortgage Credit: A Historical Perspective." *Housing Policy Debate* 7, no. 1: 147–74.

Leach, J. 2000. "Statement of Chairman of the Banking and Financial Services Committee, Hearings on Predatory Lending Practices, U.S. House of Representatives, Committee on Banking and Financial Services." May 24.

Leeper, D. 2008. "Neighborhoods: The Blameless Victims of the Subprime Mortgage Crisis." Testimony before the U.S. House of Representatives Government Oversight Committee: Domestic Policy Subcommittee. May 21. http://domesticpolicy.oversight.house.gov/documents/20080522110137.pdf.

Leonnig, C. 2008. "How HUD Mortgage Policy Fed the Crisis: Subprime Loans Labeled 'Affordable.'" *Washington Post*, June 10, A01.

Levitin, A., and J. Goodman. 2008. "The Effect of Bankruptcy Strip-Down on Mortgage Markets." Georgetown University Law Center. Research Paper No. 1087816. February 6.

Levitt, A. 2008. "Regulatory Underkill." *Wall Street Journal*, March 21, A13.

Lin, Z., E. Rosenblatt, and V. Yao. 2008. "Spillover Effects of Foreclosures on Neighborhood Property Values." *Journal of Real Estate Finance and Economics* 36, forthcoming.

Livermore, G. 2001. "Real Estate Information in a Wired World." *Mortgage Banking*, April, 81–88.

Loan Performance, Inc. 2006. *Market Pulse: December 2005 Data*. San Francisco: Loan Performance, Inc.

Lowenstein, R. 2008. "Triple-A Failure." *New York Times Magazine*, April 27.

Lucchetti, A. 2008. "Moody's Aims to Buff Image by Revising Policies." *Wall Street Journal*, May 15, C2.

Mallach, A. 2006. *Bringing Buildings Back: From Abandoned Properties to Community Assets; A Guidebook for Policymakers and Practitioners*. New Brunswick: Rutgers University Press.

——. 2008. "Tackling the Mortgage Crisis: 10 Action Steps for State Government." Washington, D.C.: Metropolitan Policy Program at the Brookings Institute. May. http://www.brookings.edu/papers/2008/0529_mortgage_crisis_vey.aspx.

Mason, D. 2004. *From Buildings and Loans to Bail-Outs: A History of the American Savings and Loan Industry, 1831–1995*. Cambridge: Cambridge University Press.

Mason, J. 2007. "Dealing with the Rating Agencies: Market Crisis Update." October 9. http://www.criterioneconomics.com/docs/20071009%20Market%20Commentary.pdf (accessed July 13, 2008).

Mason, J., and J. Rosen. 2007. "Where Did the Risk Go? How Misapplied Bond Ratings Cause Mortgage-Backed Securities and Collateralized Debt Obligation Market Disruptions." http://ssrn.com/abstract=1027475 (accessed May 14, 2008).

Massey, D., and N. Denton. 1993. *American Apartheid: Segregation and the Making of the Underclass*. Cambridge: Harvard University Press.

Matasar, A., and D. Pavelka. 1998. "Federal Bank Regulators' Competition in Laxity: Evidence from CRA Audits." *International Advances in Economic Research* 4: 56–69.

Mayer, M. 1998. *The Bankers: The Next Generation*. New York: Truman Talley Books.

McCluskey, O. 1983. "The Community Reinvestment Act: Is It Doing the Job?" *Banking Law Journal* 100, no. 1: 33–57.

McCoy, P., and E. Renuart. 2008. "The Legal Infrastructure of Subprime and Nontraditional Home Mortgages." February. UCC08-5. Cambridge: Joint Center for Housing Studies.

Mikelbank, B. 2008. "Spatial Analysis of the Impact of Vacant, Abandoned, and Foreclosed Properties." Unpublished manuscript. Cleveland: Cleveland State University Housing Research Center. June.

Milligan, J. 2004. "Learning the Hard Way: The History of the Antipredatory Lending Law in Georgia Is a Case Study in How Well-Intentioned Lawmakers Came Close to Closing Down the Mortgage Market." *Mortgage Banking*, September.

Mishkin, F. 2008. Speech at the U.S. Monetary Policy Forum on "Leveraged Losses: Lessons from the Mortgage Meltdown." New York Federal Reserve Board of Governors. February 29. http://www.federalreserve.gov/newsevents/speech/mishkin20080229a.htm.

Missal, M. 2008. "Final report of Michael J. Missal, Bankruptcy Court Examiner." United States Bankruptcy Court for the District of Delaware. Washington, D.C.: Kirkpatrick and Lockhart Preston Gates Ellis, LLP. February 29. http://www.klgates.com/FCWSite/Final_Report_New_Century.pdf.

Moody's Corporation. 2004. *2003 Annual Report*. New York: Moody's.

———. 2008. *2007 Annual Report*. New York: Moody's.

Moody's Investor Service. 2005a. *Moody's Default and Recovery Rates of Corporate Bond Issuers, 1920–2004*. New York: Moody's. January.

———. 2005b. *Moody's Default and Loss Rates of Structured Finance Securities: 1993–2004*. New York: Moody's. July.

Morgenson, G. 2008. "A Road Not Taken by Lenders." *New York Times*, April 6.

Mortgage Bankers Association. 2003. "Standard & Poor's to Disallow Georgia Fair Lending Act Loans." http://www.mortgagebankers.org/NewsandMedia/PressCenter/32153.htm (accessed June 14, 2008).

———. 2008. "Stop the Cram-Down Resource Center Puts a Price Tag on Bankruptcy Reform." January 15. http://www.mortgagebankers.org/NewsandMedia/PressCenter/59343.htm.

Moskowitz, E. 1987. "Pluralism, Elitism, and the Home Mortgage Disclosure Act." *Political Science Quarterly* 102: 93–112.

Myrdal, G. 1944. *An American Dilemma: The Negro Problem and Modern Democracy.* New York: Harper and Row.

National Conference of State Legislatures. 2003. "Banking and Financial Services: Predatory Mortgage Lending." http://www.ncsl.org/programs/banking/bankmenu.htm (accessed June 24, 2003).

National Consumer Law Center, Consumer Action, Consumer Federation of America, Consumers Union, Leadership Conference on Civil Rights, National Association of Consumer Advocates, National Fair Housing Alliance, and the Empire Justice Center. 2008. "Summary of Consumer Comments to the Federal Reserve Board on Unfair Mortgage Lending Practices." April 9. http://www.nclc.org/issues/predatory_mortgage/content/hoepacommentsapril08summary.pdf (acccesed June 10, 2008).

NeighborWorks. 2008. 2007 Annual Report. http://www.nw.org/network/pubs/annualReports/documents/NWA07Annual.pdf (accessed June 2, 2008).

New York Times. 2003. "Spitzer Threatens to Sue U.S. Regulator over Loan Exemption." *New York Times,* December 13.

Nier, C. 1999. "Perpetuation of Segregation: Toward a New Historical and Legal Interpretation of Redlining under the Fair Housing Act." *John Marshall Law Review* (Spring).

Novak, W. 1996. *The People's Welfare: Law and Regulation in Nineteenth-Century America.* Chapel Hill: University of North Carolina Press.

Onaran, Y. 2008. "Banks Subprime Losses Top $500 Billion on Writedowns." *Bloomberg,* August 12.

Pavlov, A., and S. Wachter. 2006. "Aggressive Lending and Real Estate Markets." Unpublished manuscript. Philadelphia: Wharton School of Business, University of Pennsylvania. December 20.

Pence, K. 2006. "Foreclosing on Opportunity: State Laws and Mortgage Credit." *Review of Economics and Statistics* 88, no. 1: 177–82.

Pennington-Cross A., A. Yezer, and J. Nichols. 2000. "Credit Risk and Mortgage Lending: Who Uses Subprime and Why?" Working paper No. 00–03. Reston, Va.: Research Institute for Housing America.

Pew Charitable Trusts. 2008. *Defaulting on the Dream: States Respond to America's Foreclosure Crisis.* April.

Quercia, R., M. Stegman, and W. Davis. 2007. "The Impact of Predatory Loan Terms on Subprime Foreclosures: The Special Case of Prepayment Penalties and Balloon Payments." *Housing Policy Debate* 18: 311–46.

Quinn, J. 2008. "Loan Programs Will Leave Some Students Behind." *Washington Post,* May 25, F01.

Reiss, D. 2006. "Subprime Standardization: How Rating Agencies Allow Predatory Lending to Flourish in the Secondary Mortgage Market." *Florida State Law Review* 33: 985–1065.

Roche, D. 2008. "How Far Will Deleveraging Go?" *Wall Street Journal,* November 8, A-11.

Rodrik, D., and A. Subramanian. 2008. "We Must Curb International Flows of Capital." *Financial Times*, February 25.

Rosen, R. 2002. "Is Three a Crowd? Competition among Regulators in Banking." Paper presented at the 2002 Federal Reserve Bank of Chicago Bank Structure Conference, May 8.

Rosengren, E. 2008. "Current Challenges in Housing and Home Loans: Complicating Factors and the Implications for Policymakers." Speech at the New England Economic Partnership's Spring Economic Outlook Conference on Credit, Housing, and the Consequences for New England. May 30. www.bos.frb.org/news/speeches/rosengren/2008/053008.htm.

Rumberger, R. 2002. "Student Mobility and Academic Achievement." *Eric Digest*. EDO-PS-02-1. Chicago: Clearinghouse on Elementary and Early Childhood Education. June.

Rutherford, J. 2007. "Letter to Ms. Nancey A. Morris, Secretary, Securities and Exchange Commission." Comments on proposed rules on rating agencies: File Number S7-04-07. March 8. http://www.sec.gov/comments/s7-04-07/s70407-17.pdf (accessed May 3, 2008).

Scholtes, S., and F. Guerrara. 2008. "Home Equity Loans Threaten Regional Banks." *Financial Times*, June 9.

Schultes, R. 2008. "BIS Sees Need for Change; CEO Knight Backs a Series of Overhauls for Securitizations." *Wall Street Journal*, May 30.

Scott, K. 1977. "The Dual Banking System: Model of Competition in Regulation." *Stanford Law Review* 30: 1–49.

Securities and Exchange Commission. 2008. *Summary Report of Issues Identified in the Commission Staff's Examinations of Select Credit Rating Agencies.* July 8. http://www.sec.gov/news/studies/2008/craexamination070808.pdf.

Securities Industry and Financial Markets Association. 2008. *Mortgage Related Issuance.* New York: SIFMA. http://www.sifma.org/research/pdf/Mortgage_Related_Issuance.pdf (accessed April 20, 2008).

Shlay, A., and G. Whitman. 2004. "Research for Democracy: Linking Community Organizing and Research to Leverage Blight Policy." http://comm-org.wisc.edu/papers2004/shlay/shlay.htm (accessed July 15, 2005).

Silver, J. 2003. "Findings from an Analysis of Subprime Lending in Six Cities." Washington, D.C.: National Community Reinvestment Coalition. September 22.

Simon, R., J. Hagerty, and G. Zuckerman. 2007. "New Century Halts New Loans: Nervous Creditors Underline the Angst over Subprime Mortgages in the U.S. Market." *Globe and Mail*, March 9, B-7.

Simon, R., and S. Patterson. 2008. "Borrowers Abandon Mortgages as Prices Drop." *Wall Street Journal*, February 29, A3.

Smith, G. 2008. "Foreclosures in the Chicago Region Continue to Grow at an Alarming Rate." Chicago: Woodstock Institute. March.

SMR Research Corporation. 2005. "The Home Purchase Market of 2005." http://www.smrresearch.com/HP2005.pdf (accessed June 12, 2006).

Snowden, K. 1994. "Mortgage Rates and American Capital Market Development in the Late Nineteenth Century." *Journal of Economic History* 48, no. 3: 671–91.

———. 2008. "Mortgage Companies and Mortgage Securitization in the Late Nineteenth Century." http://www.uncg.edu/bae/people/snowden/Wat_jmcb_aug07.pdf.

Solomon, D. 2008. "U.S. Pushes a European Method to Help Banks Make Home Loans." *Wall Street Journal,* June 17, A3.

Spader, J., and R. Quercia. 2008. "Mobility and Exit from Homeownership: Implications for CRA Lending." Working paper. Chapel Hill: University of North Carolina Center for Community Capital. January. http://www.ccc.unc.edu/documents/MobilityAndExit_final.pdf.

Spiegel, Der. 2007. "Saxony State Bank Saved from Possible Collapse by Sale." December 13. Spiegel Online. http://www.spiegel.de/international/business/0,1518,523170,00.html.

———. 2008. "Banking Crisis Topples Governor of Saxony." April 14. Spiegel Online. http://www.spiegel.de/international/germany/0,1518,547267,00.html.

Squires, G. 2003. "The New Redlining: Predatory Lending in an Age of Financial Service Modernization." *Sage Race Relations Abstracts* 28, nos. 3–4: 5–19.

Standard & Poors. 2005. "S&P Comments on Risk in Newer Mortgage Products, as Discussed at Industry Event." Press release. New York: S&P. April 6. http://www2.standardandpoors.com/spf/pdf/events/SPCommentsonRiskin NewerMortgageProducts.pdf (accessed June 20, 2008).

———. Undated. "SPIRE: Standard & Poor's Interest Rate Evaluator." Brochure.

State Foreclosure Prevention Working Group. 2008. "Analysis of Subprime Mortgage Servicing Performance." Data Report No. 1. February 2008. http://www.mass.gov/Cago/docs/press/2008_02_07_foreclosure_report_attachment1.pdf (accessed June 23, 2008).

Stein, K., and M. Libby. 2001. *Stolen Wealth: Inequities in California's Subprime Mortgage Market.* San Francisco: California Reinvestment Committee. November.

Stiff, D. 2008. "Housing Prices Collapse Inward." Case-Shiller, http://www2.standardandpoors.com/spf/pdf/index/052708_Housing_bubbles_collapse.pdf.

Stock, R. D. 2001. "Predation in the Subprime Lending Market: Montgomery County." October. Project 1097. Dayton, Ohio: Center for Business and Economic Research, University of Dayton.

Tholin, K. 1993. "Sound Loans for Communities: An Analysis of the Performance of Community Reinvestment Loans." Chicago: Woodstock Institute.

Tomlinson, R., and D. Evans. 2007. "The Ratings Charade." *Bloomberg Markets,* July.

U.S. Commission on Civil Rights. 1961. *Housing: 1961 Commission on Civil Rights Report, Book 4.* Washington, D.C.: U.S. Government Printing Office.

U.S. Department of Housing and Urban Development. 1997. *U.S. Housing Market Conditions.* Winter.

———. 2000. *Unequal Burden: Income and Racial Disparities in Subprime Lending in America.* Washington, D.C.: HUD.

U.S. Department of Justice. 2001. *Fair Lending Enforcement Program*. January, www.usdoj.gov/crt/housing/b1101.htm (accessed May 23, 2003).

U.S. Department of Treasury and U.S. Department of Housing and Urban Development. 2000. *Curbing Predatory Home Mortgage Lending*. Washington, D.C.: Treasury and HUD.

U.S. General Accounting Office. 2004. *Consumer Protection: Federal and State Agencies Face Challenges in Combating Predatory Lending*. GAO-04-280. January.

——. 2005. *Mortgage Financing: Actions Needed to Help FHA Manage Risks from New Mortgage Loan Products*. GAO-05-194. Washington, D.C.: Government Accountability Office. February.

——. 2006. "Federal Housing Administration: Proposed Reforms Will Heighten the Need for Continued Improvements in Managing Risks and Estimating Program Costs." GAO-06-868T. Washington, DC: Government Accountability Office. June.

U.S. Office of the Comptroller of the Currency. 1999. "Letter to Chief Executive Officers of National Banks, Department and Division Heads, and All Examining Personnel, OCC 99-10." Cover letter for Interagency Guidance on Subprime Lending. March 3. http://www.ffiec.gov/ffiecinfobase/resources/retail/occ-bl-99-10_interag_guid_subprime_lending.pdf (accessed June 20, 2008).

——. 2003a. "Avoiding Predatory and Abusive Lending Practices in Brokered and Purchased Loans." Advisory Letter 2003–3. February 21. http://www.occ.treas.gov/ftp/advisory/2003-3.pdf.

——. 2003b. *Economic Issues in Predatory Lending*. July 30.

——. 2008. *OCC Mortgage Metrics Report: Analysis and Disclosure of National Bank Mortgage Loan Data, October 2007—March 2008*. June. http://www.occ.treas.gov/ftp/release/2008-65b.pdf.

U.S. Office of the Comptroller of the Currency, Board of Governors of the Federal Reserve System, Federal Deposit Insurance Corporation, Office of Thrift Supervision, and National Credit Union Administration. 2006. *Interagency Guidance on Nontraditional Mortgage Product Risks*. September 29. http://www.federalreserve.gov/newsevents/press/bcreg/bcreg20060929a1.pdf (accessed June 20, 2008).

U.S. Senate Joint Economic Committee. 2007a. *The Subprime Lending Crisis: The Economic Impact on Wealth, Property Values, and Tax Revenues, and How We Got Here*. Washington, D.C.: Joint Economic Committee. October.

U.S. Senate Joint Economic Committee. 2007b. "Sheltering Neighborhoods from the Subprime Foreclosure Storm." April 11. http://jec.senate.gov/index.cfm?FuseAction=Reports.Reports&ContentRecord_id=c780213f-7e9c-9af9-761d-fd7e597b5cfe&Region_id=&Issue_id= (accessed June 23, 2008).

U.S. Supreme Court. 2007. *Watters, Commissioner, Michigan Office of Insurance and Financial Services V. Wachovia Bank, N. A., et al.* No. 05–1342. Argued November 29, 2006—decided April 17, 2007. http://www.supremecourtus.gov/Opinions/06pdf/05-1342.Pdf (accessed March 22, 2008).

Vale, L. 2007. "The Ideological Origins of Affordable Homeownership Efforts." In *Chasing the American Dream: New Perspectives on Affordable Homeownership*, edited by W. Rohe and H. Watson. Ithaca: Cornell University Press.

Vandell, K. 1995. "FHA Restructuring Proposals: Alternatives and Implications." *Housing Policy Debate* 6, no. 2: 299–383.

Van Order, R. 2000. "The U.S. Mortgage Market: A Model of Dueling Charters." *Journal of Housing Research* 11, no. 2: 233–55.

Walter, J. 1995. "The Fair Lending Laws and Their Enforcement." *Federal Reserve Bank of Richmond Economic Quarterly* 81, no. 4: 61–77.

Warren, E. 2007. "Unsafe at Any Rate." *Democracy* no. 5 (Summer). http://www. democracyjournal.org/article.php?ID=6528.

Warsh, K. 2007. "Market Liquidity: Definitions and Implications." Speech at the Institute of International Bankers Annual Washington Conference. Washington, D.C.: Federal Reserve Board of Governors. http://www.federal reserve.gov/newsevents/speech/warsh20070305a.htm (accessed May 5, 2008)

Weiss, M. 1989. "Marketing and Financing Home Ownership: Mortgage Lending and Public Policy in the United States, 1918–1989." *Business and Economic History* 18: 109–18.

Werdiger, J. 2007. "Subprime Woes Hit Norwegian Brokerage." *New York Times*, November 29.

Wesbury, B. 2008. "Testimony to the House Committee on Financial Services on the Economic, Mortgage, and Housing Rescue Bill." April 9. http://www. house.gov/apps/list/hearing/financialsvcs_dem/wesbury040809.pdf (accessed May 10, 2008).

White, A. 2008. "The Case for Banning Subprime Mortgages." Valparaiso University Legal Studies Research Paper No. 08-06. http://ssrn.com/ abstract=1133609 (accessed July 2, 2008).

Will, G. 2008. "Alice in Housing Land." *Washington Post*, May 15, A15.

Woodstock Institute. 2008. "2007 Foreclosure Report: Foreclosures Continue to Grow at an Alarming Rate." March. http://www.woodstockinst.org (accessed May 12, 2008).

Wyly, E., and S. Holloway. 2002. "The Disappearance of Race in Mortgage Lending." *Economic Geography* 78: 129–69.

Wyly, E., M. Moos, H. Foxcroft, and E. Kabahizi. 2008. "Subprime Mortgage Segmentation in the American Urban System." *Tijdschrift voor Economische en Sociale Geografie* 99: 3–23.

Yellen, J. 2008. "Opening Remarks to the 2008 National Interagency Community Reinvestment Conference." San Francisco. March 31. http://www.frbsf. org/news/speeches/2008/0331.html#17.

Index

Recovery and Enforcement Act
(FIRREA) (1989), 44–46, 56–57,
59–60
Financial Products Safety Commission, proposed, 207
First American Corporation, 106
Fishbein, A., 63
Fitch Ratings, 104, 110n3, 111; leverage
over state policy makers, 172–73
Fixed-rate mortgages, 7, 10, 31
Fleet Mortgage Group, 124
Florida, 11–12, 69, 113, 114, 148–49
Ford, Gerald, 51
Foreclosures: emotional effects of,
145–47; HOLA and, 29; increased
rates in 2007–2008 crisis, 135–40;
loan-to-value ratios, 73–74; preda-
tory lending and, 82, 84; public
policy responses to, 183–92; second
homes, 113. *See also* High-risk
lending, economic and social costs of
Fort, Vincent, 172, 173
Foster, C., 145
Frank, Barney, 182–83
Fraud, mortgage brokers and, 103–5
Freddie Mac. *See* Federal Home Loan
Mortgage Corporation
Frederickson, D., 21–22
Free-market ideology. *See* Deregula-
tion
Fully amortizing, fixed-rate mortgages,
7, 10, 31

Garn, Jake, 52
Garn–St. Germain Act (1982), 44
General Accounting Office, 180
Geodemographic marketing tech-
nology, 83
Georgia Fair Lending Act (GFLA),
172–73, 178, 209
Germany, 197
Gillen, K., 80, 81
Gilleran, James, 178
Ginnie Mae. *See* Government National
Mortgage Association
Global financial stability, effect of
high-risk lending on, 158–62

Global savings glut, 99–100, 120–21
Golding, E., 103, 114
Goodman, J., 185
Gorton, G., 3
Government National Mortgage
Association (Ginnie Mae), 35–36, 41
Governments, effect of high-risk
lending on, 4, 152–53, 162
Government-sponsored enterprises
(GSEs). *See* Federal Home Loan
Mortgage Corporation; Federal
National Mortgage Association;
Government National Mortgage
Association
Gramlich, Edward, 180, 181
Great Depression, 10, 25, 28–29, 197
Green, R., 30, 103, 114
Greenlaw, D., 148, 159
Greenspan, Alan, 160, 180
Gruenstein-Bocian, D., 81

Hays, R. A., 6
Hermanson, S., 102
Hershaff, J., 81
High-risk lending, alternative mortgage boom, 68–72; appreciated
housing values, 92–94; exotic loan
products, 84–88; federal regulations, 180–83; low- or no-down-
payment loans, 88–92; securitization
and, 94–98. *See also* Public policy,
1995–2008
High-risk lending, cash-out refinancing boom, 11–12, 68–72; at New
Century Financial, 126; public
policy and dual mortgage market,
72–78; race and dual mortgage
market, 78–83; technology and
market segmentation, 83–84. *See also*
Public policy, 1995–2008
High-risk lending, economic and
social costs of, 3–4, 133–66; to
borrowers, 141–47; to community
reinvestment programs, 165–66;
foreclosure rates and, 135–40; to
global financial stability, 158–62; to
lenders and investors, 147–49;

Author Biography

Dan Immergluck is Associate Professor in the City and Regional Planning Program at Georgia Institute of Technology in Atlanta. Professor Immergluck is the author of two previous books and more than twenty peer-reviewed research articles, as well as numerous policy reports, on issues such as mortgage lending patterns and practices, bank and mortgage regulation, fair lending policies, housing market analysis, foreclosures, and related public policies. He has testified before Congress, the Federal Reserve Board, and state and local legislatures and agencies, and his work has been widely cited in the recent policy debates regarding the mortgage lending crisis. He has been quoted and his work has been cited widely in the media, including in the *New York Times*, the *Wall Street Journal*, the *Boston Globe*, the *Chicago Tribune*, the Associated Press, and many other news outlets. Dr. Immergluck serves on the board of the Woodstock Institute and on the Research Advisory Council of the Center for Responsible Lending.